Getting Rich In

COMMODITIES, CURRENCIES OR COINS

—Before Or During The Next Depression

Getting Rich In

COMMODITIES, CURRENCIES OR COINS

—Before Or During The Next Depression

ROBERT VICHAS

ARLINGTON HOUSE · PUBLISHERS
165 HUGUENOT STREET · NEW ROCHELLE, NEW YORK 10801

Third Printing, Nov. 1976

Copyright © 1975 Robert P. Vichas

MANUFACTURED IN THE UNITED STATES OF AMERICA

Library of Congress Cataloging in Publication Data

Vichas, Robert P
   Getting rich in commodities, currencies, or coins before or during the next depression.

   Includes index.
   1. Commodity exchanges. 2. Speculation.
3. Investments. I. Title.
HG6046.V52   332.6'45   75-5600
ISBN 0-87000-284-8

**This book
is dedicated to
the source of all wealth!!**

Acknowledgments

AUTHORSHIP INCURS MORE INDEBTEDNESS THAN ASSETS. NOT ONLY DO ideas have consequences, they also boast antecedents. To trace and allow proper credit to the sources of every notion would require another volume, perhaps two or three. I humbly acknowledge, *in toto*, my indebtedness to the originators of the ideas encompassed in this publication but, of course, accept responsibility for concatenating them in an ordered (or even disordered) sequence and for resultant thoughts emanating from their juxtapositional relationships.

Most recently I have benefited enormously from contact with numerous individuals in the commodity futures industry—too multitudinous to list here. Several—Ray Kaye, Paul Jones, Joe Ellis, Tom Kaye, Dr. Hans Sennholz, among many others—will recognize an idea or story as theirs. Mr. Martin Gross, senior editor of Arlington House, has offered both encouragement and beneficial suggestions.

Particularly I thank the following persons for reviewing portions of the manuscript: "Nick" Nickerson, grain and meat specialist, and member of the MidAmerica Commodity Exchange; Saul Weber, broker and egg specialist with Riley-Faulkner, Inc.; Chuck Strong, former grain-elevator manager and now registered representative and lumber specialist with Peavy Company; Rodney Young, housing-module manufacturer and secretary-treasurer of American Commodities Exchange, Inc.; Dr. R. W. Bradbury, professor of economics and international economics expert,

University of Florida; and doubly to Ms. Dolores Vichas both for reading parts of the text and for secretarial assistance.

Additionally, personnel and agents of several exchanges have been extremely cooperative and generous with time and materials.

I wish to thank the following: Bob Kornfeld, president of Robert Kornfeld Associates, Inc., New York City, public-relations firm for the New York Mercantile Exchange; William L. Pollock, vice-president of R. S. Weeks & Associates, Chicago, public-relations firm for the MidAmerica Commodity Exchange; Ms. Larissa Nicolayev, director of marketing, Pacific Commodities Exchange, Inc., San Francisco; John J. Capobianco, director of education and trade relations, New York Coffee and Sugar Exchange, Inc.; F. J. Brennan, secretary, New York Cocoa Exchange, Inc.; Ms. Kate Lewis, public relations, Chicago Board of Trade; Roderick Turnbull, director of public affairs, Kansas City Board of Trade; and the International Monetary Market, Chicago.

Introduction

LIFE IS FULL OF EXCITEMENT, LOTS OF ZIP, AND ZAP! JUPITER IS STILL IN your third Solar Sign of Aquarius—a great period for commodity, currency, and coin futures! That can really cause things to happen!

You are driven to success. I see your ambitions full of fire and enthusiasm! Uranus moves into your Sun Sign. You will accomplish the unusual this year. Uncertain uncertainties are reduced to certain uncertainties.

Because Neptune and Lunar Node are moving together, you must keep your financial affairs in order. There is necessity for money management and risk analysis. Money is often made and lost in mysterious ways. Do not overtrade. Conserve capital by retaining some in reserve—a contingency fund.

Too, financial equilibrium is indispensable. Neptune is subtle. Let profits run. The Lunar Node is outrageous. Cut losses.

If your Sun Sign is Taurus, you will be successful in commodity, currency, and coin futures. Bulls make money.

If your Sun Sign is Leo, others will be impressed by your progressive and aggressive attitude. They will lionize you when you multiply an unimportant sum into huge amounts.

However, if your Sun Sign is Sagittarius, you must decide which role to pursue before you commence trading commodity futures. Becoming a high-flyer—I mean a real shooter—you could end up with the wrong end of the horse.

Scorpios should especially take care in selecting their registered representative, tax consultant, and financial adviser. They can be badly stung.

If Saturn is in your seventh Solar Sign of Gemini, and you are either a beginning beginner or an advanced beginner, keys to successful trading are secretly ensconced throughout the text. Therefore, nothing less than complete perusal of the book will satisfy you.

However, if you don't know the exact time of your birth, you may have been unsuccessful in commodity markets. There are only two categories of traders—beginners and winners. If you are an old-time loser, then your status is "advanced beginner." Study the entire manual, especially those areas where you are weakest.

Errors can be costly. Keep records. Be accurate. Develop a trading plan; stick with it.

Traders with split personalities, under the influence of Gemini, should mercilessly tear out losing traits and integrate successful characteristics into a winning personality. Learn more about the psychology of trading in the following pages.

If Libra dominates your personality, maintain financial balance. Trade spreads and straddles or engage in arbitrage.

Some individuals may strive for freedom, for financial liberty, for new horizons. International diversification of assets seems the lesser of all evils. Part of your wealth is held in foreign assets. Can you hedge against losses? See Chapters 16 through 19.

Do you desire to transact in big numbers? Try currency futures. Section E will get you started.

In your favorite crystal ball, a man wearing a dark suit appears. He carries a bulging brief. His countenance is stern. You see the letters "IRS" tattooed on his forehead. Quick! Read Chapter 19.

But all of this may be old stuff. You understand technical analysis in Section B. You intellectualize some on fundamental analysis in Section C, but you may have overlooked one important aspect of markets discussed in Chapter 12.

Further, you know about trading plans, money management, risk analysis, and straddling in Section D. Sections E and F are not your bag. Nevertheless, you have not been doing as well as you would like. The answer may lie within; see Section G.

Suppose that due to governing forces of Aries, you prefer to unite together with only modest investment. Is there anything you especially need to discover before becoming betrothed to a club or fund? Before joining in community sing, follow the bouncing ball in Chapter 21.

By the way, if dancing is an avocation, definitely learn the Commodity Fox-trot in Chapter 13. It's the latest for swingers.

On the other hand, you may be only searching for a good story. Your Capricornian curiosity leads you to explore crags but not to the point of plunging. As they say in Chicago, "This book's just right for you, sweetheart."

One final prediction: After Uranus moves into your Sun Sign, I foresee great changes in your affairs following the first of the month—more excitement, moving around frequently, unexpected opportunities. Others will be impressed by your progressive and knowledgeable attitude. You are a leader. A real winner! There is electrical force and drive within.

Of course, be practical; don't make the mistakes of inexperience. Success comes by solving problems. Stand aside and analyze your reasoning processes. Never imitate. Be original. You have genius!

One word of caution: Never invest during Moon Wobbles!

Contents

Illustrations

Figures

Tables

Page

SECTION A

The Psychology and Mechanics of Commodity Trading

CHAPTER 1
Harry's System and the Royal Road to Riches

For of all sad words
of tongue or pen,
The saddest are these:
"It might have been!"

—John Greenleaf Whittier

HARRY HAD A SUREFIRE SYSTEM FOR BECOMING RICH. HE MIGHT HAVE BEEN a millionaire many times over. "Why, I could have bought that piece of land back in 1942 for a song. That's where they're building that new jet airport. Why, if I had bought that land back then, I'd be a multimillionaire today. I coulda retired like a king." The truth is that if Harry Hindsight had actually owned that piece of land, it would still be a week patch or probably the unofficial dump. The airport would most likely have been built elsewhere.

Of course, Harry is not the only one with 20/20 rear-view vision. The other day I was talking with a Harry-type personality. "If I'd bought that September cocoa last June, I could have made $100,000 in less than two months." Oh, what a world this might have been!

The purpose of this text is fourfold: The first section, an overview, spotlights self-examination. Are you really psychologically prepared to become a successful commodity trader? Second, if you decide to stick with me beyond the first three chapters, then the bulk of the book will show you how to trade profitably and put dollars in your pocket. (You probably already know something about these markets even if you have never traded in them.) This book is written for people of action.

The third purpose is to reveal secrets and tips on multiplying an unimportant amount of money into an important sum. The fourth message's aim, the most significant one, focuses on keeping wealth once you have accumulated it. Many otherwise successful traders have lost their possessions down to an embarrassing level.

This Reality

Self-delusion is probably the most mesmeric sport in which an aspiring trader can indulge. To avoid the hard facts of research, financing, trading, and conserving capital, a prospective trader will often fabricate a picture of what he thinks a successful speculator does—how he actually operates. No one likes to admit being wrong!

The self-deluded high-flyer envisions himself striding into the broker's office, consulting the teletype briefly, then proceeding to trade while onlookers lionize him in astonishment and amazement.

Just look at that high roller! Fifty cars of pork bellies! Twenty contracts of silver! Forty of Maine potatoes! Then, one hundred of eggs! Think of it! He just bought 2¼ million dozen of eggs! After four hours of fervid and effusive trading, he totals up his net earnings—$8,700 for the day after commissions. "Not a bad day!" Afterwards he imperiously trots out of the brokerage house at 3:01 P.M. (EST), tumbles into his new Bentley, trundles off to the club for lunch. Oh, what a life this one might have been!

Many speculators (representatives and brokers, too) project such dreams as wish fulfillments. These dreams seem real for a while because of intensity of desire that they be real. But they soon fade away. The barren sensorial state is a real letdown. Here we need self-honesty. The light of truth! Self-delusion should be avoided. Otherwise, trading becomes a compulsive habit that can lead to bankruptcy.

Actually trading is a business—one that should be approached scientifically. Like all businesses, it will yield income to the pursuer in direct proportion to the attention and energy he devotes to it. The market is fast-moving; fortunes can be acquired before you can say Jack Robinson. They dissipate just as rapidly.

Success in these markets depends upon only a small number of factors. Degree of prosperity can be measured by the extent to which you are awake—or asleep. A trader must accept certain limitations if he operates through normal, competitive channels. Everyone can be wealthy with 20/20 hindsight. Here you transact within the womb of time. Your unborn riches emerge from your ability to perceive coming events correctly. Triumph hinges on 20/20 foresight. Later on, I will spell out exactly how you can develop predictive and cognitive skills.

Market of the Future

As far back as we can discern in history, man has always been obsessed with coming events. Kings, dictators, presidents, generals, rebels have always had an immediate, intense interest in near-term prospects. Businessmen peer into the future to project capital expenditures, to plan marketing tactics. Students try to secure their futures through boot-licking and apple-polishing (a learned response carried over into adult life). Contrary thinkers capitalize on *their* projections—antipodal to the opinions of their multitudinous cousins—of tomorrow's prices.

Commodity markets reflect what the price structures of goods will be in the future. This is why these markets are sometimes referred to as *futures*. This market can be bought or sold for the future. If you are a reasonably accurate predictor, it may be just the right market for you.

Of course, timing is important. You cannot have a celestial time-sense, like those who have been prophesying the end of the world for several decades. I fully agree with them! The world is going to the dogs! But it has been headed in that direction for at least five thousand years. If I cannot prognosticate a reasonably accurate date for the evolvement of the "new order," it will not put a dime in my pocket—certainly not a silver dime.

Futures contracts seldom have lives exceeding a year. Amassing wealth means forecasting next week's and next month's action. Many people living today have acquired millions of dollars in these volatile markets. Like the customer, sitting in his broker's office a few months ago, who suddenly threw his papers airborne and shouted, "I'm a millionaire! I made it! I'm a millionaire!" Finance offers no counterpart to the thrill of winning in these markets, of reaching important objectives.

There is the story of a sales engineer who dabbled in the market when he was not plying his principal trade. By the time he had reached his late twenties, he had assembled enough cash to purchase a seat on a major exchange and, thenceforth, devoted his attentions to speculating on his own account and for some large clients.

Within a few years he had both accumulated and lost large sums of money. But each time he reached a new frontier of wealth it was always higher than the previous peak. Each time he was financially down, his lows mounted progressively higher.

He was learning to accomplish two things: to speculate successfully, and to preserve his wealth. Each time his successes scaled the heights more rapidly than before. He required nearly five years to stabilize his first million dollars. He climbed to $12 million within another three.

Individuals living today have mobilized millions speculating in these risky markets, but *many more have lost*. In fact, some estimates indicate that 85 percent of those who invest in commodity futures eventually lose their capital. But most people are born losers. They learn losing habits during youth and never put any sustained effort into changing their life's patterns, which accounts for the fact that approximately 85 percent of this country's wealth is controlled by less than 15 percent of the people.

They say that only 5 percent of us become financially independent by the time we reach age sixty-five. Eighty percent of the sixty-five-year-olds in this, the world's richest country, have less than $600 in the bank. Can you imagine that? At current rates of inflation, exceeding 10 percent annually, much spending power is filtered out within a few years after retirement. But never mind those people, this book is not written for them. What about you?

No one ever can rendezvous with an important amount of wealth using only his own funds (or his own brains). He must leverage his money. The English call it "gearing." The term well describes the benefits of leverage. Later we will discuss leverage and other advantages of trading commodities. But right now let's return to this theme: "end of the world."

The Safest Asset

The world is going to the dogs—but this tendency prevailed long before you and I were around! I recently visited Herculaneum—near Pompeii in Italy—and was admiring the beautiful remains of this rich, Roman residential community preserved under volcanic ashes. This small town of approximately five thousand inhabitants, situated about four miles east of Naples on the lower slopes of Mount Vesuvius, consisted of private dwellings of the nobility.

Menace of destruction first heralded in A.D. 62, when a seismic convulsion badly damaged many edifices. The town was finally buried under muddy lava in the tremendous eruption of Vesuvius in A.D. 72. Eighteenth-century excavations yielded a wealth of valuable relics. As I stood admiring the city's attractive remains, I mentally drifted backwards in time to speculate on the fortunes of the escapees, who had left behind perhaps a significant portion of their material assets.

How is life different today? With the December 1972 earthquake in Managua, Nicaragua, numerous fortunes—small and large—were destroyed. Many people will never recover the value of their earthly possessions. However, most of us may never experience uninsured losses of property engineered by the destructive forces of nature. There are more common ways of forfeiting wealth. How can you protect yourself from governments, thieves, bureaucracies, envious neighbors, exploiting relatives, and whoever else covets your hard-earned wealth?

Let me ask you a question that I have often posed to students of finance. Which investment form do you think is the safest: gold? silver? dollars? Swiss francs? real estate? stocks? government or private bonds? some other medium? Of course, a prudent investor will diversify instead of relying on any single investment vehicle; but any one of these media is subject to confiscation—through taxation, inflation, or expropriation—and to loss by theft, swindle, bankruptcy, or default.

32

So how does one preserve his accumulated wealth—and obtain more of it? Should he place his trust in government—his own or some other, in a system, or in his friends and relatives, or in his competitors?

You, my friend, are the best protector of *your own* wealth—you and those with whom you align yourself: your immediate family (in some cases), your business associates, your financial advisers, and all others whom you permit to orbit in your world. You are the *center* of *your* world.

You have the right to select your friends and associates (and enemies, if you are so foolish). If they act in harmony with your purpose of accumulating wealth, you will be successful to the degree you are able to direct and influence them. Choose carefully. Study carefully. Study may lead you to select only one or two to orbit in your financial world. Numbers are unimportant; working together toward *your* common goal *is* important.

How much wealth you will possess in a few years depends upon your decisions now. Whether your objective be $1 million, $10 million, $100 million, or $1 billion, the steps in reaching your goal successfully remain the same. Substance is formed by individual and collective mental attitudes.

Before the Next Depression

In a subsequent chapter I will touch upon the next great depression now foreseen by many eminent individuals. Meanwhile, what should you do to prepare and protect your property? There are two points frequently overlooked in discussing any crisis. The first centers on the wealth you have already assembled. If your finances are lilliputian, wizened and marasmic, and you expect to have little more than a few bucks in the bank, a heavily mortgaged house, and an automobile or two, then forget it. This book is not for you. You do not have anything to preserve, my friend.

If you seriously desire to accumulate a large sum of money and are willing to act in a courageous, decisive, self-reliant manner, then read on. Your thoughts of action will crystallize into circumstances of wealth and financial freedom.

The second point is not to fear the coming depression. Remember that chaos presents opportunities to move ahead which no other situation offers. If you are aware of the events leading up to the collapse, your knowledge and analysis will clearly place you in the middle of those 5 or 10 percent who are looked upon as financial whizzes. You may even preen your feathers and perch in an aerie with that elite and supernal 1 percent.

Your immediate objective is to acquire wealth faster than inflation and taxes (and your children) take it away from you. If you are not satisfied with your present level of wealth procurement, then to accelerate the accumulative function you must allocate a portion of your assets to a high-risk, high-return market. Of course, a prudent, intelligent investor will employ his money wisely. He knows that in order to make money he must assume risks. He minimizes those risks while maximizing his profits.

Commodity futures trading is probably the only market in the world where both small and large investors can quickly leaven an unimportant sum of money into a substantial fund. Although futures trading was organized more than one hundred years ago in Chicago, most investors "discovered" this market only in the last five or ten years. It is one of the quickest routes to wealth. Although the risk factor is high, these markets offer the possibility of returns greater than probably all other liquid markets in the world. They yield profits both in good times and in bad times.

Before the next depression you will want to be liquid and nimble enough to take advantage of the opportunities and bargains that will surely appear. Wealth in just any form is inadequate protection. Wealth in a form that can readily be converted into other assets may open unforeseen vistas of financial independence.

This book may make you aware of a whole new range of opportunities. If you have never traded commodity futures because of fear and doubt of these markets, then you will surely know whether these markets suit your temperament by the time you have finished reading Chapter 3. If you are now trading commodities, this book may help you become a successful trader and encourage you to pursue your activities more aggressively.

Many traders quit at the first sign of failure. They stop when success is almost assured and rapidly succumb to adversity. "He who would accomplish little must sacrifice little; he who would achieve much must sacrifice much; he who would attain highly must sacrifice greatly."[1]

The Royal Road

The futures market is not one to be taken lightly or casually. (Shouldn't you always take money matters seriously?) Retaining and building your wealth is serious business—unless, of course, you are satisfied to retire on social security and a few bucks in the bank.

The reality of it all is that the road to riches will involve some definite action on your part. Forget about yesterday's losses. Hindsight is valuable only for the experience you draw out of the past. The trick is to develop foresight.

The dollar is worth only one-fourth of its value of twenty-five years ago; there have been over twelve hundred devaluations in the world since World War II; sad people with "blue chip" stocks have learned what the "blue" means; and rumors of more controls, higher taxes, and increasing rates of inflation flow freely.

Has your real wealth increased? Now don't tell me you are worth more today than, say, two years ago unless you have accounted for that cruelest of all taxes—inflation. Remember that inflation rates vary even in different sectors of the economy.

1. James Allen, "As a Man Thinketh," in *Inspiration Three* (New Canaan, Conn.: Keats Publishing Co., 1973), 1:124.

Inflation is measured not only in terms of rising prices but also in terms of deteriorating quality. Keep in mind, too, that your European vacation two years ago cost about 30 percent *less* than it would today. Now recalculate your net worth. Recall that I said *real* net worth. This is reality.

Trading commodity futures does not warrant a royal road to riches. It is a road—well, perhaps only a bridle-path or by-way for some—and somewhere down the pike there is a pile waiting to be plucked by the person who has psychologically prepared himself to assume possession over a portion of it. It is not the queen's highway to riches. But I do believe that one of the shortest access routes to wealth is to trade commodity futures conservatively.

However, the trip is not free. There is no money-back guarantee. I recall the astonishment of an acquaintance who had immigrated to the United States several years ago. He was absolutely overwhelmed by all the seemingly "free" things our society offers. It appeared that everywhere he turned, one firm or another was eagerly trying to "give away" its merchandise.

During his first several months in this country, he devoted much of his free time to answering advertisements, collecting trading stamps, gathering all advertised free goods. After several months he sadly realized that even in the richest country on earth, there is still no such thing as "something for nothing."

Everything has its price. After reading the next chapter you should know whether you are the type of person who is willing to pay the price of becoming a winner. Before you become a winner you will be tested many times. You may lose a large sum of money. However, if you can discern a trend in the commodities markets and enter it with the proper attitude and sufficient funds to finance minor fluctuations, there is no place in our economy where a greater return can be reaped!

CHAPTER 2
Winning in
Commodity Futures
Transactions

*So use all that is called Fortune. Most men gamble with her, and gain all,
and lose all, as her wheel rolls. But do thou leave as unlawful these winnings, and deal with Cause and Effect, the chancellors of God. In the Will
work and acquire, and thou hast chained the wheel of Chance and shall sit
hereafter out of fear from her rotations. A political victory, a rise of rents,
the recovery of your sick or the return of your absent friend, or some other
favorable event raises your spirits, and you think good days are preparing
for you. Do not believe it. Nothing can bring you peace but the triumph of
Principles.*

—Ralph Waldo Emerson

"Approximately 85 percent of the people who invest in commodities eventually lose," parrot some authorities. These figures may
be correct. But let me remind you that buyers of war bonds lost in real
terms due to the first, elephantine post-World War II inflationary surge;
owners of stock in Rolls Royce (or even IBM if purchased at high
prices) are big losers; some who "invested in" real estate from certain
land-development companies are not particularly pleased with their purchases; owners of savings accounts of declining real value are in the
same position as many possessors of profitless government and corporate
bonds, and so forth, *ad nauseam.* Do you get the point?

Most "investors" are foozlers anyway because they have been reared
to think like losers. Of course, unproductive rituals can be replaced with

winning ways. You must be willing to pay the price. Determine at the outset whether you are willing to sacrifice much to gain much. Examine the profile of a winner.

The Decision to Win or Lose

They say the secret to success in financial markets is to buy low and to sell high to the next fellow who wants to buy low. That philosophy is on a footing with the advice of scare-mongers who project linear models far into the future and tell us that we will one day run out of both space and resources.

Solutions to these problems will be found. I have faith in government. If the government does not foment a major war to annihilate half the world's population, it will probably abrogate the right to live beyond age thirty.

Losers usually misjudge events, distort facts, and panic. Winners, first of all, decide to claim victory. Do you want to be a winner?

"Anybody who says his book can teach you how to bargain and haggle isn't telling the truth. You learn to wheel and deal by wheeling and dealing, and to master these techniques you are going to have to pay a price."[1] If you trade commodities, you are aware of tuition costs. The *raison d'être* of this book is to lower your tuition fee.

Thunderbolts in commodity speculation have earned their reputation. They have planned to triumph. They have goals which they do not compromise. However, they also recognize that not every situation ranks equally profitable. When originating a position, they project not only potential profits but also degree of risk.

Successful people focus sharply on goals. They pursue fulfillment of needs with energy and direction. They make their own decisions over control of their lives and property. They decide what they wish to protect, then proceed to safeguard it.

In other words, the champion is aware of the circle of influence he has projected into space. He willingly defends his territory. He does not let others take advantage of him. He asserts himself. "It's sad to say, but most people are simply too lazy to assert themselves. They are rarely willing to take risks or to give up what they have gained. They fear getting less."[2]

Formation of Habits

Most persons have patronized defeatist habit patterns from the onset of earliest training. Do you challenge that statement? Next time you're

1. David S. Viscott, *How to Make Winning Your Life Style* (New York: Dell Publishing Co., 1972), p. 222.
2. Ibid., p. 98.

out shopping, listen carefully to the comments and reprimands of parents and relatives to children. They project negative thoughts.

And this bombardment of negativity continues throughout life. The individual receives abnegatory, resigning impressions from tutors, class-mates, and subsequently, fellow workers.

It almost seems as if there is a conspiracy to develop and sustain a can't-do attitude in individuals. Conditioning continues through acquies-cent song lyrics, television programs, commercials tailored for imbeciles, discourses of misdirected fanatics, and pressures from friends, relatives, neighbors, social contacts, and society in general to cradle a posture of immaturity.

If the dissident still is not convinced by this nugatory "wisdom," his local, amiable political candidate will reassure him, "Friend, you don't have to worry about your life. We'll take care of it for you. We know better than you what is good for you."

Some authors estimate that 90 percent or more of our decisions are foisted upon us by others. The wife, children, in-laws, Jonsey the neigh-bor, probably account for two-thirds of the inputs in the decision-making process. I don't have to spell it out with examples. You know exactly what I am referring to.

Some decisions are forced upon us by legislative decree: taxes, pre-scriptions (from Vitamin A to hard drugs), seat belts, census information, conscription, investment decisions, etc. As I wrote before, most people are duffers *ab ovo*. So it should not surprise us that most individuals who invest in commodity futures markets do lose. The fact that they bungle has little to do with commodity speculation. They are willy-nillies. They have been paying the table all their lives. Before examining this win-lose attitude in commodity investing, I will present you with a brief introduction to risk analysis.

Risk Assumption in Profitable Trading

Analysis usually originates with the comment that there are three types of investors: risk-lovers, risk-averters, and those who are indif-ferent, or neutral, to risk. It is unlikely that such distinctions actually prevail in the real world.

Those who maintain neutral behavior toward risk have probably long been buried; risk-lovers either require treatment or have already been restrained. I believe we all express risk-aversion in varying degrees. Choosing rationally, we prefer to minimize rather than maximize risk.

Why does anyone want to assume risks in the first place? Because we are acquisitive creatures, we want more. Anyone can receive a little in this life without risking much. The bigger the stakes, the greater the chances one must accept with the experience.

Suppose I offer you two assets. Forsaking originality, I will simply call them Asset A and Asset B. As an investment vehicle, Asset A offers to return 5 percent annually. Asset B promises a yearly yield of 15 percent. Which asset will you choose? If you are not very prudent, not having inquired about risk, predictably you will select Asset B. Now let me provide additional information.

Analysis reveals that the odds are 95 percent in your favor that Asset A will return 5 percent a year with equal chances of receiving back your original investment at maturity.

Reasonability of collecting an annual return from Asset B during its life approximates fifty-fifty. Equal odds favor repatriation of your original investment in due time. Undoubtedly you will now tend to prefer Asset A. Do you follow me?

However, if Asset B promises the potentiality of recouping an annual yield of 80 percent, you may elect to hazard loss of your original investment, trusting to double or triple your money quickly.

In other words, although you prefer to invest in a riskless asset, you will assume a certain level of risk provided the stakes are high enough. You are a risk-averter. Therefore, you expect to be paid adequately to invest in a chancy proposition. This type of behavior is diagrammed in Figure 1.

On the vertical axis we gauge risk. The higher we edge away from the origin, the greater the risk—that is, the danger of *not* realizing anticipated returns on an asset increases as we travel upwards on the vertical axis.

Various rates of return are measured along the horizontal axis. The farther we move away from the origin (toward the right), the greater the rate of return computed as a percentage of investment.

Assume that point A represents a riskless asset. Without risk, such an asset will extract a low yield, say, 3 percent.[3] An absolutely riskless asset, illustrated in Figure 1, promises a 100 percent guarantee that failure is impossible. We will definitely receive return of original investment.

Point B designates an asset that taps higher income. It encompasses increased risk; that is, the prospect of partial or complete loss rises the higher we move upward in the diagram.

Let us say that the odds are six to one against ever losing invested funds. But the contingency exists. To induce you to invest, you insist upon higher return, say 18 percent, to compensate for services. Because you have assumed risks, providing a service, you must be paid. You may consider 18 percent fair payment under reigning conditions.

Now let us examine Asset C. Asset C lies directly to the left of Asset B. Both Assets B and C match degree of risk. The return on Asset C,

3. The nominal rate of return consists of the real rate plus an allowance for inflation. Because the rate of inflation and, therefore, the interest rate, may be astronomically high by the time you read this book, these rates are meaningless in an example, while the real rate of return tends to stabilize over long periods of time. For example, an 8 percent interest rate and a 5 percent inflation rate produce an actual return of 3 percent; while a 13 percent interest rate coupled with a 10 percent inflationary rate still yields only a 3 percent real return.

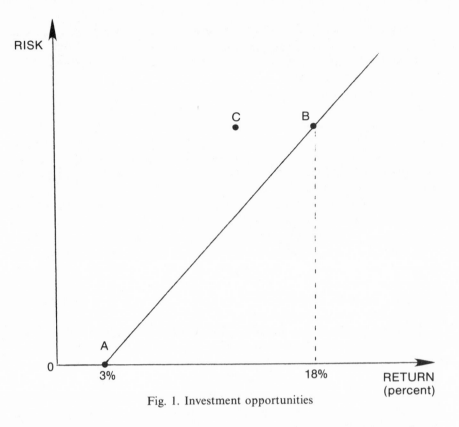

Fig. 1. Investment opportunities

however, is less than the yield on Asset B. You would reject Asset C as an implausible investment. You prefer Asset B. It carries equal risk but annexes a higher rate of return.

In the world of reality, all investments ensphere some magnitude of risk. Most investments are a great deal riskier than the ordinary investor is led to believe. The real financial condition of many corporations is hidden to the ordinary investor through window-dressing, inadequate knowledge about management, inept analysts reporting on the firm's condition, eager brokers responding to their own interests, and just plain fudging of facts.

The risk factor in commodity trading, vis-à-vis other investments, has been vastly overstated and misrepresented. The commodity markets are relatively simple in operation, most competitive in nature, most open in information. The difference between commodity and other markets is sense of time. Profits and losses occur very rapidly. It is like condensing a twenty-four-hour day into five minutes. All activity appears to accelerate.

Another often-repeated myth centers on the belief that all trades are equally risky. First of all, let me point out that risk assumption was the original purpose for creating futures markets. The intention was to shift risk away from the producers and into the hands of speculators. When you purchase a futures contract you have assumed the risk of price fluctuations. However, not every trade carries an equal scale of risk.

As an informed trader, you decide how much risk you are willing to assume. There are, of course, techniques for reducing risks through diversification and straddles, but I am not referring to these methods at present.

For example, let us say that you consider the egg market a volatile one. Your examination of this market suggests that the price of eggs may move upwards by 10¢, but odds are equal that price may move downwards 5¢. You are risking 5¢ to earn 10¢.

In the live hog market you calculate that the price of hogs should rise by 8¢. There is an equal chance price will fall by 2¢. In the second trade you risk 2¢ to acquire an 8¢-per-pound profit. These simple examples illustrate that you can control the extent of risk you are willing to assume.

To this point we have approached the notion of trading and risk assumption on a rational basis. The rational trader carefully analyzes his prospective trades and makes some assumptions about the degree of risk involved. This trader is acting like a winner. He has control over his situation. We presume he has adequate funds to finance his convictions about the future. The loser, on the other hand, takes a bandwagon approach to the market. Let us examine this win-lose attitude over a trading cycle.

Optimists or Pessimists

Ordinarily, a person thinks in terms of buying—never selling. An investor usually looks at the speculative medium from the viewpoint of a buyer. In commodity trading a speculator both buys and sells. Most persons, nevertheless, fail to fully comprehend the rationale behind a short sale.

How can you sell something you do not own? When you buy, you expect to sell when the price is higher. So let us say that you sell when the price is higher and buy when the price is lower. It is the same process but in reverse order. If you do not understand now the process of short-selling, it is unimportant. The mechanics of short sales will be thoroughly covered in another section of the book.

The point here is that most investors think in terms of rising prices and want to buy. We term these persons optimists. They probably account for three-fourths of our population.

By the same token, high-risk-averters greatly outnumber those who express a low aversion to risk. "On the average, low risk averters have larger per capita investment capacities than high ones, mainly due to their much greater success in speculative markets."[4] What effects do these classifications have on commodity markets?

4. Jack J. Hayden, *What Makes You a Winner or a Loser in the Stock and Commodity Markets?* (Larchmont, N.Y.: Investors Intelligence, 1970), p. 15.

Let us lead off by assuming that the general market has been in a downtrend but is now unveiling support buying. It is becoming evident to some analysts that an incipient uptrend may have drawn breath in a particular commodity.

The first group of buyers to initiate trades in this market situation will be professional short-term traders. They reflect a low degree of risk aversion. They are realists. As the upward trend becomes more pronounced, additional buyers enter the picture.

Now optimists with a low aversion to risk inaugurate long positions. As the market continues to bristle, more optimists purchase contracts. The more apparent the rise in prices, the more likely higher-risk-averse optimists will become buyers and support the trend. As prices pitch upwards so do expectations that prices will rise even more.

On the sidelines sit high-risk-averse optimists. They are counting the profits they could have made had they entered the market earlier—Harry Hindsights with 20/20 rear-view vision. Still they hesitate to plunge into a position. They want to be sure. Through all of this price movement they experience deeply emotional sensations. The higher price gyrates, the more their emotions stir. Their state of optimism continues to build.

Finally, this class of speculators reaches a state of optimism sufficiently great to bring them to an emotional decision to enter the market. Expectations run high. The public has been sucked in. In their sleep state they have woven into their web of dreams unrealistic expectations about future riches in order to push themselves across their psychological buying thresholds.

When the general public becomes aware that an upward price trend is in progress, their combined buying power pushes futures prices up very dramatically.[5] At this point earlier buyers sell (or offset) previously purchased contracts. The market is transferred from strong hands to weak hands. Suddenly there are no longer any buyers. Price collapses.

However, some of these extreme optimists are stubborn characters. They may have sold out earlier but buy back into the market again on price dips. In fact, even higher-risk-averse speculators will consider the price retracement an opportunity to buy at "bargain" prices. Because of greed they are afraid to miss out on these bargains.

On the other side, risk-averse pessimists will commence selling contracts short. They enter into short positions. When a downward bent finally gets under way, the swing usually requires less time to complete than the uptrend. More investors tend to be buyers rather than sellers.

Larger profits are more likely generated quickly on the downside by nimble and alert traders. Chartists know these facts. Analysts watch volume, open interest, as well as chart formations. These valuable tools will be discussed early in the book to quickly place in your hands important analytical concepts.

5. See the discussion on "blowoffs," page 119.

Learning to Win

But if you are a nonstarter, these tools will be of limited value. Your emotional state will predominate. You will convince yourself that a trend is not under way until it has nearly reached its peak. You will refuse to accept large profits. You will settle for small profits, and probably incur large losses as well, unless you possess the tremendous self-control needed to override the sterile habits you have developed and rehearsed for many years. Are you a winner?

Now if you are an also-ran, and after reading this book you decide to embark on, or continue, commodity trading, don't blame markets, sources of information, or me for your *faux pas.*

The disease of ineffectualness is already programmed into your psychological patterns. If you are not a champion but sincerely desire to become one, you must rewrite your program to bypass previously learned negative habits.

While you rethink your own situation, examining attitude and aptitude, I will provide an overview of commodity-trading mechanics. By the time you finish perusing the next chapter, you will have decided either to try for big stakes or aim for that $600 cash in the bank at age sixty-five plus a few dollars in social security payments.

CHAPTER 3
The Simplicity of Trading Futures

If you don't panic in commodities once in a while, you don't understand the situation.

—"Nick" Nickerson

ONE OF THE ABLEST ANALYSTS I KNOW HAS BEEN ACTIVELY TRADING commodity futures on his own account for the past seven years. He has forecasted correctly many market moves, on some of which I personally profited. While he has an intuitive feel for the market and usually anticipates changes in trends, his own personal trading record leaves something to be desired.

One day he confided to me: "Everything I've ever done has been easy for me to learn. I've always been successful in every undertaking. I made three-quarters of a million in real estate. But you know, Doc, this is the first thing I've ever tackled that I couldn't completely lick."

Are his personal decisions being thwarted by a mysterious *doppelgänger* or is he just a flibbertigibbet? Later in this chapter I will tell you about the real market bogey. Can you overcome it?

This chapter answers some basic questions about the mechanics of trading. What is a futures contract? How is an order filled, and how long does it take? How often does a speculator trade? What do all those figures mean, and did I earn a profit? Is there any danger of being delivered actuals? Can I limit my losses? After covering these and other points, I will tell you the story of a Chicago recluse named Ishmael and his friend Dionysus.

Tomorrow's Transactions Today

There are sixteen times as many Americans trading in the stock market as the two million who speculate in commodity futures. But these two million transact over $200 billion yearly in contract value—considerably more than the total value of stocks transferred on the New York Stock Exchange.

More than half the commodity transactions are handled on the 125-year-old Chicago Board of Trade and between one-fourth and one-third of trade volume flows through the fifty-four-year-old Chicago Mercantile Exchange. Eleven other commodity exchanges around the country absorb most of the remaining business. (Not all twenty-three licensed commodity exchanges are active.)

Through daily accounting and a system of defense funds, the industry's self-regulation protects the public speculators' funds on deposit. Commodity commission houses must separate customers' assets from their own. Because of these safeguards, effected over the last hundred years, traders do not lose money in commodities due to house failures.

On the other hand, stock commission houses can borrow against margined accounts and use these funds to pay ordinary business debts. When a stock commission house is forced into liquidation, the stock trader fares little better than ordinary creditors. The new government "insurance" fund, Securities Investor Protection Corporation (SIPC), only partially protects some stock traders. Carefully reading the law will verify that commodity traders are better protected, through self-regulation, than stock traders, in spite of so-called government guarantees and regulations.

The SIPC "guarantees" the safety of investment accounts up to $50,000, of which a $20,000 maximum can be in cash. The SIPC does not guarantee profits. Margined accounts are most vulnerable to substantial losses under SIPC-forced sellouts of stocks and bonds. "SIPC officials confirm that margin customers face the possibility of losing their stocks and bonds, receiving the leftover cash instead."[1]

A commodity speculator is not obsessed with owning the cash product. Actuated by price changes in the future, he sniggles, snags, and snares the profits produced by price palpitations. Supporting the futures contract is an actual product.[2] In the commodity futures contract inheres

1. Philip Greer, "Protection Costs Investors," *Atlanta Journal and Constitution*, Oct. 14, 1973, p. 4-E.
2. The term *actuals* signifies commodities on hand, ready for shipment, storage, or manufacture. The term is used in the *spot*, or cash, market.

an agreement to accept delivery if a trader is *long* and to make delivery if he is *short* within a specified time in the future. If the trader does not desire to make or take delivery, then he must *close out* his position prior to delivery date.

Speculators do not make up the only players of the game. If markets existed exclusively for the pleasure of speculators, futures markets would soon disappear as a business tool. The rationale behind commodity markets is to provide a place where producers and purchasers of agricultural, processed, refined, and manufactured products can shift the risk of price fluctuations to risk-takers. Business profits are more easily calculated and business costs anticipated in the presence of these markets. The effect of these markets modifies seasonal price movements and lowers the price of end products to the public.

Farmers, elevator operators, meat packers, exporters, producers and users of silver, copper, lead, zinc, propane, and a number of other products employ these markets to *hedge* their costs and protect their profits. They do not primarily trade futures for the purpose of profiting on price periodicity—and I emphasize the word *primarily*.

Although we retain no interest in hedging operations in this book, you should at least know the meaning of the term. Hedging is a "protective procedure designed to minimize commodity marketing and processing losses that are due to adverse price fluctuations."[3]

While you should recognize that commercial interests figure as a significant element in the market, through careful and thorough study you can gain sufficient expertise to compete with the mightiest. Data are easier to acquire than in most other financial markets, prices are established through an open auction and are immediately disseminated throughout the world, the mechanics of initiating and closing out a trade are simple, and the mechanism functions rapidly.

Trailing a Trade

Having established an account with a broker,[4] suppose that you decide to buy one contract (fifty troy ounces) of platinum. Must you wait until a willing and able seller comes along? If you have set a price very far away from the "going price" of platinum, you may have a long wait. But if the current price is reasonable, you may decide to buy one platinum contract *"at the market."* The order will be executed promptly and at the best possible price the pit broker can obtain.[5]

3. *Understanding the Commodity Futures Markets* (New York: Commodity Research Publications Corp., 1973), p. 19.
4. Information on opening an account will be covered in a subsequent chapter.
5. The term *pit broker* may be misleading because on some commodity exchanges trading actually transpires in a pit comprised of descending steps, while on others trading occurs around rings. Platinum, coffee, and sugar, for example, are traded at rings; see the accompanying photographs of the New York Mercantile Exchange and the New York Coffee and Sugar Exchange.

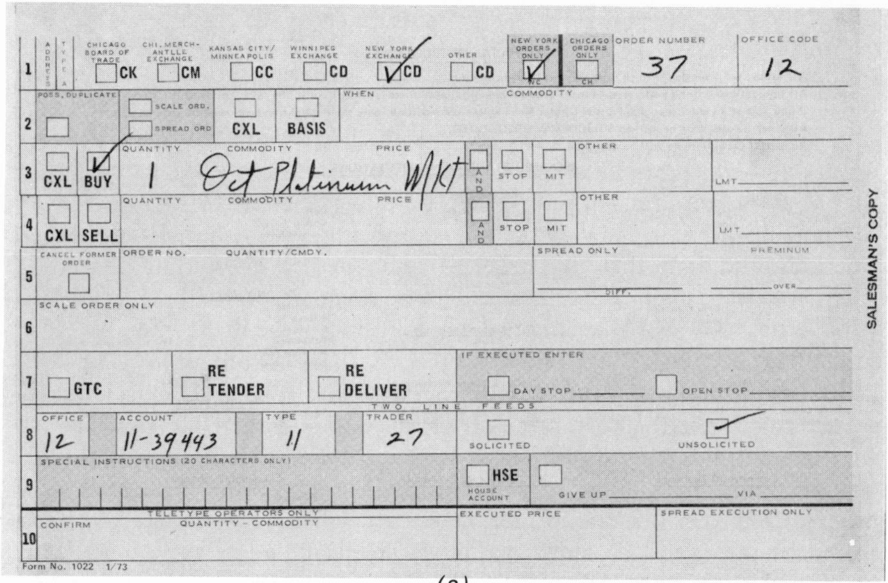

1 ADDRESS TYPE A CHICAGO BOARD OF TRADE CK CHI. MERCH-ANTILE EXCHANGE CM KANSAS CITY/ MINNEAPOLIS CC WINNIPEG EXCHANGE CD NEW YORK EXCHANGE ✓CD OTHER CD NEW YORK ORDERS ONLY ✓ WC CHICAGO ORDERS ONLY CH ORDER NUMBER 37 OFFICE CODE 12
2 POSS. DUPLICATE SCALE ORD. SPREAD ORD CXL BASIS WHEN COMMODITY
3 CXL BUY ✓ QUANTITY 1 COMMODITY Oct Platinum PRICE MKT AND STOP MIT OTHER LMT
4 CXL SELL QUANTITY COMMODITY PRICE AND STOP MIT OTHER LMT
5 CANCEL FORMER ORDER ORDER NO. QUANTITY/CMDY. SPREAD ONLY PREMIUM DIFF. OVER
6 SCALE ORDER ONLY
7 GTC RE TENDER RE DELIVER IF EXECUTED ENTER DAY STOP OPEN STOP
8 OFFICE 12 ACCOUNT 11-39443 TYPE 11 TRADER 27 TWO LINE FEEDS SOLICITED UNSOLICITED ✓
9 SPECIAL INSTRUCTIONS (20 CHARACTERS ONLY) HSE HOUSE ACCOUNT GIVE UP VIA
10 TELETYPE OPERATORS ONLY CONFIRM QUANTITY - COMMODITY EXECUTED PRICE SPREAD EXECUTION ONLY
Form No. 1022 1/73
SALESMAN'S COPY

(a)

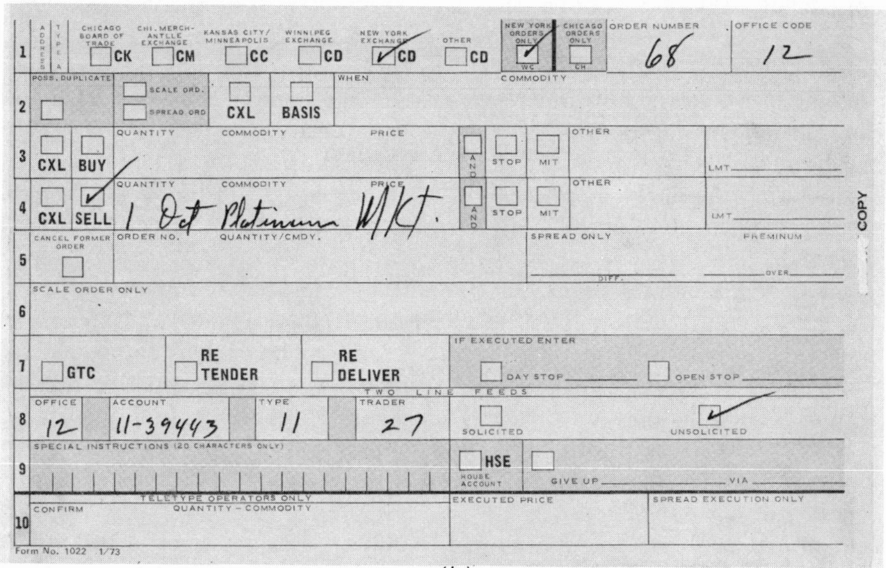

1 ADDRESS TYPE A CHICAGO BOARD OF TRADE CK CHI. MERCH-ANTILE EXCHANGE CM KANSAS CITY/ MINNEAPOLIS CC WINNIPEG EXCHANGE CD NEW YORK EXCHANGE ✓CD OTHER CD NEW YORK ORDERS ONLY ✓ WC CHICAGO ORDERS ONLY CH ORDER NUMBER 68 OFFICE CODE 12
2 POSS. DUPLICATE SCALE ORD. SPREAD ORD CXL BASIS WHEN COMMODITY
3 CXL BUY QUANTITY COMMODITY PRICE AND STOP MIT OTHER LMT
4 CXL SELL ✓ QUANTITY 1 COMMODITY Oct Platinum PRICE MKT. AND STOP MIT OTHER LMT
5 CANCEL FORMER ORDER ORDER NO. QUANTITY/CMDY. SPREAD ONLY PREMIUM DIFF. OVER
6 SCALE ORDER ONLY
7 GTC RE TENDER RE DELIVER IF EXECUTED ENTER DAY STOP OPEN STOP
8 OFFICE 12 ACCOUNT 11-39443 TYPE 11 TRADER 27 TWO LINE FEEDS SOLICITED UNSOLICITED ✓
9 SPECIAL INSTRUCTIONS (20 CHARACTERS ONLY) HSE HOUSE ACCOUNT GIVE UP VIA
10 TELETYPE OPERATORS ONLY CONFIRM QUANTITY - COMMODITY EXECUTED PRICE SPREAD EXECUTION ONLY
Form No. 1022 1/73
COPY

(b)

Fig. 2. Sample orders: *a*, buy; *b*, sell

Let's say that you telephone your broker and request him to "buy one October platinum at the market." He writes out the order on a form similar to the one presented in Figure 2, then reads the order back to you to make sure it has been clearly understood and correctly interpreted.

As soon as you hang up the instrument, he telephones directly to the trading floor. The floor receives a steady stream of futures orders via telephone, wire, letter, and direct contact. (Many commodity commission firms employ direct telephone lines to the floor instead of depending on a wire service, as most stock houses do. The intermediate step means that your broker transmits the order by direct teletype or private wire to the branch office in New York, Chicago, Kansas City, San Francisco, or wherever, and from there the order is telephoned to the trading floor.)

Order clerks man telephones and pass along orders to brokers. When your order has been telephoned to the floor, the desk man (women sometimes are employed) answers the call (see photograph I a). The desk man writes out your request. He asks the *registered representative* (your broker) for the customer's (your) account number. He will then assign another number to the order for quick identification purposes, repeat the entire instruction to your broker for verification, time-stamp the order (notice the time-stamp mechanism on the desk, right side of photo, to record the exact minute the order is received), and then hand a copy of the order to a runner.

On some exchanges, order-desk operation may be diversified to accommodate a larger volume of orders through a division of tasks. On the New York Mercantile Exchange, for example, there are usually at least two clerks at a desk so that if one acts as a runner, the other can watch the phones. The runner scurries to the trading ring (or pit) with your order. In photograph b, runners are approaching the pit brokers; the telephone clerks are at the rear (or upper portion) of the photograph. (Notice that the dark-haired clerk in photograph a is on the fringe of the trading ring in photograph b after handing the broker your order to be executed.)

Since it is a market order, the broker will immediately note prices and will attract the attention of a seller through hand signals[6] and an open outcry. (Photograph I c depicts trading activity.) The trade is completed.

An observer of the New York Mercantile Exchange records the transaction. Notice the data on the chalkboards in the upper portion of photographs I c and I d. Information, transmitted to a computer, the price at which the trade was consummated, will be flashed on screens, tickers, and boards across the country.

If the pit broker is not too busy, he soon notifies a runner of the completed transaction. Within minutes information is telephoned (see photograph I d) to your registered representative. You have bought one contract of platinum.

On the New York Mercantile Exchange, qualified floor traders can trade on the exchange even if they are not members; however, they must be affiliated with a member firm. Members own a seat on the exchange,

6. Palm turned inward denotes buying; outward, selling. See Photograph II for hand signals employed on the Chicago Board of Trade.

but all orders must be processed by a *clearing member*. Clearing members trade and also serve as the financial channel to "clear" trades of nonclearing members.

When selling your platinum, your broker will write out an order on a blank similar to the one shown in Figure 2, and repeat the above operation. Where large numbers of orders are consummated every minute, your one contract will not even make a ripple in the market. In an active month several thousand contracts may change hands daily. Thinner markets do not enjoy this degree of liquidity. If you have earned a profit and want to retrieve your funds, notify your broker. He will contact his accounting office. Funds will be wired or air-mailed the next business day in most cases.

Up, Down, and Sideways

The length of time you remain in the market depends on your objectives, how soon they are met, and your own temperament. You may find it easier to sleep if you are "not in the market" overnight. You may prefer to *day-trade*. To day-trade means to buy and sell the same contract the same day. At day's end you have no market position. Day-trades carry reduced commission.

At the other extreme, you may have deciphered that a long-term trend is under way. In that situation hold, even add to, the position, not taking profits until the trend has distinctly exhausted itself. Several months may elapse before closing out your contracts.

Most capital gains, nearly all capital losses, are short-term ones. It is difficult to establish long-term capital gains in order to take advantage of preferential tax rates. However, in Chapter 19, I will instruct you in techniques to reduce tax liability.

Mostly we have talked about buying. It is pleasanter to think "up." Discerning an uptrend, you will want to buy, or go "long," one or several contracts.

But when the computer calculates profits or losses, it does not distinguish between an original long or short position. It only computes that selling higher than purchase price, your account is credited with profit earned minus commission. Selling at a price lower than the one at which you purchased, the computer debits your account with a loss plus commission charge. You can readily see that it matters not whether you sold first or bought first.

If the price of platinum is backsliding, you will want to sell while the price is still up. You will be *short* the market. Then, when price abates, you will buy a contract to close out, or *offset*, your position. If you sell first, you'll shout with the revolutionary who cried, "Down with up." Buying low and selling high is no different from selling high and buying low. Only the sequence of events differs.

Now if you find that the trend is neither up nor down, as is frequently the case, but prices simply bob sideways in a narrow range, you can still trade for short-term profits. Sideways movement is a tug-of-war between buyers and sellers. Neither group is strong enough to move the market decisively in one direction. Your objective and trading plan will relate to sideways market action. Positions will be held for a short duration. Overall the average transaction probably spans no more than ten days if all trades are taken into account.

Calculation of Profits, Losses, and Costs

Trading frequently will inundate you with paperwork. Confirmation notices are mailed every time a new position, or change in position, has been initiated. When the transaction is closed out, you will receive a statement of purchase and sale. At least once a month you should receive a ledger balance which recounts all open positions, cash in the account, paper profits or losses, and remaining equity. These data are not difficult to decipher.

While each commission house will enlist its own format, all statements provide certain essential information. The statement in Figure 3 states that one contract (10,000 ounces) of July 1973 New York silver, purchased on February 9 at a price of 219.90 (cents per ounce), was sold four days later at 226.00. From a gross profit earned of $610, commission and fees amounting to $45.50 were deducted. The sum of $546.50 was immediately available for withdrawal from the account.

The code letters, right-hand side, register that this notice is a statement of purchase and sale (P), consummated on Commodity Exchange, Inc. (10), a nonregulated transaction (2).

Nonregulated signifies only that certain international commodities, such as cocoa, sugar, silver, and copper, are not under the jurisdiction of the Commodity Exchange Authority. This agency, an arm of the U.S. Department of Agriculture, supervises trade in agricultural commodities, such as grains, red meats, and eggs.

However, nonregulated does *not* connote that careful safeguards and controls are not exercised over merchantry in these commodities. Although the brokerage firm must maintain separate accounts for regulated and nonregulated transactions, the same safety mechanisms for protection of the public speculator still apply.

Two other important impressions must be intromitted into this introductory chapter: (1) taking or making delivery of the physical product, and (2) range of daily price fluctuations and limitations on losses.

Fifty Tons of Sugar on Your Front Lawn

The scene: Breakfast table at Harley Hoodwink's hovel; wife is returning to the table after answering the telephone.

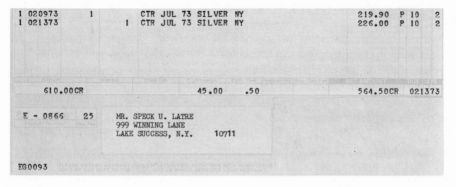

```
1 020973      1              CTR JUL 73 SILVER  NY              219.90  P 10   2
1 021373          1          CTR JUL 73 SILVER  NY              226.00  P 10   2



   610.00CR                           45.00    .50              564.50CR  021373


E - 0866    25      MR. SPECK U. LATRE
                    999 WINNING LANE
                    LAKE SUCCESS, N.Y.   10711


EG0093
```

Fig. 3. Customer confirmation of a trade

"Who was that, dear?"

"Something about delivering your sugar. It sounded like he said fifty tons, but I suppose he meant fifty pounds. What are you going to make with all that sugar?" Silence. Harley's contorted face alternately semaphores splotches of bright pink and cigar-ash gray. "You don't look well today, dear! Maybe you should stay home from the office and rest. You've been working too hard lately!"

"No, dear, the man is right. He's delivering fifty tons of sugar," Harley squeaks. "I forgot to sell out that sugar contract I bought two months ago. Quick, get on the phone and call all your friends, clubs, the church, and all the grocers in town. If it rains on all that sugar tonight, grass may never grow again on our front lawn!"

From time to time, this genre of literature pops up in print. Then the author says, "Ho, ho, ho. Did I ever put one over on you—the reader." Perhaps writing it bolsters the author's ego, but, friend, he is not granting you any favors. Your money may be a big joke for him, but it is certainly a serious matter for you. The sequence of events does not evolve exactly like the above story taken from *Fanny's Funny Fables and Other Sadistic Jokes*, but delivery can take place if you do not carefully note the expiration dates and first delivery dates of the option month in which you are trading.

Approximately 98 percent of contracts are offset prior to the time when delivery must be made or accepted. Buyers who want to accept the physical product are either in the cash business or have already established channels where they can profitably dispose of products. (An exception may be individuals who want to take possession of a precious metal, coins, or currency.) For the average trader, however, the best advice is not to speculate in the delivery month since you may wind up owning a commodity you know little about. And delivery requires immediate cash payment for the physical product!

Even producers and commercial interests have their proportion of perplexities. I once discussed imbroglios of accepting actual delivery with a former onion-grower who hedged onion futures (prior to 1954). He charged that government inspectors were bribed. Contract specifications are carefully defined; but if inspectors certify the product as better or worse than contract grade, it will sell at a premium or discount to the standard grade defined in the futures contract.

This particular grower told me that when he shipped only top-grade, carefully packed onions, price would be discounted because they "failed" to measure up to contract standards. However, when he accepted delivery, a large share of onions were rotten and not even consumable.

Whether his charge of bribery is well founded is not at issue. There *is* enough market action in later option months for even the wildest speculator. Dealing in actuals or cash market bunkers is a separate game with its own sand traps. Avoid the pitfall of trading in delivery months. Leave that action to full-time professionals.

More Horror Stories

A favorite story parroted by the weak and meek concerns the trader who was *locked in* the market and could not curtail his accumulating losses because of successive limit-down days. His deficits totaled $7 million. He committed suicide. Aside from the fact that he had violated several basic, common-sense trading rules, the question raised pivots on whether a trader can actually limit losses. Is it possible to have a situation where there are all sellers, no buyers, or the reverse case of all buyers and no sellers?

In the first place, there are limits within which daily prices can fluctuate. Established by various exchanges these delimitations are infrequently changed in tranquil markets. (Request current information before trading.)

For example, the New York Coffee and Sugar Exchange restricts price movement of sugar to 1¢ (100 points) from the previous day's closing price. Intraday, price can move down 1¢, then 2¢ up, always 1¢ of previous day's settlement price.

Each point in a sugar contract equals $11.20. At the extreme one contract can change $1120 in value from the previous day's settlement price. To pour balm on emotional price gyrations, these imposed boundaries allot speculators an overnight opportunity to reassess market fundamentals. (Photograph 3 is a picture of the "Sugar Ring.")

Most contracts in which you will probably trade are permitted a maximum change in value of roughly $500-$1,500 a day. Prices do not normally bounce by such large amounts.

On the Chicago Board of Trade, corn prices may ebb and flow 10¢ either way, $500 per five thousand bushels. On the Chicago Mercantile

Exchange, the price of pork bellies may vary up or down by 1½¢ per pound, $540 per contract of thirty-six thousand pounds.

On the Commodity Exchange, Inc., New York, copper can gyrate 5¢ from previous closing price, $1,250 per contract of twenty-five thousand pounds.[7] On the New York Mercantile Exchange, daily limit for Maine potatoes is $250 per contract of fifty thousand pounds. Of course, no limits are imposed on cash prices. Frequently limits are lifted during the last days of a contract's life.

Suppose you have purchased a contract of something. Quickly and precipitously prices wheel about. Are you stuck with a big loss? Transacting in copper, each day the market locks limit-down (i.e., no trading takes place at that price), defeat scores $1,250 daily per contract until the price descends sufficiently to attract buyers into the market. Usually, after a few days, trading ensues; you will be able to "get out of the market." The time span may endure only a couple of days.

What usually occasions, however, is that while *closing price* may be limit-down several consecutive days, *intraday trading does occur*. The typical mismanager of funds, nevertheless, will not utilize this opportunity to admit to miscarriage and stand aside for a period.

The typical blunderhead will helplessly forfeit funds, wishing for a price turnaround, because he cannot say, "Well, I made a mistake. It's better to take a small loss now and try again later."

The fumbler perseveres with the position. He chants an entirely different chorus to justify misfortune. In fact, he may become so enamored with his setback that he harps on his "hard-luck" story of how the market took money away from him. He brags in his bereavement. "The market was limit-down ten days in a row. I was losing $1,000 a day." Certainly it closed limit-down for ten days, but during eight of those days he could have curtailed his losses.

For example, when December live cattle last year reached a peak of 61¢, continued heavy buying was anticipated with the impending withdrawal on September 12 of the price freeze on beef. The market collapsed. Several limit-down days trotted out. By the time price had dropped to 58¢ on the third day, market weakness was apparent.

Considerable trading did occur on the third day. A trader with a long position could have sold out that day with a total decrement of $1,000-$1,200 per contract, even if he had bought a contract near the market's top. He would have sacrificed only his original security deposit (margin money). If that much thrashing takes bread off the table, he should not have been speculating.

7. Effective July 1, 1974, the International Monetary Market offered a half-sized copper contract (ticker symbol CR) of 12,500 pounds. Trading limit is 5¢, or $625 per contract. After two consecutive limit-up days, limit is raised to 7½¢ on the third day, to 10¢ on the fourth consecutive day. At date of writing, the London Metal Exchange anticipates reducing copper contracts from twenty-five metric tons to twenty-five thousand pounds.

Now let's examine an extreme case. Suppose, being short wheat, price is locked limit-up every day. It is impossible to buy wheat contracts to offset your position and unmoor losses. What can be done?

An astute trader will try to buy in another market. Wheat is traded in Chicago, Minneapolis, and Kansas City. (Photographs of the Kansas City Board of Trade appear further along in the book.) Although the product is not identical, hedge may not be perfect, failures may be quartered or quarantined or even completely unfrocked.

Another method: contract an opposite position in the product of a commodity, or a related or substitute good. Assume that instead of speculating in wheat you are in a losing pork belly trade. Try buying live hog contracts. Being related, the two markets tend to roll imperfectly together.

With international commodities, such as sugar, silver, or cocoa, for example, it may be possible to take an opposite position in a London market. Arranging a foreign-order execution, a relatively simple matter, is justified when the situation calls for immediate action. These cases are rare. They are not the rule. If you believe otherwise, you have been misled. Nevertheless, with the possibility not altogether ruled out, alternatives exist. Smart money knows these avenues of retreat.

In spite of all the misleading tales and horror stories you have heard, none of them ever once mention the real market bogey. All books focus on trading mechanics, the exchanges insist that the public be properly informed on the risk of losing money, but not one of them ever hints at the real *doppelgänger* or flibbertigibbet. The following story illustrates the point.

The Flea That Became a Lion

It is rumored that on Riverside Drive in Chicago there resides a recluse by the name of Ishmael. He lives alone with his personal ticker and spends his days scanning and scrutinizing the symbols on the ticker tape. His only companion is a flea with whom he has made friends. He calls the flea Dionysus.

One day a fat cat passes by. Dionysus jumps on his back. The cat mercilessly scratches at his pelt. He deals the flea a tremendous blow. The flea flees to his friend for protection.

It so happens that Ishmael had studied under a sanyasi during his worldwide travels and had become somewhat of a thaumaturgist himself. He looks down at the flea and grumbles: "I'm tired of you running to me every time you get into trouble. Can't you see I'm busy with more important matters? You'll have to learn to protect yourself." Then, with a swish of his straight-edge, a presto, and a shazam, he changes the flea into a cat.

The flea that became a cat no longer has to flee from his new furry friends. He is now their equal. He is as big as they. But one day, Dionysus, the flea that became a cat, encounters a dog. The dog, in hot pursuit, chases the cat back to Ishmael's place, with one leap the cat lands in Ishmael's lap. In fact, he rips the ticker tape Ishmael is holding in his hand. The tape parts between EF and LHG.[8]

"Now listen," growls Ishmael, "I don't have time for your insignificant problems." Then with a swish, a presto, and a shazam, he transmutes the cat into a dog. Not only is he a big dog in the neighborhood, Dionysus now also possesses the power to chase fat cats that dare challenge him.

In spite of his new circumstances, he still lacks the respect he craves. The neighbors know the real truth. They malign, "Don't pay any attention to him. He's only a flea that became a dog." Of course, Dionysus knows that people ridicule him. He tries hard to ignore the gossip.

One afternoon, after Ishmael finishes studying his commodity charts, he and Dionysus go for a walk around the zoo. Being egocentric, the dog wanders too close to the lion's cage. With a swipe of his paw, the lion draws blood on Dionysus's hind leg. Yelping and whimpering, with tail between legs, he scampers to his friend and benefactor.

By this time Ishmael is thoroughly irritated with Dionysus. "I'm going to solve your problems once and for all time," he admonishes sternly. With a swish, a presto, and a shazam, he transforms Dionysus into a lion.

No creature was ever more enraptured with his own self-importance. Everywhere he paraded he would assert, "Look at me. I'm king of the ring and wit of the pit!"

But the neighbors know the truth. They all deride him. "Don't worry about that lion," they laugh. "He can't hurt you. He's only a flea that thinks he's a lion."

Finally, no longer able to bear the humiliation, Dionysus concludes that if he can rid himself of Ishmael, the one who has each time made him successively bigger and more powerful, his only remaining problem will be solved. He awaits his opportunity to corner Ishmael. When the proper moment arrives he leaps at Ishmael with the intent of eliminating him with his powerful muscles. The recluse senses what is happening and with a swish, a presto, and a shazam, he changes Dionysus back again into a flea.

The market can elevate the messenger or porter to high financial status, but it also possesses the power to humble the mightiest. The humbling power of the market makes the speculator tremble with fear and demands respect from the most successful.

Most traders lose in this market because of fear of loss. Fear paralyzes the decision-making process. Fear causes even the most brilliant to doubt his abilities and to trade from the wrong side of the market.

What do most traders fear losing? Most of them are convinced it is their money they fear to squander. It is not money but the ego which is exposed. We all accept losses nearly every day: an overpriced gift, a bad

8. EF and LHG are ticker tape symbols for January eggs and February live hogs.

buy, spoiled fruit at the bottom of the basket, the contents of the can failing to live up to the label, a seemingly jinxed lawn mower, and so forth.

We live with all these mistakes and probably never think about them a third or fourth time. We do not suffer mortification if someone cons us into buying an unneeded engine tune-up, or a package vacation tour that turns into a nightmare. But nowhere in our material world do we come nearer to facing ourselves than we do in trading commodity futures. A speculator, like a frontiersman, either learns to defend himself or is destroyed by a vicious bear, or like the matador who steps the wrong way, he is gored by the bull.

The market is as much a test of an individual's mettle as it is a test of his skills. This book will teach you something about the skills you can develop; the rest depends upon you. Now, my friend, if you are prepared to become an initiate, let's get down to specifics.

SECTION B

Forecasting for Profits

CHAPTER 4
Charting the Future
for Profits

The thing that hath been, it is that which shall be; and that which is done is
that which shall be done: and there is no new thing under the sun.

—Ecclesiastes 1:9

I PREFER TO ENTERTAIN WITH STORIES AND GENERALITIES. BUT IF
you intend to deal in futures successfully, then nothing less than hard
work will suffice initially. The next five chapters, devoted to discovering
basic technical tools, are followed by four introductory chapters on market
fundamentals.

If you elect to skip hard work and opt to put theory into practice, then
hedgehop to Chapter 13. I really do not care how you read this book.
Dash through it if you wish. Dabble around if you are the nervous type.
Donate it to the local branch of the public library if you feel charitable. Or
trade without ever bothering to study and lose all of your money. After
all, it is *your* money. You have a right to dispose of it as you desire.

Seeds of the Past

A study of commodities begins by recording daily action, because daily
action registers the activities of thousands of persons. It summarizes
their inhibitions, lunacies, expertise, analytical abilities, financial objectives, and everything else that enters into a decision to buy or sell. Not

theory—not what they *may* do under different conditions—it replays how they acted in actual real-life conditions of the now.

A study of market action is not a dissertation on prices and demand and number of cows in feedlots—these things only outwardly reflect the thoughts and conduct of people. A study of market action is an investigation of people interacting in the general market. Since we cannot insert people into test tubes to research their psychological behavior in a laboratory, we can only use proxies. Prices provide a means to measure the results of people's reactions, so let us begin where we can.

Predictions of Tomorrow

Will charting past price behavior lead a trader to accurately forecast future price action? One extreme view says yes. The trends established yesterday will likely continue in the same direction tomorrow. The other extreme asserts that price is determined by logical and illogical inter-actions of buyers and sellers now, not by history.

Futures prices are tomorrow's prices today. Price charts are pictographs of the struggle between sellers and buyers. Recognizing that events occur neither accidentally nor in isolation, that a certain historical periodicity plagues the pursuit of human pleasures, technical tools furnish excellent timing devices.

Generally, the direction or trend of the market is determined through fundamental analysis—through a study of the factors that affect demand and supply over relatively long intervals of time. Picking the day and hour to originate an actual trade is best accomplished through the application of technical devices. Chartists essentially observe technical aspects of the market.

Certain chart formations reappear at frequent enough intervals so that their structures are well known. The balance of this chapter will introduce you to these formations on actual charts which have not necessarily been picked for clearest representation. Contrived diagrams usually manifest differently from real cases. Bar-chart analysis will haunt this chapter and the next; reversal-chart analysis the one following.

Bar charts may be purchased or constructed on either an arithmetic or a ratio scale. (While ratio-scale charts are superior, for simplicity, all charts contained herein are on an arithmetic scale.) On the vertical axis in Figure 4, prices are mapped; on the horizontal axis only trading days are logged. Omit weekends and holidays to avoid gaps in the chart. Note the high and low daily price for the commodity, and mark a vertical line on the chart covering the distance between extreme prices of the day. Register the closing price with a short horizontal line intersecting the vertical one. Bar charts can be constructed on a daily basis for maximum detail, or weekly for less detail, or even monthly for continuation charts. All charts here are daily ones; these are the types with which you will be mostly working.

Secrets of the Formations

The purpose of probing known patterns is to aid in determining when a trend reversal takes its first breath of life. In the next chapter I will discuss trends, but let us launch our inquiry into some reversal patterns important in short-term and intermediate trend analysis beginning with the M or W formations, also known as *double tops* or *bottoms* and *triple bottoms* or *tops*.

An *M formation*, arising at the end of an intermediate up-movement, such as the one in Figure 4, unfolds when a commodity treks to a high level, retreats appreciably, then returns to the level of the first peak before finally turning downward for a major decline.

The first advance, consistent with expectations, is accompanied by higher volume (more about volume in Chapter 8), which tells us that new buyers are coming into the market at a rate faster than older buyers are closing out their positions and taking profits. When the market loses its momentum—the number of buyers is exceeded by sellers—the price falls back.

The break in price presents a second "opportunity" to buy the commodity at lower prices. The strong demand of new buyers again propels the price upward to match the previous high. At this point many short-term traders will take profits at the level of the old high; but should the old high be significantly penetrated, negating the double top, these same traders will reinitiate their positions.

At the second high, a double top is formed. Volume frequently is lower at this second top than at the first one. Increased profit-taking suggests that more positions are being closed out than new ones being instituted until the selling pressure overwhelms the bulls and price softens. Mani-

Fig. 4. Double-top formation (Source: Commodity Research Bureau, Inc., One Liberty Plaza, New York, N.Y. 10006.)

festing impotence, buying power cannot loft prices decisively into higher ground. Subsequently, support on the bottom side is broken when prices penetrate the area of the previous low, the valley formed by the middle part of the *M*.

At the other end of the scale, a *double bottom* incarnates like the letter *W*. Prices descend to form the left side of the *W*, then attempt to rally under renewed buying, but slump on low trading volume again to *test* the previously formed bottom. If prices recoil, after the second bottom, on increasing volume, above the previous high formed by the middle section of the *W*, the bottom has been successfully proved (see Figure 5). However, if prices do not surpass the previous near-term high, together with increasing volume, then the market may try a third test to fashion a triple bottom.

A *triple bottom,* similar in appearance to the *M* formed at the top, materializes less frequently in intermediate and long-term trends. It may pop up often during periods of consolidation. (They are especially prevalent in reversal charts, discussed in Chapter 6.) The third bottom, most likely, will be accompanied by low volume. The conclusive test is that the bottom support area endures; prices thrust through the previously established high; volume of contracts and open interest also pick up.

A *triple top,* forming a *W* at trend's top, is similar in characteristic to the double top—actually a triple bottom turned upside down. Triple tops cannot be anticipated. The third time a top is tested, price may catapult into higher ground; the triple top will look more like a double bottom as the original long-term trend peregrinates upward.

Fig. 5. Double-bottom formation (Source: Commodity Research Bureau, Inc., One Liberty Plaza, New York, N.Y. 10006.)

Direction of the Triangles

Even during its formation, a double top or bottom is not easily distinguishable. It may really be a large triangle. During its formation an *ascending triangle* (Figure 6) resembles a double top. Each time price rises to a certain level, sellers close out positions. Prices decline. However, in the distribution process, strength of buyers heaves prices up anew to the same level. Once more selling takes place. But strong demand prevents prices from reacting as low as previously. *De novo* they rebound. As it becomes evident that bottom prices are trending upwards, more new buyers are attracted. Finally prices slam through the tops.

By definition, an ascending triangle consists of a horizontal top extremity and ascending, or rising, bottom edge, which slopes upward to form an apex with the horizontal portion. An ascending triangle "predicts" probable direction of prices on breakout. Volume should pick up

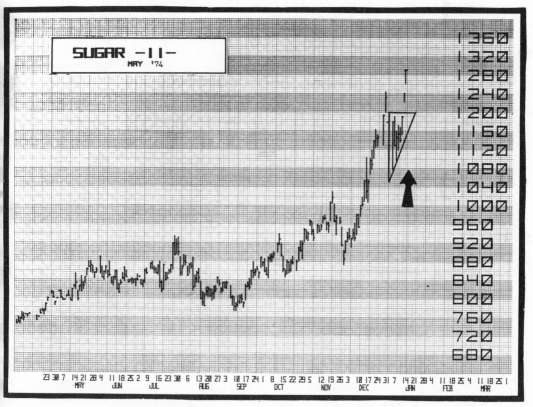

Fig. 6. Ascending triangle (Source: Commodity Perspective, 956 Hillcrest Road, Elgin, Ill. 60120.)

on each rally as the apex is neared. If it does not rise on the breakout, then you will want to reevaluate your evaluation of the formation. It may not even be a triangle but only a figment of an overactive imagination!

A *descending triangle* (Figure 7) points toward the opposite direction. Its lower boundary is horizontal; the upper confine falls toward the apex. It portends a breakout on the downside. Market conditions countervail those creating an ascending triangle. Obviously selling forces predominate. Successive rallies exhibit weakness as lower highs evince. Of various consolidation patterns mentioned in this chapter, these last two are most reliable; namely, in an uptrend, the ascending triangle is the most reliable pattern to follow, while in a downturn, the descending triangle is the most reliable.

By this time you may have observed that prices generally move sideways during formation of these various chart patterns. During creation of these patterns, competition between buyers and sellers prevails until one group or another dominates and establishes the direction of price movement. When prices undulate in one direction, then crab-walk horizontally, this interruption in trend signals a period of *consolidation*—either a period of reaccumulation in an uptrend or one of redistribution in a downtrend. Or the top formation identifies a reversal pattern, the termination of a trend, an area of distribution. Or a bottom formation, also a reversal pattern, underscores an area of accumulation. Further comments on *congestion* areas—that is, sideways price movement—are forthcoming in the next chapter.

Triangles generally develop as a consolidation pattern—that is, a temporary interruption in the trend—but on occasion develop at major trend junctures signaling a reversal. The last triangle reviewed, the *symmetrical triangle* (Figure 8), is sketched to consist of converging downward-sloping and upward-sloping boundary lines; namely, an acute triangle. This pattern has also been contextually depicted as a *coil*.

As the apex is approached, over time, the trading range narrows, and, like a coil spring being wound tighter and tighter, prices finally snap through the confines of the triangle. Trading volume tends to diminish as the apex is approached and then accelerates sharply as prices spring away. Unfortunately, the formation itself gives no clue as to the ultimate direction of the big leap.

Even after prices break out, there is always the possibility of a false move and deceit not discovered until after some losses have accumulated. No chart formation is completely reliable. With this one, and all others, seek confirmation from other indicators.

Closely related to triangles are *flags* and *pennants*. Flags unfurl frequently in certain commodities and are important in reversal-chart analysis, discussed in Chapter 6. A flag formation—a small, compact parallel-

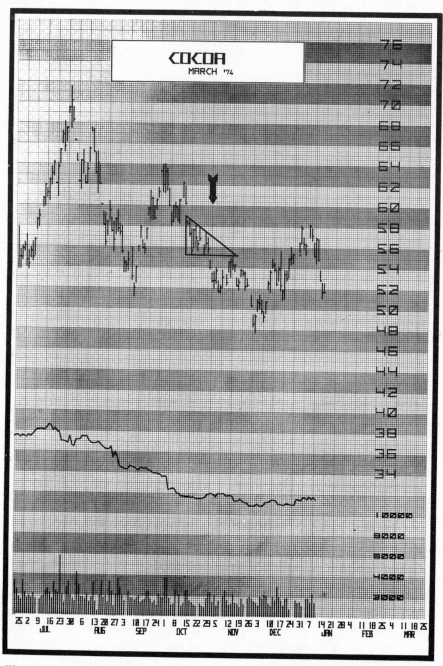

Fig. 7. Descending triangle (Source: Commodity Perspective, 956 Hillcrest Road, Elgin, Ill. 60120.)

Fig. 8. Symmetrical triangle (Source: Commodity Perspective, 956 Hillcrest Road, Elgin, Ill. 60120.)

ogram on the end of a long pole—implies that the pattern evolutes after precipitous market action. A pennant resembles a small, symmetrical triangle on the end of a pole but with two of its sides slanted in the same direction (see Figures 9 and 10).

Both of these formations tilt in a direction opposite to the general trend. These patterns tend to form rather quickly and are fairly easy to recognize with a little practice. After a steep movement upward, prices consolidate to form a flag within a narrow price range. Usually the flag points downward. The breakout on the upside continues in the direction of the trend already in progress. In a downtrend the flag rests upside down. The mast extends *above* the flag; the flag itself points upward. When prices break through, the downtrend will remain intact.

No important differences reign between a flag and a pennant. The pennant's boundary lines converge, while the flag's lines tend to remain equidistant. They usually slant downward in an up-market, upward in a down-market; in other words, both are half-mast patterns and are characteristic of sharp moves.

Fig. 9. Flag pattern (Source: Commodity Perspective, 956 Hillcrest Road, Elgin, Ill. 60120.)

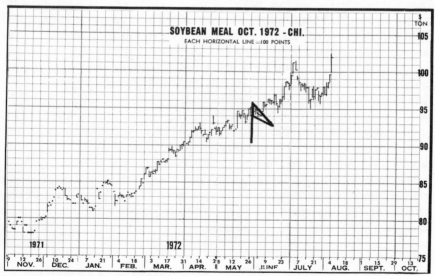

Fig. 10. Pennant pattern (Source: Commodity Research Bureau, One Liberty Plaza, New York, N.Y. 10006.)

Message of the Reversal Patterns

In addition to ascending and descending triangles and flags, an important and tricky formation, the *V*, exists in both an upright and an inverted form. Tricky because it is one-half of an *M* or *W*, the *V* pattern means that the trend has suddenly reversed without warning or time enough to take early advantage of change. When it is first molded, the natural tendency is to wait, to determine whether the bottom *(V-formation)* or top *(inverted-V)* will be again tested to sculpt a double bottom or top. Instead of giving the speculator a "second chance," the new trend emerges directly from a single bottom or top (see Figure 11).

The *V*, probably more typical than the inverted *V* (although the latter sprang up frequently during 1973), predominates in emotional markets. Also residing in combination with flat bottom patterns, it is not always readily singled out as an integrated structure.

The *flat bottom*, also known as the *dormant bottom*, a flat extended bottom shape, shown in Figure 12, represents a long, inactive period in the palladium market. A combination may originate with a *V* followed by a long flat period of inactivity. The opposite, where the *V* presents itself after an inactive period, tricks the investor into believing that prices are headed downward, that the formation was not really a flat bottom one. Then activity suddenly vivifies. Prices zip in the other direction—upward. When prices zip, the unaware investor gets zapped.

Accompanied by a low volume of activity, the structure arises in thinly traded markets. The few buyers and sellers resist allowing price to move far in either direction. This state of affairs can continue for some time.

Similar to the flat bottom arrangement, the *rounded bottom*, also known as a *bowl* or *saucer* model, depicts a fairly long struggle between buyers and sellers until predominance of buyers determines the trend direction. A rounded bottom appears in Figure 13. *Rounded tops*, also referred to as *inverted bowls,* are quite uncommon.

One difficulty with rounded bottoms: as they wend their way around, a spurt of buying activity over several days may give the impression that the long-awaited uptrend has commenced. Afterwards, prices will drop back to approximately the same level. In Figure 13, September corn erupted in a premature burst during the second half of December. Price abated and did not reach a comparable level until April's end—four months later. These eruptions can tempt an eager trader.

The most celebrated layout, *head and shoulders*, is usually cited as most common, either because, in fact, it does appear with a certain regularity, or because chartists have extremely active imaginations which have been programmed to identify every third assortment as H & S. We will begin with an H & S top illustrated in Figure 14, an intermediate swing in copper.

Composition of the left shoulder, accompanied by a strong rally climaxing an extensive advance, is then followed by a brief price relapse.

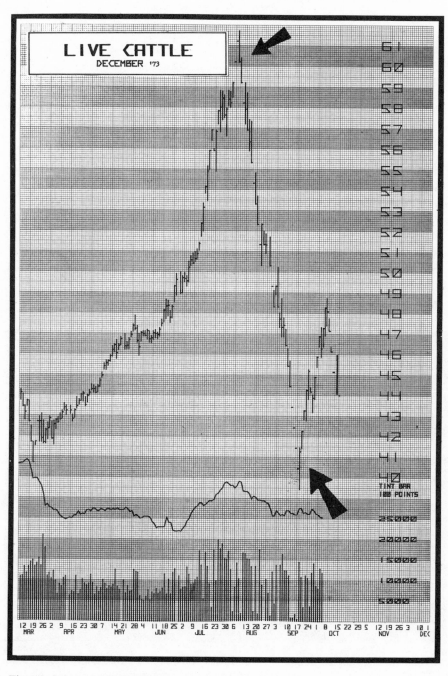

Fig. 11. Inverted-V and V- formations (Source: Commodity Perspective, 956 Hill-crest Road, Elgin, Ill. 60120.)

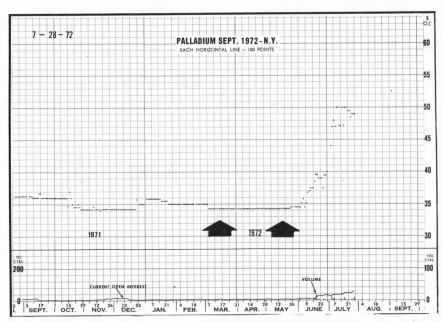

Fig. 12. Flat bottom (Source: Commodity Research Bureau, Inc., One Liberty Plaza, New York, N.Y. 10006.)

Fig. 13. Rounded bottom (Source: Sibbet-Hadady Publications Incorporated, 380 East Green Street, Financial Building, Suite 200, Pasadena, Calif. 91101.)

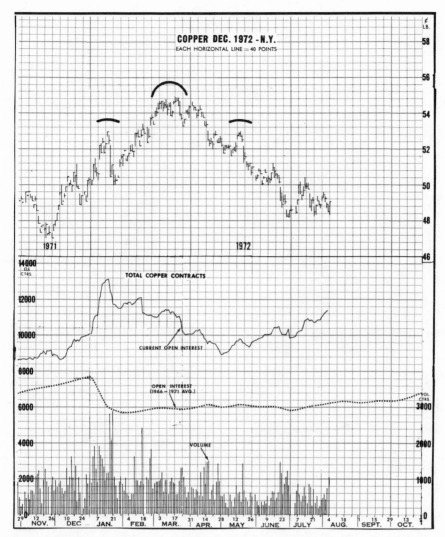

Fig. 14. Head and shoulders top (Source: Commodity Research Bureau, Inc., One Liberty Plaza, New York, N.Y. 10006.)

When the next rally surpasses the highest price of the left shoulder and molds the head portion, an even sharper retreat ensues. In the ideal H & S specimen, the second reversion will approximately match the dip which silhouetted the left shoulder. The third rally fails to touch the high head price. Prices wane; the right shoulder is sculpted.

A touted feature of the H & S pattern is its *neckline*, or, as Anthony Reinach properly calls it, an *upper chestline*. The neckline, or upper chestline, derived by drawing a line across the bottoms of valleys on

71

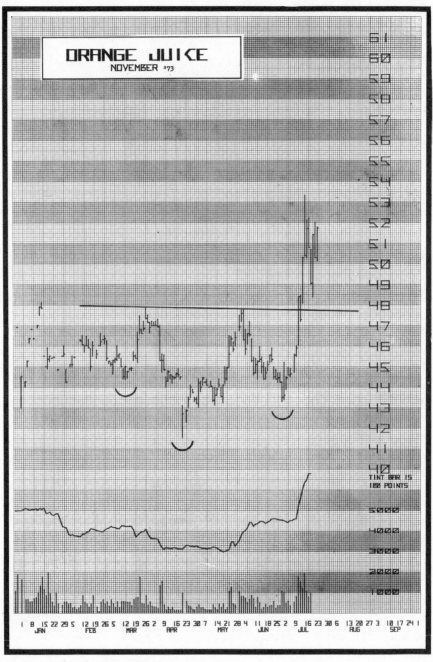

Fig. 15. Head and shoulders bottom (Source: Commodity Perspective, 956 Hillcrest Road, Elgin, Ill. 60120.)

either side of the head, is extended to the right. After shaping the right shoulder, breaking through this upper chestline confirms the downtrend.

A difficulty in authenticating an H & S pattern, the large number of mutations provide fertile ground for the (ch)artist. The freakish offspring may exhibit two left shoulders or four shoulders altogether, a little head, or it may be hunchbacked, be afflicted with partial paralysis, display shoulder-droop, or have shoulders clear up to its ears. Quite a few variations, therefore, exist. Reinach has classified twenty-seven clear-cut possibilities.

The H & S reversal pattern also surfaces after major declines. The H & S bottom, simply an inverted top, stands on its head (see Figure 15). The left shoulder unravels after an extensive tumble followed by minor price revival. The next descent, even sharper, carries price lower than the previous valley. Then price rebounds to the peak fashioned by the left shoulder. This second reaction and rally frame the head. The right shoulder is created by a third price dip which fails to equal the decline of the head portion. As prices revivify and penetrate the upper chestline, volume, too, picks up in the accompanying breakout.

These schematisms also loom during consolidation periods. As a reversal prototype they are reliable if they can be properly branded. Not infrequently, traders will anticipate the final formation of an H & S pattern and initiate positions before the breakout is confirmed. A false move, or unconfirmed breakout, will cost the speculator some dough. An alternative plan, waiting for definite confirmation, means foregoing some potential profits. As they say, half a bagel is better than a hole in the middle.

This chapter has introduced you to some basic and most common patterns sought by chartists. Their formation reveals struggle between buyers and sellers; the direction of the trend hinges on the stronger group. As you become more interested in the sport of charting, adeptness will depend upon considerable practice, careful scrutiny of quantities of charts, then more study. Other aspects of chart-reading include trend analysis and significance of gaps—both of which are adumbrated in the next chapter.

CHAPTER 5
More Charting for More Profits

No man who is correctly informed as to the past will be disposed to take a morose view of the present.

—Thomas Macaulay

THE PATTERNS SURVEYED IN THE PREVIOUS CHAPTER ARE CONGESTION areas; that is, structures forged when prices do not decidedly dance in one direction or another. What succeeds before, during, and after a price movement? At the bottom of a cycle buyers are *accumulating* positions in anticipation of an upswing. This period of acquisition may be rather protracted in the case of rounded bottoms. However, when there is sufficient optimism to impel prices across the Rubicon, a trend is born.

After a rapid ascent prices may retreat somewhat during a *consolidation* period. Further consolidation may persevere after the regression, or prices may spurt quickly upwards again without sculpting much congestion detail. This plateau is an ordered sequence of *reaccumulation*. The chart may evince considerable "work"—a wide expanse of consolidation—or practically none.

At the top of an advance, patterns of *distribution* churn out as profit-takers close out trades, uninformed newcomers buy, and bears establish short positions. On the way down, further regions of consolidation, or *redistribution*, spawn as the market adjusts to new prices. These congestion zones are probed by technicians to prognosticate the trend likely to emerge from the arena of sidewise price action.

With knobs still on bar-chart analysis, trends, gaps, and further trading advice will dominate the pages of this chapter.

When Is a Trend a Trend?

In commodity trading fewer losses will sprout if a trader can determine the direction of the trend, stay on the right side of it while trading, and stand aside during transition periods. Simple advice? Yes! Can't anyone see whether the drift is up or down? Yes, but . . . The closer you focus on your charts, the narrower your time horizon, and the greater your predilection for trying to pick tops and bottoms, the harder it is to see the forest for the trees.

Trends are of three types: *uptrend, downtrend,* and *sideways trend.* Within the major, or primary, trend pulsate intermediate-term trends and short-term, or minor, trends. Profits accrue by identifying the trend, staying with it as long as possible, and exiting when it has ended. Minor trends in commodities will usually endure only a few days before there is a small technical correction. The duration of longer swings varies widely.

To draw a *trend line*, and project it into the near-term future, requires concatenating at least two points. To locate an incipient uptrend, pin down two bottom reversal points. The interesting feature of this method is that the line drawn along a straight-edge tends to define the support level of prices as they make headway upward (refer to Figure 16).

When first drawing trend lines on your charts, sketch them in lightly with a No. 3 pencil and extend them about a week forward until they are technically justified. It is interesting to observe the validity of a long-run trend line and the frequency with which intervening price swings approach to a point of tangency and then parry without penetrating it. This phenomenon happens so often that a correctly inscribed trend line is an extremely valuable technical tool.

Initially, however, it may be necessary to cast several test-lines on the chart until sufficient action verifies the limits of an intermediate-term, and eventually a longer-term, trend line. The more often bottoms recur along the trend line, the greater is its technical importance. If a trend line has been tested repeatedly, the more likely the direction has permanently reversed after a trend line is ultimately gapped.

When a trend line is drawn rather steeply, I tend to be skeptical of its validity. Usually I end up retracing it along a flatter plane. The steeper the direction line, of course, the more easily sideways movement can honeycomb it. On the other hand, if trading activity materializes considerably above the trend line, then prices must move a substantial dis-

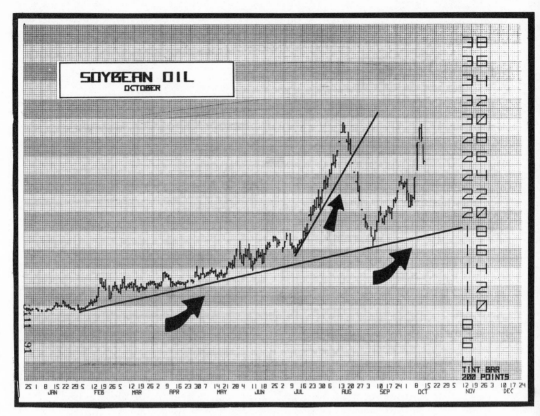

Fig. 16. Uptrend (Source: Commodity Perspective, 956 Hillcrest Road, Elgin, Ill. 60120.)

tance downward to traverse it and signal permutation in the mainstream of prices.

Reversal of a trend can also be matched with a topping formation—for example, head and shoulders. Penetration of the trend line and upper chestline, a double-chart confirmation of direction shift, attests to the need for an examination of other indicators and factors.

Once prices take a header through the uptrend line, the advance has expired. At an appropriate time a downtrend line can be drawn. Downtrend lines are determined somewhat differently. The straight line more than likely harnesses price tops together. Figure 17 illustrates construction of a downtrend line. The same rules apply as before but in reverse. The downtrend line remains viable until it has been impaled. Directional turns of major movements are usually accompanied by deviations in trading activity.

Besides the above two tests of validity—the number of times the trend line is approached and its steepness—a third test is the length of time

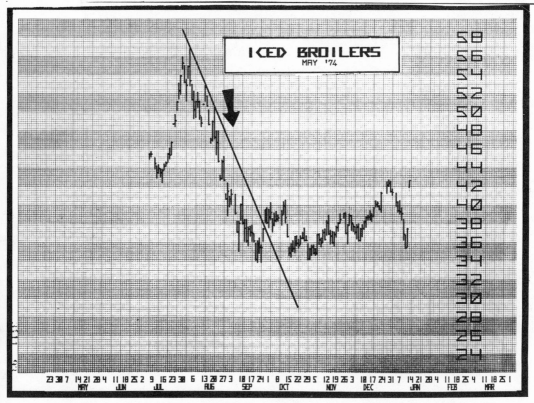

Fig. 17. Downtrend (Source: Commodity Perspective, 956 Hillcrest Road, Elgin, Ill. 60120.)

trends prevail. A minor trend may be defined as price flows (advances or declines) of 3-10 percent. An intermediate-term play may be defined as 10-50 percent for advances and 10-33 percent for declines. A major trend may be defined as exceeding 50 percent for advances and over 33 percent for declines. (If you're curious about the odd figure of 33 percent, notice that if crude coconut oil advances from 30¢ to 45¢, prices rise by 50 percent; but a price descent from 45¢ to 30¢ measures a reflux of 33 percent.)

Trend channels may also be constructed with a little care and common-sense application. In an uptrend, the direction line is drawn by uniting successive bottoms. After a trend has been under way for a sufficiently long period, you will notice that it seems to bump into an imaginary resistance line—an upper level. The upper limit may be penciled in by conjoining several tops. This upper limit may be subject to an occasional revision until it has been clearly delineated. The derived trading channel possesses obvious benefits for the nimble short-term trader.

There are two methods of interpreting price undulations within the channel. To the extent that rallies fail to reach the upper limit, there is weakness in the trend. At the other extreme, a sustained penetration of the upper limit of the channel suggests a *trend acceleration*, which typifies the final stages of a bull market. Channel lines can also be constructed in downtrend markets; the above observations, in reverse, apply.

Previously I alluded to the suitability of a ratio, or logarithmic, scale for recording price action. How does a ratio scale modify the shape of trend lines? For minor trends there is no trenchant dissimilarity. For longer-term trends, a straight line on an arithmetic chart will transfigure into a curved line on a logarithmic chart. As shown in Figure 18,

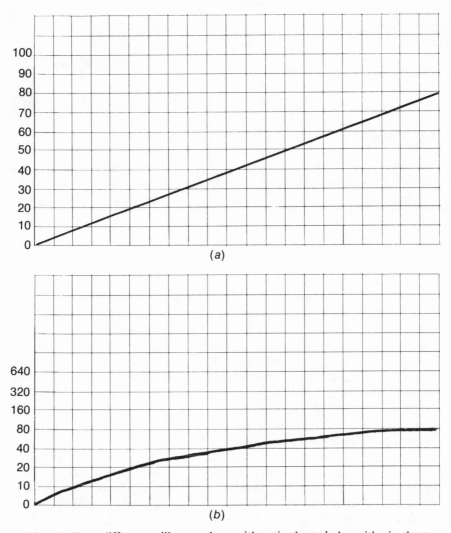

Fig. 18. Chart differences illustrated: *a*, arithmetic chart; *b*, logarithmic chart

on an arithmetic chart the distances between prices on the vertical scale remain constant; on a logarithmic scale, the percentage change on the vertical scale remains constant.

Did You Say Gaps or Gasps?

Another critical chart characteristic is the *gap*. A good gap man can convert these blank spaces into cash in *his* account. Gaps are holes in the chart, or as the technician says, a gap is a price range where no trading has taken place.

In the precedent inquest on trend lines, the issue of false breakouts cropped up. Recurrently I have observed that a breakout does not penetrate the trend line by caracoling through it but by leapfrogging it, thereby creating a small gap. The regularity of this occurrence posits that when prices gap above the intermediate trend line, the trend has reversed. Glance at Figure 17 or at a number of other charts to disinter other circumstances similar to the one recited.

With a *runaway gap*, as shown in Figure 19, the market practically gasps for breath as it skips upwards in leaps and bounds. Trading volume accelerates when the runaway is at top speed. These gaps suggest that market progression still has a substantial distance to rise.

Runaway gaps are usually stationed about half-way up an intermediate or longer-run trend. If the speculator can identify the runaway gap correctly, he can estimate the extent to which the market may budge. Easy to identify in retrospect, runaway gaps are sometimes misinterpreted as exhaustion gaps.

Exhaustion gaps, too, represent the same type of events as the runaway gap; however, while runaway gaps tend to raft about halfway during a trend, the exhaustion gap signalizes the end of a trend. In Figure 20, soybean prices have ascended precipitously, opening several gaps on the way up. A situation of many buyers and few sellers causes price to skip until profit-taking creates a congestion area. Running headlong into a wall (of sellers), price bounces off the barrier and retraces itself far enough to fill in the exhaustion gap. Of course, while the exhaustion gap proclaims that it is time to take profits, it *does not* herald that a trader should reverse his position. The long-run trend may still stand intact or some time may lapse before marking a change in course.

An exhaustion gap seldom spaces out alone in a precipitous move. At least one runaway gap often precedes it. Obviously, therefore, after the first runaway gap, each sequent gap becomes suspect.

There is a popular notion that all gaps must be filled (or closed), which means that in a subsequent rally or reaction trading takes place at prices corresponding to the "hole." Gaps are frequently but not always filled. No rule states *when* they will be closed. Exhaustion gaps are usually fairly quickly filled, like March 1974 soybeans in Figure 20. Runaway gaps require more time. They may never be stoppered if the contract expires.

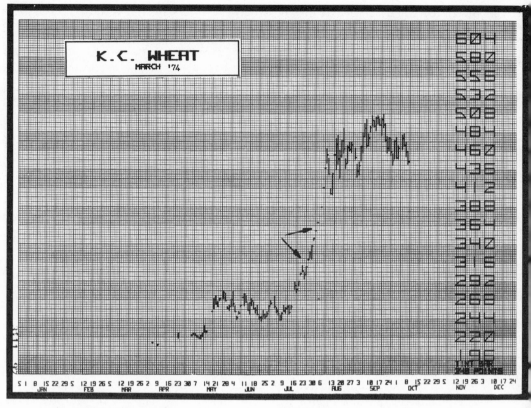

Fig. 19. Runaway gaps (Source: Commodity Perspective, 956 Hillcrest Road, Elgin, Ill. 60120.)

The third type, the *breakaway gap*, develops subsequent to maturation of a formation from which prices "break away." They flaunt themselves at the termination of either bottoms or tops but mostly after consummated topping action. Normally the downside gap is more strung out. The longer the gap, the greater the expectancy that the ensuing move will be extensive. In Figure 21, silver coins exhibit a breakaway gap after molding a head and shoulders bottom. Notice, too, in the chart, attendant runaway gaps and exhaustion gap followed by an unveiling of a downside breakaway gap, after the small topping configuration, trailed by more runaway gaps on the downside.

What Kind of Island Is That?

A climax pattern, such as island reversals, key reversal day, or two-day reversal, may telegraph the end of a move. Accompanying a climax top is high volume and a last-ditch effort to penetrate new high ground antecedent to a price slump. On the bottom side, there will be an unsuccessful at-

Fig. 20. Exhaustion gaps (Source: Commodity Perspective, 956 Hillcrest Road, Elgin, Ill. 60120.)

tempt to maintain a thrust into lower prices, and either a high or low volume may accompany this effort.

An *island reversal* is a trading range separated by an exhaustion gap on one side and a breakaway gap on the other. The island reversal in the Japanese yen contract shown in Figure 22 clearly illustrates this reversal pattern. In this example the trading range consists of a single day before collapse. If you will return to Figure 21, try to detect the island reversal in the silver coins chart. Retroaction may last three or four trading days and form a V-shaped island. Even major reversal patterns, such as head and shoulders, may be set apart by gaps on both sides.

Another evidential reversal pattern, the *key reversal* day, is formed by a trading range that besieges new high prices but then surprisingly closes below the previous day's settlement. Two examples emerge in Figure 23. At the bottom of the first major decline, the low end of the price range plunges into new low ground, but price settles *above* the previous day's close.

The top pattern erupts at the third peak in the diagram. The trading

Fig. 21. Breakaway gap (Source: Commodity Research Bureau, Inc., One Liberty Plaza, New York, N.Y. 10006.)

range bursts into new highs, but on the key reversal day price retreats *below* the previous day's close to signal the debut of a sharp reaction in prices.

The *two-day reversal* pattern arises at the end of a trend. Generally, a two-day reversal originates as a key reversal, a foin into new territory (either high or low), but instead of closing near the bottom of the range, price settles at the high of the range in a two-day reversal *top*. Price finishes at the low end of the range in a two-day reversal *bottom*. During the next day's trading, the highest price is tested again in a top; the lowest price is tested again in a bottom pattern. But price closes at the opposite end of the range. That is, in a two-day reversal *top*, the second day's concluding price will be at the bottom of the range. In a two-day reversal *bottom*, the second day's closing price will be near the top of the range similar to the example in Figure 23.

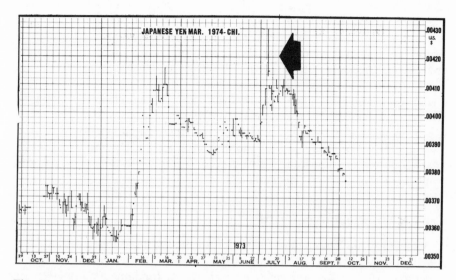

Fig. 22. Island reversal (Source: Commodity Research Bureau, Inc., One Liberty Plaza, New York, N.Y. 10006.)

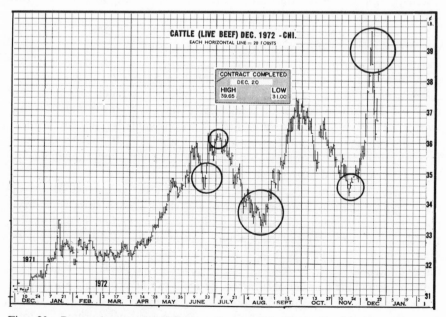

Fig. 23. Reversal patterns (Source: Commodity Research Bureau, Inc., One Liberty Plaza, New York, N.Y. 10006.)

Two other patterns also apparent in this chart should be brought to your attention. The *middle-of-the-range* close draws attention to the right of the chart. As the name suggests, closing price is midway between the day's highs and lows. The *narrow-range* day, exhibited at the top of the first peak, is a trading day when daily high and low prices are close together; it occurs after several wider-range days. Both of these patterns demonstrate indecisiveness, while action during the next day or two shows signs of decisiveness.

For practice you may wish to discover other formations in this chart. At the far right, notice that a change in the intermediate downtrend occurs at a gap which is followed by runaway gaps, then an exhaustion gap, and then another breakaway gap on the downside again. The more you study charts, the better opportunity you create to put those dollars where you want them—in your own pocket.

Can I Really Profit from Charts?

Altogether too often, more is read into charts than appears in simon-pure substantiality. A successful trader neither pursues purely technical aspects of the market nor relies exclusively on fundamentals or even on cycles and waves. In fact, most successful speculators will *use* all of these tools as vehicles for gathering information, but winning trades originate internally. Details on this aspect of the decision-making process are relegated to a subsequent portion of the book.

One widely known rule concerns the extent of a price reaction. How far will prices retrace before resuming an upward course? No one can predict the extent of a swing. It may progress much farther than anticipated. However, in intermediate and short-term trends, *a 50 percent retracement* is considered an objective. The extent to which prices reach this midpoint tests the degree of strength or weakness of the play. Sometimes the rule works well. Most of the time it is difficult to pinpoint. My advice is not to lean on mechanical approaches to market analysis. If they really performed all that well, profits would disappear because everyone would apply similar analytical procedures.

Another interesting observation is the length of each fluctuation, or wave. Where there is irregular up or down activity, each successive wave *tends* to be of equal duration. Don't look for perfect fits. In Figure 24, March cocoa demonstrates the viability of this guide. Wave measurement does provide the trader with an idea of the magnitude of each swell. Its disadvantageous feature—two or three fluctuations elapse to establish a pattern—limits the number of times the concept can be profitably employed.

Good action tends to develop out of long periods of congestion. Where formations are of a broadening type—in other words, where there is a long period of consolidation—a more dynamic advancement ensues. However, during a period of reaccumulation the trader sometimes expects prices to

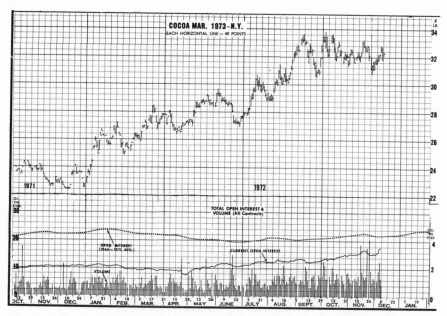

Fig. 24. Wave lengths (Source: Commodity Research Bureau, Inc., One Liberty Plaza, New York, N.Y. 10006.)

continue their ascendant course but is deceived with a sudden trend reversal known as an *end run*. These are really *traps*, and prices will just as suddenly turn again in the direction previously anticipated.

For example, an up-movement hesitates, forms a congestion area of reaccumulation; and suddenly prices flutter downward briefly. If the downmovement quickly stalls, and further congestion occurs, price action will likely revert to flow with the major trend.

Generally, once prices break through a congestion area—really a resistance area—this resistance region becomes a support plateau on the way up. On the way down, however, the support layer now becomes a belt of resistance. If the zone is not penetrated, prices may not continue their downward course. Most of these patterns appear on other types of charts and invite similar interpretations. They are even more clear-cut on reversal charts.

CHAPTER 6
Point and Figure
Your Profits

A selfish man willingly undergoes troubles for the sake of the self, he suffers hardship and privation without a murmur, simply because he knows that what is pain and trouble, looked at from the point of view of a short space of time, are just the opposite when seen in a larger perspective. Thus what is loss to the smaller man is a gain to the greater.

—Rabindranath Tagore

BAR CHARTS ARE EXCELLENT FOR LONGER-TERM TRENDS. THEY REVEAL A wealth of information to the alert analyst. But some short-term traders prefer a supplementary tool that furnishes additional intraday detail—in effect, a broadening of the bar chart. Such particulars further indicate market strengths and weaknesses, and are especially suitable for the day-trader. This simple technique is becoming increasingly popular among commodity speculators.

The best method for learning this wizardry is by doing. There are several rituals, variations of these routines. With continued application of this charting method, you will devise adaptations, develop market insight, and, in some cases, an intuitive foreglimpse of price shifts *before they crystallize.*

Tic-Tac-Toe

To obtain a complete tableau of price direction and changes during the day, record every "tick," or price variation. This method has the disadvantage of consuming reams of chart papers. Detailing the events in an extremely active market can overwhelm beginner and pro alike. Nevertheless, the final result is a graphic image of the past. When strips of graph paper outrun surface area, after several months of charting the same option, fasten them to the walls for the big picture.

We will begin with an examination of December 1973 live cattle. Each cent is divided into one hundred parts called *points*. The minimum price movement, or *tick*, varies with the commodity traded. For live cattle the minimum change is two and one-half points. Each point equals $4. For purposes of chart construction, however, we will employ five-point squares; that is, each square, or X, will be worth $20 per contract.

Daily data input may be obtained from several sources: (1) subscribe to a diurnal service that mails out intraday price changes; (2) visit your broker's office every day and record each change as it appears on the board or screen; (3) hire a chartist (perhaps a university business student) to visit the brokerage firm four or five hours daily to construct charts; (4) purchase copies of charts from a broker who maintains them (this information, also, can be quickly relayed over the telephone for updating); (5) purchase charts from a service. If none of these sources is practical, I will pipeline you into a method to construct a point-and-figure chart from daily quotations in your favorite quotidian, but the resulting chart will be less diffuse in detail.

In Figure 25, a blow-by-blow account of December live cattle action during three trading days, each X tallys five points. The columns embody up-and-down action. Movement to the right reflects time, but not in the normal sense. Transition along the horizontal axis accommodates *market-time*. But this "time" may be fast or slow. Unrelated to clock-time, it cannot be adequately explained or illustrated in ordinary terms. The only manner to match market action with time in the usual sense is to log dates and to separate each day by darkening the square which chronicles either closing or opening prices.

Construction of a point-and-figure chart, or reversal chart, is simple; the technique is readily mastered. If you decide to become a full-time professional speculator, I suggest that you install a "personal ticker" in your home or office. It will permanently record all prices. You can update charts carefully at your convenience.

For each .05¢ change, mark an X in the appropriate square. Suppose that several consecutive prices are: 44.40, 44.45, 44.47, 44.50, 44.60. Tattoo an X on your chart corresponding to 44.40 and 44.45. Because 44.47 is less than the next square's value, 44.50, ignore it. Do not record another X until price reaches the next square's equivalent, 44.50.

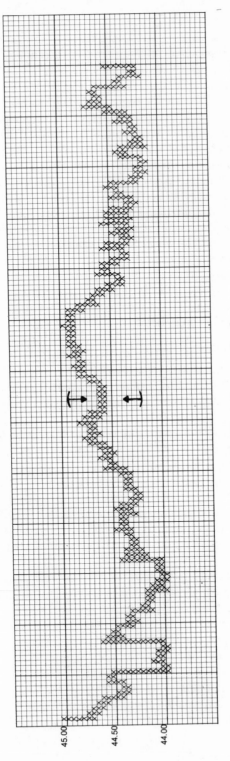

Fig. 25. Action on a 5 x 5

With the above prices, you will have Xed in five squares upward in one column. Although no actual trade existed in space 44.55, record it anyway. Do not skip squares. Assume that all price action is continuous rather than discrete.

The above prices stand for cents per pound—44.40¢, or $0.4440. If the two extra decimal places confuse you, think in terms of hundredweight— $44.40 per cwt.

Now suppose that price dips slightly to 44.55, then 44.45 and 44.40. Swing to the next column; chalk up Xs for four squares down. Continue downward until price starts upward again. To conserve paper, and some space, fill in at least two squares before transferring to the next column.

After reaching price 44.40, assume that it ascends to 44.45, reverts to 44.40, advances to 44.45, falls to 44.40 and 44.35. Record 44.45 in the next column and 44.40 below it. Shifting one column to the right, cross squares corresponding to 44.45, 44.40, and 44.35. In other words, you can catalog an upward and downward price change in the same column.

Notice, in the accompanying chart, several columns with only two Xs representing prices 44.55 and 44.60. This brief sideways action (which may have lasted only ten minutes or endured for an hour) depicts the tug-of-war between buyers and sellers. The standoff indicates that neither group, at that time, desired to commit sufficient financial muscle to move prices up or down by very far. It represents a brief period of consolidation.

Using a method similar to the one in Figure 25, a pit broker mentally "graphs" the day's price action and is said to have a "feel of the market." Practice charting over several months; it may well be worth the "pain and trouble."

Some speculators prefer less detail. One system records larger price changes. Each square registers ten points (or even twenty points) instead of the five-point system shown in Figure 25. A trader who is not interested in every small price reversal may consider a thirty-point reversal adequate on a ten-point chart.

For example, after live cattle had risen to 44.60, they reversed to 44.40 before resuming their upward course to, say, 44.80. On a thirty-point reversal chart, no record of the dip would show between prices 44.60 and 44.40. (Only a thirty-point reflux to 44.30 merits attention on a thirty-point reversal chart.) As if the mini-fluctuation never occurred, an observer assumes that prices moved directly upward to 44.80.

On the other hand, if price retreats from 44.60 to 44.30, then wheels about to 44.40, onward and upward to 44.80, that price scenario will occupy three columns. For a clearer indication, let us employ an X when the price drifts upward, an O when it courses downward. Figure 26 identifies the same data posted in Figure 25. But now that each square represents ten points, reversals are recorded only when prices have retreated a full thirty points. A thirty-point reversal chart not only contracts the total picture but eliminates minor price aberrations.

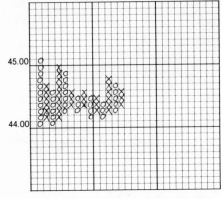

Fig. 26. Compressed action on a 10 x 30
(Fig. 25 reduced to a 10 x 30 chart)

The extent of solicited detail depends upon the speculator's trading plan and objectives, price volatility, and the speed of the market. For example, a couple of years ago when grains were more quiescent, it was common to construct ⅛¢ charts with a three-eights reversal. This detail would have inundated the trader during 1973. In fact, grains no longer fluctuate in one-eighth increments on major exchanges but in ¼¢ additions. For the grains, possibly a 1¢ chart with a 3¢ (or 1 x 3) reversal suffices.

Due to mercurial situations and mutable interests, no rule applies every year to every complexity. For a guideline, however, the following suggestions will help a lame dog over the stile. In creating your own charts: for live cattle, live hogs, pork bellies, iced broilers, and eggs, a 10 x 30 chart usually proves adequate; however, in the more volatile egg and pork bellies markets, you may want to simultaneously maintain a 20 x 60 chart. Any larger-scaled chart can be constructed from data taken directly from a smaller-scaled one. For corn, oats, wheat, flaxseed, rapeseed, and soybeans, try a 1¢ x 3¢ scale. Employ a 5 x 15 point-reversal for sugar. Copper, cocoa, and frozen concentrated orange juice trade well from a 20 x 60 point-reversal. Most recently, a ½¢ x 1½¢ has worked well for silver, and either a $4 x $12 or a $6 x $6 for U.S. silver coins. Lumber and plywood will chart on a 10 x 30 point basis. Experimentation will reveal appropriate graduations in accordance with your requirements and market conditions for the particular commodity you are dealing in.

The *XOV* Mystery

Because of their widespread application, the symbols *X* and *O*, probably a carry-over from the game tic-tac-toe, have become entrenched; no cabalistic sign or mysticism is intended. In fact, while explaining chart interpretation to you, I will introduce a third variation of *V*s and inverted *V*s, and will employ *X*s and *O*s in a different context later in the chapter. If the price is falling, substitute a *V* for an *O*; for rising prices, an inverted *V* for an *X*.

Figure 27, December 1973 eggs, graphs the decline of egg prices from their 1973 high. Each square represents twenty points; each point equals $2.25; sixty points are required for a reversal. The price trend points downward.

90

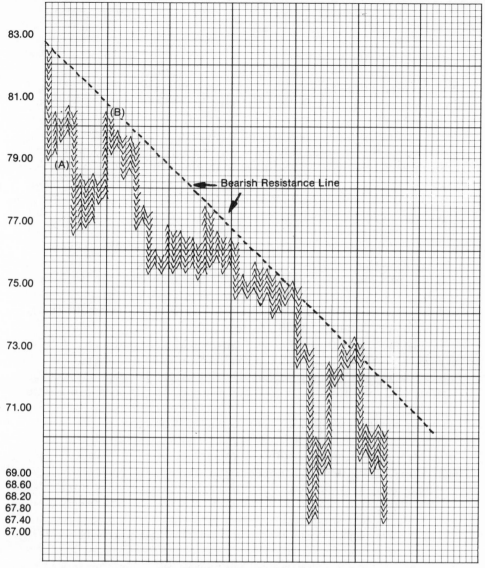

Fig. 27. Bearish resistance line

After a few days of price action, a *bearish resistance line* can be constructed at a 45-degree angle. Moving up one square above the top inverted *V*, extend a 45-degree line downward. This line forms the upper limit of the channel within which prices will probably fluctuate in their downward course. As long as prices remain below this line, the downtrend is intact. On the other hand, a breakout above this line is no guarantee that the trend has been broken. It may be a false breakout. No technical tool is completely valid. It acts as a guideline and abets in operating the trading plan.

How do you know the trend is down? When do you sell short? A major sell signal at point (A) will alert you to a possible short position. Point (A) indicates that prices have fallen below the previous low. Lower bottoms and lower tops suggest possible short sales, provided that the major trend is down. Should you sell short at 79.60 or wait?

For verification, wait until the price rises to test the previous top at 80.60. Notice that the next column of *V*s rises only to 80.40, point (B), and does not break through the bearish resistance line. Since the price does not exceed 80.60, the sell signal at point (A) has not been negated. The trading plan is to sell against the next major rally following completion of *V*s in the column at point (A). That is, sell December eggs short at point (B) and place a stop-loss *above* the bearish resistance line. Since daily egg prices do tend to fluctuate widely, place the stop far enough above to allow for normal intraday gyrations.

In this particular case, the position generates immediate profits. A substantial down-movement has supervened. As price shrinks, accrued profits can be protected with a trailing stop-loss. (More on this technique later!) Ten cents in eggs equals $2,250—extremely profitable in short time.

In Figure 28, wheat chart action, between May 14 and June 14 1974, evinces buy signals. Notice how prices leap over the downtrend line; *O*s indicate a gapped opening. Because buying is not possible on opening, strategy calls for purchases on pullback at price (A). Action is favorable to pyramid. Initiate, say, fifty thousand bushels with a stop-loss 10¢ below. Each 10¢ change is worth $500 per five thousand bushels.

The bullish (ascending) triangle signals another opportunity to either originate a new position or add to an existing position. At point (B), position another thirty thousand bushels; move the stop-loss up 6¢.

After a short-term top, consolidation occurs until a column of inverted *V*s exceeds recent tops. On the first pull-back, at point (C), add twenty thousand bushels, move stops up 10¢, follow price with a trailing stop-loss.

For the intermediate term, take profits on fifty thousand bushels at (D); hold fifty thousand for longer-term play with a stop-loss below the long-run trend line, which you can construct by connecting bottoms under (A), left of (B), intersecting about four rows up from the bottom formed to the left of (C), and extend it upwards. The long-run trend is still intact in mid-June. When price returns to point (E), begin rebuilding your position in twenty-thousand-bushel increments.

Another triangle, though imperfectly formed, can be observed in, Figure 29, June 1974 Chicago silver. The ½¢ breakout on January 11 portends the gap-opening of January 14. For short-term strategy, buy on the first pullback after opening. Events subsequently revealed that price reined in very slightly.

Figure 29 also illustrates variations in the reporting system of *V*s and inverted *V*s. It provides additional information for decision-making. To begin in the first column, an *X* documents the previous day's closing price

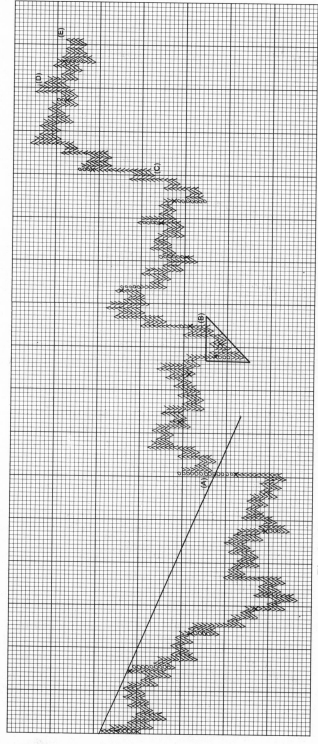

Fig. 28. Buy signals in the wheat pit (Chicago July '74 wheat 1 x 3¢)

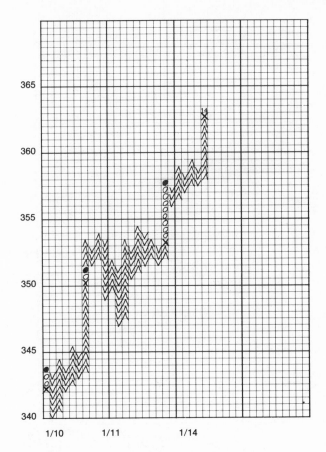

Fig. 29. Reporting variations (June 1974 Chicago silver ½ x 1½¢)

(January 9). On the next day (January 10), June silver opened 150 points higher than the previous day. To indicate that a gap in price occurred between the close of trading at 2:25 P.M. (EST) on January 9 and the opening bell at 10:00 A.M. (EST) on January 10, *O*s are employed. The opening price itself is indicated with a blackened *O*. (If there is an opening range of prices, then more than one *O* will be darkened.) To log the end of a trading day, the date may be shown such as the "14" in the last column.

Figures 30 and 31 present two examples of reversed formations. In Figure 30, after the price of September 1973 Swiss francs steadily climbed from the middle of January to the first part of March, prices began to decline until the middle of June. Sell signals are identified with three successive lower bottoms. However, the major uptrend line has not been violated. With the steady influx of buying power, the first buy signal is recorded on June 14 followed by additional bullish signals. (There are SFr 250,000 in each contract on the IMM. Read Chapter 16.)

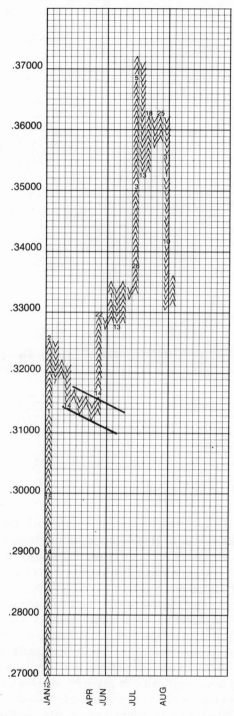

Fig. 30. Reversal pattern in Swiss francs (September Swiss francs)

95

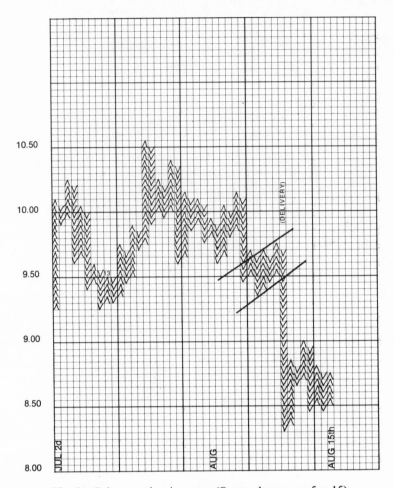

Fig. 31. Price reaction in sugar (September sugar 5 x 15)

In Figure 31, the reversed formation occurs in September world sugar #11 during a price reaction. Higher bottoms and higher tops initially suggest the market is turning around. However, the sell signal at 9.40 is reconfirmed at 9.30. Price continues downward for another cent). (A 1¢ change in sugar is worth $1,120 per contract.)

These last two formations point out the treacherousness of analyzing a single formation in isolation from other facts. Chart patterns are subsidiary tools and do not in themselves guarantee successful trades. Other technical factors, such as trend of the market and scale of charts, cannot be overemphasized. Additionally, variations and combinations of these patterns complicate penetration of the mystery of Xs and Os and Vs. With study you will recognize that each commodity tends to develop its own peculiar chart formations; interpretation is not necessarily identical for soybeans and for gold.

Tops and Bottoms

Picking the tops and bottoms of a price swing can be difficult if not outright dangerous. Nevertheless, a fascinating game, it attracts its proportion of participants. Certain formations repeatedly display themselves and add to the excitement of the challenge. The September 1973 cocoa contract charted in Figure 32 furnishes several examples, during month-of-August trading, for our analysis.

At point (A), an example of a double-top, market action cannot pierce 83.20 on its second try. Action conveys a sell signal at 82.00. At 79.20, a quadrubottom (point [B]) alludes to an end of the down movement; but a breakthrough at 79.00 confirms further downside action.

A double top at point (C) and triple bottom at point (D) illustrate similar action. In fact, prices then continue nearly straight down to 63.60 before any significant rally transpires. (A 10¢ price movement in cocoa, traded on the New York Cocoa Exchange, amounts to $3,000 per contract. Exchange photographs are exhibited elsewhere.)

At roughly midpoint, the upward tilted flag suggests another 10¢ remains in the downward course. But the descending triangle subsequently bodes a decline even below 63¢.

Before examining a couple of trading situations, I promised to disclose how to construct a reversal chart without plotting every intraday tick. This method furnishes only limited detail. It does provide slightly more information than a bar chart. From your daily newspaper, record the opening price of the commodity you are tracking. If price opens higher than the previous day's close, proceed to the high-of-the-day column. Assume that prices first continue upwards after opening. Observing the day's low, move to the next column; record the appropriate number of *V*s downward. If the closing price is up from the day's low, shift another column to the right, register inverted *V*s, mark the closing price.

If, on the other hand, price opens lower, assume that it continues downward after opening. After completing the column of *V*s, check the previous day's high prices; record corresponding inverted *V*s in the next column to the right. With this system each day's action will occupy at least two, possibly three, columns on your point-and-figure chart. A brief period of practice—of doing—will clear up any questions. In fact, you cannot learn and retain the information in these three chapters by just reading. The only shortcut is: Practice! Practice! Practice!

Profitable Interpretations

Now let us employ chart-reading techniques already learned to interpret short-term profit potential in two commodities—copper and live hogs.

The portion of December 1973 copper in Figure 33 charts a rather wide bottom during August and September. Previously, copper had reached a contract high of 90.40 in mid-July. With a little imagination, most of the

97

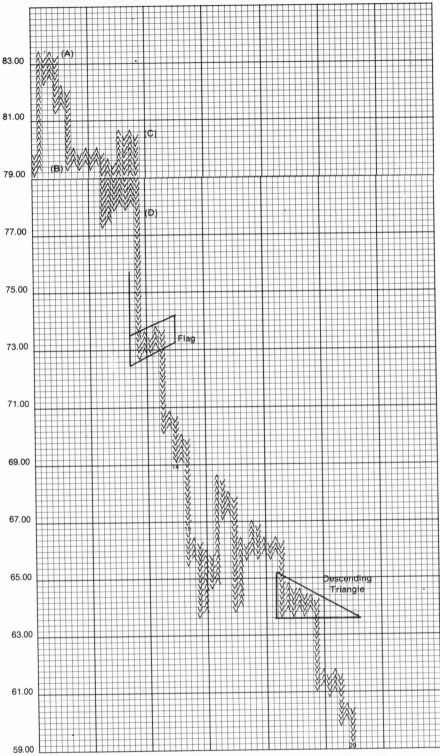

Fig. 32. Bearish cocoa action (September cocoa 20 x 60)

98

entire bottoming action forms a huge *W*. Notice, also, the triple bottom at 74.60. These two basic formations, coupled with large amount of "work," imply that a substantial bull move may be under way.

Breaking out of the downtrend line, copper is bought at 79.00. The fast runup of price appears to stall at point (B), forming a double top. Since the top is not taken out together with a weak sell signal at point (C), profits on all or part of held positions can be taken around point (D). (Each 1¢ per-pound price change equals $250 per contract.)

It is now desirable to stand aside and wait for a fourth test of the bottom at 74.40. Nevertheless action remains above the major downtrend line. At first blush, the near-term quadrubottom at point (E) seems to be broken. However, a steep price ascent after the sharp break connotes market strength. Buy signals at (F) and (G) confirm both the original *W* bottom and inability to sustain subsequent reaction. Purchases at 79.60 would have enjoyed a protracted upward advance to 89.00 before any correction occurred. New contract highs were again established in October at 92.40. By December, copper prices exceeded $1 per pound.

Difficulty arises when prices are followed too closely. Efforts to interpret every minor reaction within a major trend absorb mind energies. The patient, calm, strong-willed trader would have taken substantial profits out of the copper market if he had correctly interpreted the broad base being formed as the start of a new major move and possessed adequate funds to sustain positions.

The recorded portion of the February 1974 live hog chart, in Figure 34, reflects another type of bottom—a *V*-shaped formation. After a limit-down day on October 29, live hogs, on October 30, opened slightly higher and feigned a rally. The rally failed. Prices broke through the previous low.

In a second show of strength, the new rally, surpassing the earlier attempt, imparted a buy signal. Escape from a triangle dispatched subsidiary evidence that a bottom had manifested. The market, having closed limit up on the thirtieth, bestowed supplemental confirmation. A speculator might have initiated a speculative position at 44.60. A more cautious person would tend to wait—to determine whether the bottom at 43.50 would again be proven.

(Notice use of the letter *L* to indicate a limit move. A limit move equals 150 points—1½¢—or $450 per contract of thirty thousand pounds of hogs. Letters, colored pencils, or other markings may be useful to the chart reader. Nevertheless, be cautioned against chart clutter and losing sight of your original intent.)

During the next three days—October 31, November 1 and 2—accumulation evinced. This accumulation of long positions provided the base for the subsequent upward move. With the new buy signal at 46.50, on the fifth, the ratio of risk-to-possible-profit appears low. It is unlikely that prices will move back through the previous three days consolidation. Stop-loss protection can safely be placed 100 points lower. The downside risk

99

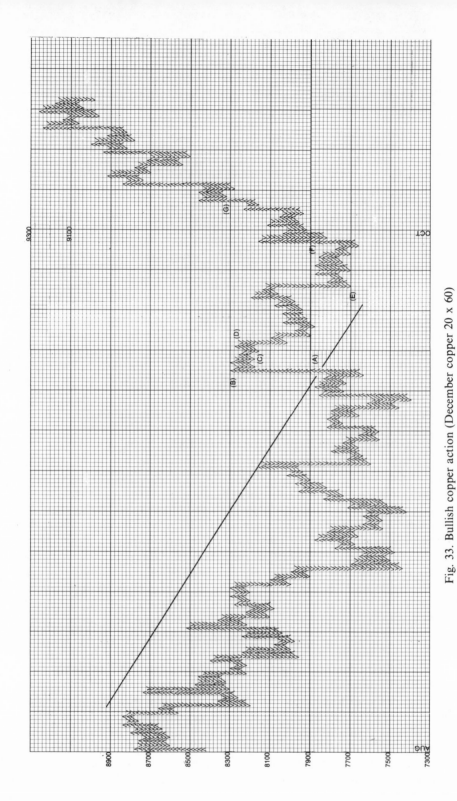

Fig. 33. Bullish copper action (December copper 20 × 60)

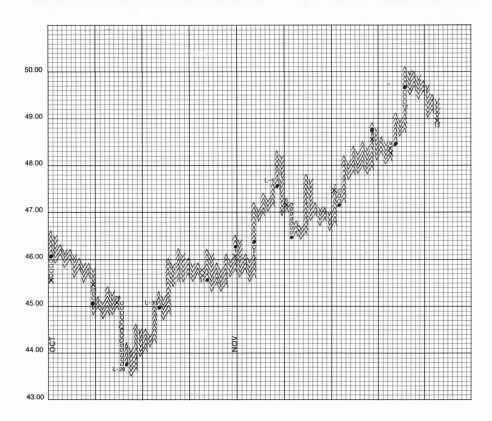

Fig. 34. V-shaped bottom (February live hogs 10 x 30)

seems to be a potential $300 loss. An objective on the upside exceeds 50.00. The potential-loss-to-potential-profit ratio is better than 1-to-3.

February hogs closed limit up on the fifth. Price reactions of the sixth and seventh provided new buying opportunities to add to a winning position. Prices fell slightly short of the 50.40 objective; but it is always better to leave something in the market and take out a large profit in the middle. As the old saw warns—"Bulls make money, bears make money, but hogs get butchered"—don't try to pick tops and bottoms. You may be wondering how I selected a price objective of 50.40. Here is how it is done.

Price Objectives

Determining the extent of a price movement is not an exact science, or even an art, but the method described below does provide a vague guideline. Treat it as another input of information—only one of several factors. As a general rule, the wider the base the greater the potential move in a bull market.

The difficulty with the method is time. I have already mentioned that time is measured on the horizontal axis of the chart, but I am referring to market time. Calculated in terms of days and/or weeks—that is, clock time—

it has no invariable relationship with ordinary time. In fact, an entirely new and different concept is required. Rather than delve into my new theory of time, I will only relate that once calculated by any of the following methods, there is no way of determining when or how rapidly that price objective will be met.

The first method is to linearly measure the width of the entire base. With a straight-edge, determine distance from its first column, left-hand side, across a line marking the 46.00¢ price, to where that line intersects the last row of inverted *V*s. Turning the ruler upwards, from a base line of 46.00, mark the vertical distance that corresponds to the base's horizontal width. Having measured correctly, your vertical mark will lie at 50.40.

A second method is to count the number of columns which comprise basing, or accumulative action, of the thirty-first, first, and second. This action creates a springboard for a subsequent rally. The base is eighteen columns wide. Because it is a thirty-point, three-square, reversal chart, multiply eighteen times three, which equals fifty-four squares. Each square matches ten points; ergo, 54 squares totals 540 points, 5.40 cents. Add this figure to the lowest point of the base—that is, add 5.40 to 45.30. Price objective by this system adds up to 50.70.

In both cases, actual top price falls slightly short of estimated objectives but near enough to furnish a reliable guideline. As one broker I know would say, "That's close enough for government work."

Mix this input with other chart action, fundamentals, cash prices of hogs, stir in some intuition, and you might have taken profits at or very near the top tick.

No method is entirely reliable. Neither can a worthwhile method be mechanically implemented. If this were possible, then all trades could be computerized, risk would approach zero, profits would tend to equal risk. In spite of this apparent fact, search for the philosopher's stone continues. People perpetually pursue pie-in-the-sky; something-for-nothing still intrigues the masses.

On the other hand, many researchers busily try to reduce commodity futures trading to a mathematical science. The number of systems, models and mathematical computations must equal the number of searchers and researchers multiplied by infinity squared. This mathematical pastime promises too much pleasurableness to pass over.

CHAPTER 7
Another Path to Profits

I hardly have ever known a mathematician who was capable of reasoning.

—Plato

ALTHOUGH THE SUBJECT OF MATHEMATICS CREDIBLY DOES NOT APPEAL to most readers, many traders have been bewildered and bewitched by the variety of services and models that may be subscribed to for fees ranging from a few dollars to several hundred annually. The majority of models are founded on a system of moving averages; some of the more sophisticated ones ingest a large number of variables.

Typical models will nurture two or three weighted moving averages, daily high-low ranges, volume, open interest, percentage change of tops or closing prices, and even a "psychological" factor based on consensus of current opinion.

Essentially, all models draw a bead on the direction of the trend *after* it has manifested, and will keep you in the market as long as the tenor is unchanged. Some systems essay to anticipate changes in trend. These types, profitable to the adequately capitalized trader who can initiate every recommended position, can underlie more losing than winning trades through "selection," random or otherwise, of recommendations to speculate in.

This chapter will review the steps in constructing moving averages and then apply the technique to the creation of an oscillator. Thus you can create your own elementary advisory service. For those interested in more complicated devices, the chapter will introduce you to additional methods.

The "MA" and "WMA" Systems

Underpinning most models, however complicated their guise, lurks a set of one or more *moving averages*. The rationale behind this common feature is to determine when price reaction deviates from recent average prices. As long as the current price remains above the average price of the last ten, twenty, or hundred days, the trend spins upward. As long as the current price lies below the moving average, the trend heads downward.

The most ordinarily observed average in commodity futures trading, the *ten-day moving average,* is simply constructed. Table 1 shows February 1974 cotton prices over fifteen trading days. Cotton trades on the New York Cotton Exchange in thirty-thousand-pound units; price is quoted in cents per pound.

Even a cursory probe of the data in the table will disclose that the trend waxes up for the entire series. However, closing prices on February 7, 8, and 9 are lower than the preceding three days. A moving average, a mathematical device, smooths out these minor day-to-day fluctuations.

TABLE 1

FEBRUARY 1974 COTTON PRICES

Day and Date Traded	Settlement Prices (Cents)
Thursday, February 1	32.97
Friday, February 2	33.20
Monday, February 5	33.20
Tuesday, February 6	33.20
Wednesday, February 7	33.18
Thursday, February 8	33.15
Friday, February 9	33.16
Monday, February 12	33.35
Tuesday, February 13	33.90
Wednesday, February 14	34.30
Thursday, February 15	34.20
Friday, February 16	34.33
Monday, February 19	Closed
Tuesday, February 20	34.35
Wednesday, February 21	34.65
Thursday, February 22	35.05

For those unfamiliar with moving averages, the first step is to reduce ten days' prices down to one figure; that is, to a summary datum, or average, that provides an instant impression of price action over a ten-day period. Add together the prices from February 1 through February 14. Your total should be 333.61. Divide this sum by 10. The result is 33.361. Since the last 1 is less than 5, drop it. The ten-day average is 33.36.

To keep the average moving, or updated, add the last day's price, 34.20 on February 15, to your total of 333.61. However, because we are only interested in the most recent ten days, subtract the price of February 1, 32.97, from this sum. Your result should be 334.84. Divided by 10, the new average is 33.48.

Repeat the process for the sixteenth. The sum of the ten days equals 335.97. Divided by 10, the result is 35.597. Rounding out the output, the new average is 33.60 on the sixteenth.

The disadvantage to this method is that it gives equal weight to each day's price. The moving average assumes that the trader bestows as much importance on last week's prices as he does on yesterday's. This method simply does not conform to reality. The short-term trader's time horizon is extremely limited. Even the nature of human memory, in the course of normal events, places more import on the most recent experience.

To conform to reality, the *weighted moving average,* a superior device, too, retains the same shortcomings as any historical series of data. Assignment of various weights, largely discretionary, depends upon the propensities and predilections of the speculator. For example, you may desire to weight the most recent price ten times as much as the oldest one and weight the middle prices in descending order.

For purposes of illustration, the cotton prices in Table 1 are accorded the weights shown in Table 2.

TABLE 2

The Weighting of Table 1 Cotton Prices

Date	Price	Multiply by *Weight*	Result
1	32.97	1	32.97
2	33.20	1	33.20
5	33.20	1	33.20
6	33.20	1	33.20
7	33.18	1	33.18
8	33.15	2	66.30
9	33.16	3	99.48
12	33.35	4	133.40
13	33.90	6	203.40
14	34.30	10	343.00
		30	1011.33

The weights denote that I have equally emphasized the oldest five days because they count approximately similar in my current decision. The sixth day merits twice the importance of the fifth. The nearer to the present, the greater its significance. Yesterday's price figures ten times more in my decisions than the price of ten days ago.

To complete the calculation, divide 30 into 1011.33. The weighted average is 33.71. The weighted average surpasses the previously calculated unweighted average of 33.36 because prices have been gradually climbing. As long as prices continue to rise, the above weighted moving average will always eclipse the unweighted moving average.

You may prefer a five-day weighted moving average, or perhaps a longer series may appropriately satisfy your requirements. Commodity prices do vibrate more rapidly than the prices of most other investment forms; therefore, a shorter series usually performs best. The two-hundred-day moving average frequently employed in stock averages is useful in commodities only when analyzed along with a shorter series. A two-hundred-day moving average will not provide an adequate trading mechanism. Chart services can be purchased. Figure 35 reproduces one service recording nine- and eighteen-day moving averages.

If you want to check your own calculations for the fifteenth, the sum of weighted figures amounts to 1015.70 and yields an average of 33.86.

For the sixteenth, the sum is 1019.99; your weighted average should be 34.00. Now let us employ the above methods to create your own advisory service.

Mathematical Magic

The market technician employs moving averages to smooth out price oscillations. They can also serve as a timing signal to buy or sell a commodity. If we relate the moving average to current price, using the figures in Table 3, we can create an *oscillator* which reacts to price differences.

TABLE 3

COMPUTING AN OSCILLATOR

Date	Close	WMA	Difference
14	34.30	33.71	+ 0.41
15	34.20	33.86	+ 0.46
16	34.33	34.00	+ 0.33
20	34.35	34.10	+ 0.25
21	34.65	34.26	+ 0.39
22	35.05	34.50	+ 0.55

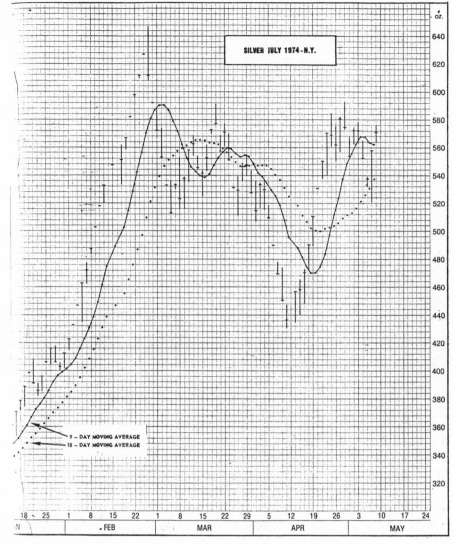

Fig. 35. Moving averages—nine- and eighteen-day (Source: Moving Averages Commodity Trend Service, 3250 Irving Park, Chicago, Ill. 60641.)

First, we will compute weighted moving averages through February 22. Next we will measure the difference between the latest closing price and the weighted moving average (WMA). If the settlement price exceeds the WMA, then the average is being pulled up, and we will record a plus difference. If the closing price were less than the WMA price, then a minus difference indicates that the WMA is being pulled downward.

The oscillator can now be plotted on graph paper. In Figure 36, I have

107

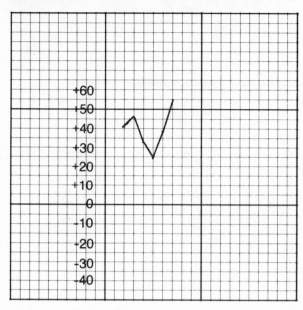

Fig. 36. An oscillator

scaled the graph for five-point intervals. Above zero, plus figures are recorded; below zero, minus figures are registered. If the settlement price had been less than the WMA, then the minus difference would have been plotted below the zero line. Connect the plotted points with a line to create continuous waves of the oscillator.

The purpose of the oscillator is to catch turning points in the market. The basic signal is penetration of the zero line. Because I have employed a ten-day weighted moving average, the oscillator is extremely sensitive to short-term moves. For longer-term moves, experiment with fifteen-day and twenty-day moving averages. You can graph three or four oscillators on the same chart and follow them with inks or pencils of different colors.

One drawback of this system, and most others, is that it functions best in a strongly trending market. During turning points and where the market is consolidating, a speculator can be whipsawed with this device through false signals.

If a major double (or triple) top or bottom forms, the first sell, or buy, indicator may be a false one. But through careful study, over a long period, coupled with other technical mechanics, this oscillator may perform as well as a run-of-the-mill service for which you have paid a substantial sum. (Naturally, the oscillator does not substitute for buying well-researched market advice, information, or models.)

One point to observe is the momentum of a move. While the uptrend is intact, the oscillator will be above the zero line. If with each wave of the oscillator, lower highs and lower lows, above zero, are recorded, this action suggests a weakening of the uptrend and provides the alert trader with a signal to prepare to take profits on his current position. If, for example, you are employing both ten- and twenty-day moving averages, one strategy would be to take profits when the ten-day oscillator indicates a weakening of the uptrend, but do not initiate a short position until the twenty-day oscillator penetrates the zero line. This system will not put you into the market as often, if you are the type who prefers to transact frequently, but may tend to put more profits into your pocket when you do trade.

The major shortcoming of any historical series is that it looks backward. The system cannot pierce the veil separating today and tomorrow. In fact, no mathematical model accurately or completely measures even today or yesterday. Models are dependent upon inputs furnished by the operator, and not all information is readily quantifiable. How other traders will react to any given set of data depends on a great many individual interpretations. Studying psychology is more relevant than becoming a polymath. These uncertainties, which sire large profits for some traders, are nerve-tingling to all.

Way of the Logicians

Sometimes an uncertainty can be reduced to a probability—that is, a certain uncertainty; this measured uncertainty is called risk. Once uncertainty becomes calculable, an investor can decide whether the possibility of a future gain is proportionately greater than the calculated loss, and if the relationship conforms to his investment plan, he undertakes to expose a portion of his capital to risk.

The difficulty is not whether some transactions will be profitless ones; a speculator expects setbacks part of the time. The problem arises in attempting to sort out the best opportunities. While *model-building* has become an engrossing pastime for many academicians, it has also been widely applied by profit-seeking speculators.

Although I cannot instruct you in the art (some audaciously claim it to be a science) of model-building in a few pages, it is beneficial to understand the rationale which underpins a system that proposes to capture the principal events affecting prices in a series of still shots of equations.

The rigor of model-building disciplines the mind to conceive of relationships that might otherwise escape it. Further, it is a shorthand system for stating the important variables and to isolate the facts most likely to influence price changes.

Let us construct a partial model for forecasting futures prices of pork bellies. By their nature, relationships focus on forecasts longer term than day-to-day price action. Let's commence by considering the consumption of pork bellies.

The first question: How many pork bellies *can* be consumed during the next three months? The number of pounds of pork bellies that *are* consumed is determined by the cold-storage stocks on hand at the beginning of the quarter, plus estimated production during the quarter, minus stocks on hand at the end of the quarter. The maximum number of bellies that can be consumed consists of beginning inventories plus production during the quarter, which, of course, leaves nothing on hand to carry forward to the next quarter, if the maximum possible quantity is consumed now during the present period.

The next question: On what does the consumption of pork bellies depend? Assuming that the Surgeon General does not announce suddenly that bacon can be damaging to one's health, consumption depends upon the price of the product (use the average wholesale price at Chicago for 12-14-pound bellies), disposable personal incomes (that is, after payment of income taxes), and the consumption of complementary products. What goes with bacon? Eggs, mostly. Ergo, the civilian consumption of shell eggs for the quarter needs to be estimated.

Now let's summarize the above assumptions in equation form.

$$C_t + S_{t+1} = Q_t + S_t$$

The above equation states that consumption (C) during this quarter (t) plus stocks on hand (S) at the beginning of the next quarter ($_{t+1}$) equals estimated production (Q) during the quarter (t) plus stocks on hand (S) at the start of the current quarter (t).

Our second equation declares that

$$C_t = f(P_t, \ Y_t, \ E_t)$$

Current consumption (C_t) depends upon, or is a function (f) of, the price (P) of bellies, disposable income (Y), and civilian consumption of shell eggs (E) for this quarter (t).

Now we also want to answer the question of how to estimate the cold-storage inventory available at the end of the quarter; that is, what determines the inventory policy of those engaged in the business?

Stocks at the beginning of next quarter (S_{t+1}) depend upon *expected* next quarter's consumption (C_{t+1}) minus future *estimated* production, and upon *probable* consumption two quarters from now (C_{t+2}) minus production two quarters from now (Q_{t+2}). To indicate that we are now referring to those people and firms who determine storage policy, we will represent their estimates by placing a ($^-$) over variables.

$$S_{t+1} = f(\overline{C}_{t+1} - \overline{Q}_{t+1}, \ \overline{C}_{t+2} - \overline{Q}_{t+2})$$

Naturally, estimates can be made from existing published information. You can assume that production expectations reflect knowledge about the proportion of the pig crop that will be marketed each quarter based on information published in the U.S. Department of Agriculture's *Pig Crop* and *Hogs and Pigs* quarterly reports. Expectations of consumption can be assumed to depend on consumer incomes projected from recent trends and prices. With these data in hand, we can state that future output of pork bellies ($\overline{Q}$) depends upon the millions of heads of sows farrowed last quarter (B) times the estimated number of pigs saved per litter (G).

$$\overline{Q}_{t+1} = f(B_{t-1} \times G_{t-1})$$

Approximately six months elapse between the date when the pigs are born (farrowed) and their reaching a marketable weight of 200-240 pounds. Variation in the size of the pig crop is the chief factor affecting total hog slaughter during any one quarter.

Each *Hogs and Pigs* contains data on previous pig crops that relate to Q_t and Q_{t+1} and B_t; that is, to estimated belly production this quarter and next and to the number of pigs farrowed. These factors, in turn, affect Q_{t+2}, belly production two quarters away. Since sows have already been bred, most of these data can be reasonably estimated. However, the number of pigs saved per litter during the quarter depends partly on weather conditions during the time of farrowing. Of course, the price of feed influences the extent to which the farmer will continue in the hog business; and if he anticipates continued high feed prices and low profits, he may discontinue his hog business altogether.

The above exercise, not intended to be a complete model, emphasizes an important aspect of commodity trading. Considerable self-discipline is required to ferret out the significant factors that affect future consumption, future supplies, and, therefore, future prices. A speculator need not be a statistician to trade commodities successfully. In fact, more than one statistician has failed miserably in these markets when he attempted to apply his favorite model.

If complex mathematical relationships drive you up the wall, do not despair. Some of the best projections spew forth from the minds of quite ordinary people who have never learned the language of mathematics and statistics. The results of any model are no better than the figures fed into it.

Notice above the frequent use of such terms as *expected, estimated,* and *probable.* These words do not imply precision. The most expensive model in the world will not improve upon incorrect estimates. Don't despair if you do not have access to the latest generation of computer equipment—you already possess the most sophisticated "computer" in the world, surrounded by your *dura mater.*

Nevertheless, try to discern as many relationships as your mind can comfortably digest to present yourself with the larger picture. Pay attention to the prices of related commodities. Note whether bacon prices are high or low in your own supermarkets, whether it is being featured, and whether people are buying more or less at the existing prices. At least, you will develop some ideas on what the market is doing without the formal framework of a model. You are really interested in making money and not in becoming enwebbed with the function and manipulation of mathematical equations.

Many models fail the test of the market because the state of statistics is such that a sufficient number of variables cannot be properly accommodated in most models. On the other hand, the human mind is capable of infinitely more minute calculations. It perceives and records details and projects them into future circumstances. The point here is that you should not become entrapped within a static framework, and, at the same time, you must discipline your thinking to comprehend as many relationships as necessary to determine whether the price of a commodity is headed up or down.

The Yezidi Phenomenon

Oftentimes a trader will either create or borrow or subscribe to a system to which he pledges undying faith. The system, no longer being a tool of the mind, becomes its crutch. He can no longer function without it and becomes confused when it fails or falters. I call this the "Yezidi phenomenon."

The Yezidis are a small group of people who reside in the Mount Ararat region. One reported aspect of their lives is their inability to transcend certain magical circumstances. A Yezidi can be entrapped within a "magic circle."

You or I or anyone, it is reported, can trace a circle in the dust around a Yezidi. If it is a completed enclosure, the Yezidi is incapable of escaping from it no matter how strenuous his efforts. Within the circle the Yezidi can move freely, but invisible barriers constrain him within it.

Even though we may try to physically pull him out of the trap, a strong invisible force will counteract our efforts. However, if we should succeed, the Yezidi will fall into a cataleptic state in which he will remain for a certain number of hours. Only two conditions will revive him from his state of catalepsis: the passage of time, or certain incantations chanted by a Yezidi priest.

Of course, he can also be freed from the circle simply by the act of someone else erasing a portion of it to permit him to escape. But he is powerless to erase it himself.

I have seen many speculators who believed that their system was the alpha and omega of trading commodity futures. They credited the system with magical powers that would transcend ordinary human reasoning. They encircled themselves with models and gimmicks in their search for a mechanical method to gain something for nothing. Naturally, the system generated correct results for a time. When the system finally failed, its creator would be stunned with the behavior of his progeny. Either time or the high priest of a new method would return him to a functioning state.

112

As I have said repeatedly, there is nothing wrong with systems and models, but they are only tools. None of them is the *sine qua non* of commodity trading. If a trading procedure could be programmed so that all positions are initiated by a computer, then our role as speculators would be reduced to a clerk's function. Profits, as well as the commodity markets, would disappear. Whether you are in the game for fun or money, you are pitting your talents against the market. And you need to utilize all the tools conjointly. How can you employ some of the principles in this chapter to fashion your own tools?

Your Own System

Thus far we have examined a number of strategies and systems that may be useful to different situations and plans. You may be inclined to build your own mathematical system, utilizing arithmetic moving averages along with other information input according to your predilections. In the first part of this chapter you were introduced to a timing device, an oscillator, which may keep you on the right side of the market.

Another useful statistical measure, *index numbers,* provides a system for recording comparative changes at different points in time. Index numbers can measure any comparative data, such as changes in gold production from year-to-year, or variations in business cycles, deviations in commodity prices, or any other quantifiable sum, reduced to a single summary figure, to register overall diversities.

Possibly the most popularized index, the Consumer Price Index (CPI), publicizes exacerbations in the cost of surviving. Other indices mentioned in this book, the Reuter United Kingdom and the Dow Jones Futures, have achieved less fame than the Dow Jones Index of leading stocks. An interesting benefit of following the Dow Jones Spot Commodity Index is that it provides an alternative to the contrived CPI. Actually indices are widely used tools which may not always be remembered as an index. Fortunately, too, they are easily constructed.

Using the figures in Table 4, let's work through a simple example to measure the change in monetary reserves of the United States from 1965 through 1972. The base year is 1965; ergo, the annual change in reserves is expressed in terms of the base year, 1965. That is, if reserves in any single year are less than the base year, the index number will be below 100; and it will be over 100 when reserves exceed the base year. Any base year can be chosen: 1914, 1929, 1948, 1960, etc. Obviously, the sorcery of it all is in selecting the base year. Choosing the correct base year will produce more favorable or less favorable results according to the wizardry of the statistician.

Here is the technique. Divide each year's reserves by the base quantity held in 1965 and then multiply that result by 100. The resulting index number furnishes a single figure to readily compare each year's progress or regress.

TABLE 4

Obtaining an Index

Year	Reserves (Billions)	Divided by the Base Year		Index
1965	15.45	15.45	X 100	100.0
1966	14.88	15.45	X 100	96.3
1967	14.83	15.45	X 100	95.9
1968	15.71	15.45	X 100	101.6
1969	16.96	15.45	X 100	109.7
1970	14.49	15.45	X 100	93.8
1971	13.19	15.45	X 100	85.4
1972	13.15	15.45	X 100	85.1

Reducing these data to a single number presents a big picture of the trend of reserves. Similarly, such unific computations can quickly reduce relative price changes, outputs, consumption, or anything else you may want to compare. Indices are especially beneficial in analyzing seasonal patterns.

Before adding more concepts to the ole tool kit, I'll make one brief observation on the Dow Jones Spot Commodity Index (changes are recorded daily in the *Wall Street Journal*), which employs 1924-26 as the base period. (A base period may consist of a single year or several years, or a moving base period may be utilized.) With the Spot Index 1924-26 = 100.

One way to measure "inflation" in one sector is to substitute the Spot Index for the Consumer Price Index.[1] Observe that between 1924-26 and August 1972, prices of commodities at the producer level increased by 67 percent. From August 1972 through May 1974, the index rose from 167 to 343—that is, prices more than doubled over a recent twenty-one-month period! A speculator's bag of tools is never overfilled until the noise of information systems clogs the channel of clear cogitation.

1. If anyone objects to the Spot Index as an inflation indicator, then he must be howling with indignation when he reads the Consumer Price Index.

CHAPTER 8
Subsidiary Kit of
Tools for Profits

Practically every individual has some advantage over all others because he possesses unique information of which beneficial use can be made only if the decisions depending on it are left to him or are made with his active cooperation.

—Friedrich A. Hayek

IN THE REPUBLIC (BOOK 5), PLATO WROTE: "THERE ARE THREE ACTS CONcerned with all things; one which uses, another which makes, and a third which imitates them." And had he written about commodity futures trading, he might have added a fourth—and one which speculates in them.

Since you have already absorbed a great deal about the technical tricks of trading, you may well say at this juncture: "So much to learn; even if I capitalize on only a portion of what I know I should earn something in this market." Adapting Plato's comments to technical analysis, we can say that a few discern and record circumstantial observations and propose distinctive rules of technical trading. A slightly larger coterie of traders profitably enlist the techniques. The majority, however, simply imitate the act of winning and never quite achieve the miraculous.

A modern author proposes: "Every successful speculator and every student of psychology knows that the mass of people are less intelligent than the few. It has been said that only 5% of the population think for

115

themselves, 10% copy the 5%, and 85% believe what they read and hear, and do what they are told."[1]

Much of what you learned in the preceding chapters is common knowledge brandished by those who fancy themselves chart technicians. Imitators have embalmed in their brain three or four basic chart patterns profiled in Chapter 4; at least it vouchsafes repartee for chinwags. However, you need to know something more to *predict* where the market is headed. Predictive skills are not easily bestowed on the casual reader. They are acquired through work, experience, and delving deeper and deeper into market machinations. This chapter opens the hatches on some servomechanics used by pros.

Volume

The Commodity Exchange Authority (U.S. Department of Agriculture) defines volume of trading as "the total of all purchases or of all sales—*not* of purchases and sales combined. Since there are two parties to every futures contract—the seller and the buyer—the aggregate of all purchases is equal to the aggregate of all sales." In other words, only one side of each transaction counts in volume data.

Volume action blows the gaff on whether speculators assent to follow existing price trends. Volume is recorded at the bottom of the Minnesota wheat chart in Figure 37. Charts can also be updated from daily volume and open-interest reports in financial newspapers such as the *Wall Street Journal.* Figure 38 reproduces this type of diurnal information.

Ab initio, there are a few basic rules that you should learn. If prices wend higher, coincidental with rising volume, increasing open interest,[2] the market is said to be technically strong. The longs are in control. Any price reaction should be of short duration.

On the other hand, if prices march upwards but volume and open interest are declining, or low, then the market is said to be technically weak because new buyers are unwilling to initiate positions. Profit-taking and offsetting of existing positions reduce activity.

Essentially the same analysis applies if the price trend is descendant. Lower prices, concomitant with rising volume and open interest, connote that the bears are in control and the downtrend is confirmed. But soft prices, modest volume, and contracted open interest pontificate a technically strong market. The general rule, therefore, is that prices tend to skate in the direction in which volume increases. Any rallies or reactions in the opposite direction can be expected to be short-lived in a technically strong market.

Referred to several times in Chapters 4 and 5 relational to pattern

1. Garfield A. Drew, *New Methods for Profit in the Stock Market* (Wells, Vt.: Fraser Publishing Co., 1966), pp. 169-70.
2. Open interest comprises the number of contracts outstanding. It will be discussed in the next section of this chapter.

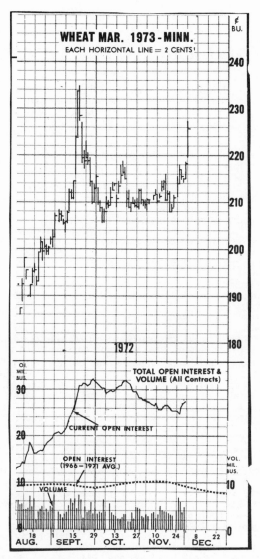

Fig. 37. Volume and open interest (Commodity Research Bureau, One Liberty Plaza, New York, N.Y. 10006.)

formation, volume generally figures most at the birth of a congestion area, but as the chart pattern unfolds volume tends to abate until the breakout. Increased volume escorts a valid breakout. For example, during the early stages of a triangle formation, volume usually is higher. As the triangle attains maturity, the trading range narrows, activity dwindles, until prices break out in one direction or another along with a fresh burst of buying or selling. The extent to which volume deviates from this pattern alerts the trader that something else may be predestined and prepares him to take advantage of the opportunity.

117

Volume and Open Interest

Grain futures trading on the Chicago Board of Trade Friday, June 14, 1974 (in thousands of bushels):

	July	Sept.	Dec.	Mar.'75	May'75	Total
Wheat	15,460	13,190	5,995	580	135	35,360
Corn	29,430	8,865	23,210	2,085	960	64,550
Oats	1,235	865	675	40	..	2,815

Soybeans: July, 18,570; August, 7,025; September, 950; November. 15,760; January '75, 3,465; March, 1,910; May, 770; Total 48,450.

Soybean oil trading totaled 7,031 tank cars of 60,000 pounds each. Soybean meal trading totaled 2,326 contracts of 100 tons each.

Open Interest (in thousands of bushels):

	Wheat	Corn	Oats	Soybeans	r-Meal	s-Oil
July	45,940	110,460	4,750	72,645	5,393	11,471
August	..	..		34,990	4,662	7,383
September ...	42,200	48,000	5,275	7,975	1,896	3,554
October	....	....		4,515	3,392
November				79,720		..
December ..	44,175	150,490	4,255		3,630	4,004
January'75 ...		.	...	30,555	1,651	3,402
March	4,805	43,365	910	13,595	1,446	1,964
May	1,030	5,855	..	3,135	293	237
Total .	138,150	358,170	15,190	242,615	23,486	35,407

r-In hundreds of tons. s-In tank cars of 60,000 pounds.

Open contracts for June 14, and changes from Thursday: **Frozen Pork Bellies** (36,000 pounds each), July 2,-428, Aug. 2,967, Feb. '75, 1,855, March 303, May 88, July 40. Total: 7,681, up 284. **Hogs** (30,000 pounds each), June 481, July 2,179, Aug. 2,699, Oct. 3,026, Dec. 1,498, Feb. '75, 567, April 200. Total: 10,650, up 550. **Cattle** (40,000 pounds each), June 995, Aug. 7,233, Oct. 5,651, Dec. 4,022, Feb. '75, 1,913, April 1,280. Total: 21,094, up 930. **Fresh Eggs** (750 cases each), June 35, July 521, Aug. 212, Sept. 1,700, Oct. 131, Nov. 202, Dec. 420. Total: 3,221, up 32. **Maine Potatoes** (50,000 pounds each), Nov. 7,059, Jan. '75, 28, March 1,247, April 268, May 1,622. Total: 10,244, up 69. **World Sugar No. 11** (112,000 pounds each), July 2,961, Sept. 3,629, Oct. 3,189, Jan. '75, 101, March 3,328, May 1,-478, July 1,501, Sept. 1,614, Oct. 1,227. Total: 19,028, down 98. **Coffee** (37,500 pounds each), July 2,080, Sept. 3,351, Nov. 538, Dec. 745, March '75, 292. Total: 7,006, up 166. **Cocoa** (30,000 pounds each), July 1,006, Sept. 1,539, Oct. 3, Dec. 2,159, March '75, 1,686, May 684, July 401, Sept. 176. Total: 7,654, down 40. **Copper** (25,000 pounds each), July 2,513, Sept. 1,841, Oct. 435, Dec. 1,369, Jan. '75, 692, March 740, May 416, July 141. Total: 8,147, up 186. **Silver** (10,000 troy ounces each), June 72, July 7,121, Sept. 7,179, Dec. 6,632, Jan. '75, 6,002, March 6,928, May 3,419, July 2,078, Sept. 828. Total: 40,259, down 163. **Cotton** (500 pound bales), July 289,400, Oct. 256,000, Dec. 725,800, March '75, 243,800, May 54,600, July 14,300, Oct. 4,400, Dec. 29,600. Total: 1,617,900, down 3,900. **Orange Juice** (15,000 pounds each), July 662, Sept. 801, Nov. 583, Jan. '75, 1,317, March 35, July 4. Total: 3,402, up 30,

Fig. 38. Daily volume and open interest report (Source: *Wall Street Journal*.)

If the trend is up and volume is rising, new buyers are coming into the market. Near the top, high prices and high volume are stimulated by those buyers who finally cross the psychological threshold, convinced that a bull market must now at last be in full swing—the late comers—plus those who went short prematurely and are now covering their short positions. To cover a short position means speculators must buy contracts to offset those they had earlier sold. Their action adds to buying power. When there are wide price fluctuations, along with high volume, this is termed a *blowoff*—the final eruption before the death knell.

Recall, also, the volume associated with forming a head-and-shoulders top. On the first peak—the left shoulder—volume was highest; on the right shoulder, volume was considerably less. It is also interesting to recognize that at times when volume dries up, it marks the end of a counter-trend. During the formation of a rounded bottom, volume is low. At the point of the breakaway gap, when prices move sharply away from the bottom formation, activity begins to pick up.

Now let us consider volume in a sidewise movement. Imagine a trading range in which volume is high at the low end of the trading range but is low as prices approach the upper end of the range. (Run that by again.) Does this action signal a strong or weak market?

Actually this action shows support-buying entering every time the price churns in the lower quartile of the range. Obviously some traders perceive the commodity as a good bargain at the lower prices. This action must be interpreted as bullish. A contrary condition—that is, if volume is high with higher prices but low with lower prices of the trading range—presages weakness, and new shorts contemplate a downward trend.

Also important on an intraday basis, volume study requires dedicating considerably more time and attention to the market than most traders can spare. Fundamentally the same rules apply on intraday as on daily volume analysis.

For example, during the market opening a heavy volume emanates from the accumulation of overnight orders generated by information fairly widely known. After a higher opening, the market can be counted on to "trade back down" for a spell. On the other hand, if the market opens lower with heavy volume, anticipate prices to rise during the mid-morning session.

What is the kinship to closing and opening prices? Let's say that prices have been trading up during the day on heavy volume. They run into resistance. During the closing hour of trading prices falter. Similar to our discussion price on gaps, a wall of sellers have stalled prices, even though they may fluctuate during the last minutes of trading. Reckon on lower opening prices the next day.

With the contraposition, prices subside on heavy volume. But the downtrend is stalled during the last hour of trading. Buyers have crossed swords with sellers toward the end of the trading session. Good prospects for a higher opening the next day!

Now let's combine the techniques in the previous chapter with volume to derive a volume oscillator. Not foreseen to betoken much effectiveness in thin markets, a moving volume curve may impart some interesting results, depending upon which commodities you trade. The method of constructing it can be quickly explained. You already know the method of moving averages.

In a faster moving commodity, construct a fifteen-day (i.e., three-week) moving average of daily trading volume. In a slower moving market, a thirty-day (six-week) moving average may appropriately serve. Experiment with both volume averages simultaneously for a while. Similar to an average price curve, the moving-average volume curve smoothes out the daily and weekly fluctuations of volume data.

You already know that with accrescent prices, volume meters activities of buyers. With decrescent prices volume gauges activities of sellers. Now on the same chart, plot also (but on a different scale) a fifteen-day moving average of prices for quick comparison.

To make the volume moving average more sensitive to short-term changes, add to your chart a five-day weighted moving average of volume. Notice when and how it penetrates the fifteen-day moving-volume curve. After an interval of observation you will be in a position to formulate your own rules and adapt them to your own trading plan. However, never try to reduce trading to a purely mechanical exercise. Mechanicalness imprisons us in an unsatisfactory state of affairs; mechanicalness must be displaced with awareness.

Open Interest

In addition to supplying information on volume, open-interest figures lend an important clue to market activity. Heraclitus (c. 500 B.C.) may well have been referring to open interest when he wrote: "Men do not know how that which is drawn in different directions harmonizes with itself. The harmonious structure of the world depends upon opposite tension, like that of the bow and the lyre." In modern lingo that means, "For every buyer there is a seller."

An "open" contract is one that has been neither liquidated by an offsetting transaction nor fulfilled by delivery. And open interest equals the number of all open commitments divided by two. In other words, *not* an aggregate of both long and short sides of transactions, it measures either all longs or all shorts outstanding at the close of business each day. For example, if open interest totals 3,000, there are 3,000 longs and 3,000 shorts.

Exactly what impends when open interest increases or decreases? Open interest *increases* if *new* buyers are purchasing from *new* sellers, or if new sellers are *selling* to new buyers. Open interest is *reduced* if *old* sellers *purchase* from *old* buyers, or if old buyers *sell* to old sellers. If you are not accustomed to the terminology you may have to think about these concepts for a while. The difference centers on whether open commitments are being initiated or offset. When a person buys one contract, open interest gains by one; when he later sells a contract he no longer has a position in the market, and open interest falls by one.

Open interest is unchanged under the following conditions: *Old* sellers purchase from *new* sellers. *New* sellers sell to *old* sellers. *New* buyers purchase from *old* buyers. *Old* buyers sell to *new* buyers. At this point you may be confused. If every buyer is matched by a seller, how do you know the market is under the control of the bulls when price flourishes and of the bears when it dips?

This question confuses not just a few. Many memorize some rules with respect to open interest and then pretend they are rationalizing by parroting these routinely learned principles. Obviously not every trader is correct in his assessment. The secret lies in whether the activity is defensive or aggressive. This point is better explicated with a scenario.

If prices thrive along with increasing volume and open interest, the market is technically strong. Rising open interest communicates that new positions are being initiated. Under these conditions it also advertises that the longs have all the money and represent the aggressive group. New buyers enter the market at different points during the trend according to their psychological biases.

Sooner or later the shorts admit their errors and offset their positions by buying, which strengthens the swing. Recall that in the summary above I wrote that liquidation of a contract *reduces* open interest. Prices up and open interest down means that the price rise is not being supported by new buying but by short covering, which adds to the technical weakness of the market.

Falling open interest also exposes the profit-taking longs who offset their positions. When buying activity dries up, prices will decline. Even precipitously! Do you understand the value of observing open interest? Don't employ it as a lone indicator; but it is a worthy subsidiary tool.

How do open-interest data unravel in a downtrend? Lower prices and higher open interest expose the shorts who flex their financial muscle and aggressively crowd the trend. How do we know that? For what other technical reason are prices declining? The longs are obviously losing money. Eventually they must cover their long positions by selling. Offsetting adds to the selling pressure, further depresses prices, and reduces open interest. When new sellers are no longer interested in entering the market from the short side and old sellers take profits, open interest is further reduced, and the market becomes technically strong.

A reminder: not all liquidation is voluntary. Traders on the wrong side of the market must support their positions with adequate security deposits; if margin calls are not met, liquidation may become involuntary. In addition to volume and open interest, some analysts await for the periodical report which summarizes the commitments of large traders and small traders.

Big Traders vs. Small Traders

Because of the value of observing odd-lot activity in the stock market, some analysts attempt to similarly interpret the *Commitments of Traders in Commodity Futures* published monthly by the USDA Commodity Exchange Authority.[3] The report affords a breakdown of open interest of large and small speculators and hedgers with outstanding commitments at the end of the month in regulated commodities.

Small traders are *not* required to file a report on their activities; but large traders—speculators, hedgers, and spreaders—must file reports of their futures transactions. The residue of open positions is attributed to "small" traders. For a large trader, anyone who holds positions equal to or exceeding a specific amount, the reporting level for wheat, corn, oats, and soybeans is 200,000 bushels; for soybean meal and oil, shell eggs, frozen pork bellies, live cattle or hogs, the reporting level is twenty-five contracts.

Table 5 portrays a page from the report on wheat futures in three markets: Chicago, Kansas City, and Minneapolis. Notice that the report provides far less detail than preferred for adequate analysis. The "theory" goes that since most losers are small traders, the safest position is on the opposite of the market. However, observe that hedging activity accounts for the largest share of the positions. Presumably the objectives of the hedger are not necessarily identical to those of the speculator. If the hedger loses in the futures market he still owns the cash product, which may yield offsetting profits.

There are other disadvantages to comparing these data to odd-lot information. Because of the nature of hedging many hedgers lose. In fact, these losses feed the financial pot on which speculators draw for their profits. On the other hand, not all hedgers are truly hedgers; many operators are sometimes hedger and sometimes speculator. Additionally, not all small traders lose.

Finally, the report shows its cloven hoof around the eleventh of each month. *Ex post facto* information promises limited value to an analyst, especially since the average commodity commitment enjoys a considerably shorter life span. By the time the report appears, traders may have already switched positions. Nevertheless, you may find some use for these figures.

3. The complete address is: U.S. Department of Agriculture, Commodity Exchange Authority, 141 West Jackson Blvd., Room A-1, Chicago, Illinois 60604.

TABLE 5
COMMITMENT OF TRADERS IN WHEAT FUTURES

CLASSIFICATION	APRIL 30, 1973		NET CHANGE FROM MARCH 31, 1973	
	Long	Short	Long	Short
Chicago Board of Trade				
Large Traders	(In thousand bushels)			
Speculative				
Long *or* short only	9,535	6,685	− 1,105	+ 320
Long *and* short				
(spreading)	18,820	17,605	+ 2,995	+ 3,710
Total	28,355	24,290	+ 1,890	+ 4,030
Hedging	51,216	46,525	+ 9,091	+ 6,860
Total reported by				
large traders	79,571	70,815	+ 10,981	+ 10,890
Small Traders				
Speculative and				
hedging	46,249	55,005	+ 7,779	+ 7,870
Total open interest	125,820	125,820	+ 18,760	+ 18,760
Percent Held By:				
Large traders	63.2	56.3	− .9	+ .3
Small traders	36.8	43.7	+ .9	− .3
Kansas City Board of Trade				
Large Traders	(In thousand bushels)			
Speculative				
Long *or* short only	1,495	2,615	− 1,330	+ 1,820
Long *and* short				
(spreading)	1,145	1,410	+ 305	− 515
Total	2,640	4,025	− 1,025	+ 1,305
Hedging	39,095	40,640	+ 5,205	+ 1,810
Total reported by				
large traders	41,735	44,665	+ 4,180	+ 3,115
Small Traders				
Speculative and				
hedging	3,095	165	− 1,850	− 785
Total open interest	44,830	44,830	+ 2,330	+ 2,330
Percent Held By:				
Large traders	93.1	99.6	+ 4.7	+ 1.8
Small traders	6.9	.4	− 4.7	− 1.8

(continued)

123

TABLE 5 (*continued*)

Minneapolis Grain Exchange

Large Traders	(In thousand bushels)				
Speculative					
Long *or* short only	0	0	+	0	–	240
Long *and* short (spreading)	0	180	+	0	+	180
Total	0	180	+	0	–	60
Hedging	20,572	14,999	–	160	–	1,067
Total reported by large traders	20,572	15,179	–	160	–	1,127
Small Traders					
Speculative and hedging	2,078	7,471	–	27	+	940
Total open interest	22,650	22,650	–	187	–	187
Percent Held By:					
Large traders	90.8	67.0	+	.0	–	4.4
Small traders	9.2	33.0	+	.0	+	4.4

SOURCE: U.S. Department of Agriculture, Commodity Exchange Authority, 141 West Jackson Blvd., Room A-1, Chicago, Ill. 60604.

Majority Psychology

The purpose of perusing the commitments of traders and similar revealing information underpins the theory of contrary opinion, which has grown out of studies of crowd psychology. The underlying premise of the theory affirms that the public, usually wrong in their assessment of the market, are the last ones aware of news, react slowly to it, and are reluctant to devote necessary resources to proper research. Chapter 2 dramatized the profile of a loser.

Less inclined to be bearish and attracted to the markets in times of ebullient excitement, the public, as they say in the deep South, just don't cotton to dull markets. They tend to buy and sell with the news rather than against it. They willingly absorb enormous losses when wrong. As the public becomes more and more fascinated with well-publicized bullish events, they eagerly buy on the first reaction after a topping formation because "it's cheaper."

Counteracting the majority, because of the theory of contrary opinion's superiority, a successful professional *cannot* score a profit by buying and selling *with* the public. Let us suppose that the general sentiment is bullish. Prices rise. All the bulls decide concurrently to take profits. Suddenly sellers are without buyers. What will happen to the price? It will drop precipitously. But the few who earlier offset positions converted a paper profit into an actual profit. What a few can do the many cannot accomplish.

The same logic inheres in the stock market. Paper profits from owning equities cannot be transmuted to actual profits without buyers. To headline that total wealth increases or decreases by billions of dollars whenever a market bounces in one direction or another is pure nonsense because it is *impossible* for everyone acting in unison to convert all stock holdings, all real estate, etc., into money. Inherent in every sale is a willing buyer.

One published compilation of market psychology appears weekly in *Consensus* (reproduced in Figure 39). Some trading systems have incorporated a similar index into their models. It is a valuable tool once you learn to operate it in your favor. The first effort, of course, is to observe yourself and the majority from a disinterested or unattached position. That step, in itself, is the most difficult to accomplish.

This chapter doubles as an introduction to subsequent advanced material that you will absorb on your path to getting rich by trading commodity futures. Little space has been devoted to these topics because they comprise an intermediate level of tactics; nevertheless, trading commodities is not confined to memorizing a few chart formations. These are only tools in a system that you must master for repetitive success.

Commodity Indices

Commodity indices telegraph the trend of the commodity markets. Data on three indices appear daily in the *Wall Street Journal,* and a weekly chart is published on Mondays. The Dow Jones Futures Index will probably be of most interest to you (see Figure 40). The index is a market average—a single indicator—pointing out the direction of futures prices on a daily basis. Taking note of the general trend sometimes helps to keep a trader on the right side of the market. However, the prices of individual commodities do turn around, and not necessarily at the same rate of change.

The Dow Jones Futures Index, as another technical tool, may be useful in determining how one commodity compares with the other ones; that is, its *relative strength.* Measuring relative strength tells us whether one commodity is stronger or weaker than the average. The theory propounds support for a long position in an uptrend if a commodity is stronger than the average, or for standing aside or going short if it is weaker than the average. The tool, however, does not function equally well for all commodities.

A relative-strength ratio is determined by dividing the closing price of the commodity by the futures average. The result may be more meaningful if it is plotted on a point-and-figure chart and then interpreted in

MARKET SENTIMENT INDEX

A BULLISH CONSENSUS OF OPINIONS

For the Week Beginning:

	Oct. 2	Sept. 25	Sept. 18
Platinum	80%	61%	44%
Potatoes	75	84	73
Oil	74	72	59
Silver	73	70	37
Sugar	66	62	34
Juice	65	57	47
Cattle	60	47	48
Corn	58	57	68
Soybeans	58	56	58
Cocoa	57	65	68
Cotton	54	53	56
Hogs	54	37	54
Pork Bellies	54	33	33
Eggs	40	39	50
Copper	40	68	47
Meal	48	72	50
Wheat	46	73	78
Plywood	42	19	38

The Market Sentiment Index reflects the opinions of professional advisors and brokers market letters as observed and recorded by our research department. The index is intended as a guide only. The "theory of contrary opinion" holds that when 85% of these analysts are bullish, it can be assumed that the market is overbought and a turn is coming. Conversely if 75% are bearish (25% bullish on the index) the market is likely to become oversold and a rally will develop soon.

Compiled Weekly By Fred Colton
Director of Research
Maduff & Sons, Los Angeles, California

Fig. 39. Bullish consensus of opinions (Source: *Consensus—National Commodity Futures Weekly,* 30 West Pershing Road, Kansas City, Mo. 64108.)

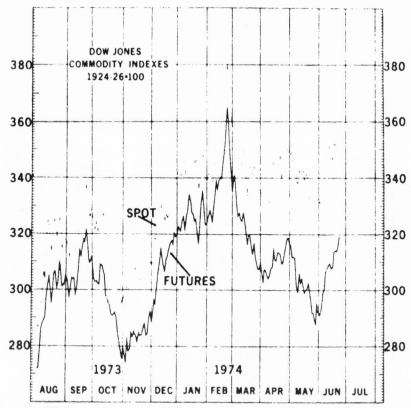

Dow Jones Futures, Friday — 319.47, up 3.51; last year, 234.67.

Dow Jones Spot — 358.39, up 3.18; last year, 243.26.

Reuter United Kingdom — 1255.6, up 4.4; last year 992.3. (1931 equals 100.)

Fig. 40. The Dow Jones Futures Index (Source: *Wall Street Journal.*)

the normal way as other charts. In Figure 41, December 1973 silver bullion (Chicago) is plotted on the left side of the chart with the relative-strength ratio on the right over a comparable period. During July, silver prices rose substantially, but the relative-strength ratio suggested that the move was running out of steam, and after formation of a triple top on July 16 began demonstrating "sell" signals. Opportunities for short sales occurred a week later.

The other indices also appear daily. The Dow Jones Spot Index summarizes average cash prices. It should be observed for tipoffs of possible

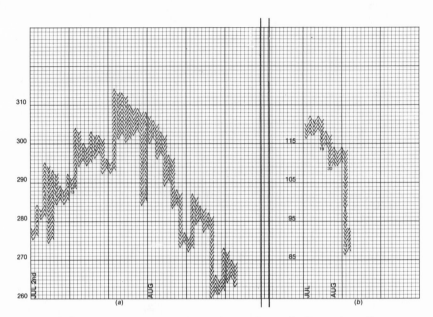

Fig. 41. Relative strength: *a*, December Chicago silver; *b*, December silver over Dow Jones Futures

new directions in the cash markets. Cash markets make the futures prices, and not the other way around. A futures price is an estimate of tomorrow's cash prices.

The Reuter United Kingdom Index primarily interests those who follow London prices. A trader may record London prices as supplementary data even though his trades are executed exclusively in the U.S. markets.

Elliott Wave Theory

One last important tool—the wave principle—will be introduced here before moving into market fundamental analysis. Although related to the cyclical fluctuations discussed in later chapters, the wave principle, developed by R. N. Elliott, is more correctly termed a natural rhythm. Certain unknown laws of nature affect the biorhythms of investors whose reactions are reflected in price-wave patterns.

Elliott observed that a bull market consists of five waves. For example, wave no. 1 is an up-wave; wave no. 2 represents the reactive wave; wave no. 3 advances to a level higher than the previous peak of wave no. 1; wave no. 4 is the second downward reaction; the final wave, no. 5, is the last upward surge of the bull market.

Elliott also accounts for the intermediate waves and ripples. The advancing waves (that is, nos. 1, 3, and 5) also encapsulate five intermediate waves. In addition, each intermediate wave is comprised of five minor waves.

Price reactions and bear markets, however, follow a different line of comportment. Primary waves nos. 2 and 4 consist of three waves in their downward movements. Bear markets act similarly; that is, they reflect a triadic pattern of waves rather than quintuplicate action experienced in the bull phase.

These waves do not occur as a matter of pure chance but reflect the operation of the natural phenomena that produce these symmetrical patterns. To disentangle the waves singles out the chief difficulty of this tool. Segregating and identifying each successive wave demands keen perception. As a practical matter, begin your study of price series in practice sessions until you have convinced yourself that this tool can place the profits in your pockets. As with all tools and techniques, treat it with the utmost respect. In fact, you should postpone utilization of technical devices until you have a basic understanding of the underlying fundamentals of demand and supply.

SECTION C

Piercing the Veil

CHAPTER 9
What Economists Do

I've found economists the most independent breed of the human species with the exception of the press. I have found that my economic advisers are not always right but they are always sure.

— Richard M. Nixon (1973)

BASIC TO A RUDIMENTARY UNDERSTANDING OF PRICE MOVEMENTS—whether your system is charts, coattailing, spirit-rapping, or holding a wet finger to the wind—are the underlying forces that induce these changes. This installment engirds an elementary introduction to economic enlightenment. It will aid you considerably in your analysis of the markets.

The difficulty with economics is that few really know what the subject deals with. Of course, it's what economists do! Once I overheard an illustrious University of Chicago graduate snap at someone who had derided him for his inability to balance a checking account. "Well, I'm not a home economist," he retorted.

Many "economists" are either statisticians or else "government economists" who volunteer their lives working out second-best or third-best solutions to government-created problems. (Whatever happened to the best?) Some business economists dedicate themselves to the construction of models. A few of these models function fairly well for a time.

What Economists Study

Most textbook definitions convey that economics is the study of the allocation of limited resources among unlimited wants. This short-run definition appropriately communicates the result of human conduct. It does not elucidate the underlying cause. Ludwig von Mises transcends the time element and advances the idea that "economics is not about goods and services; it is about human action and choice."[1]

To highlight our nature of wanting more than ever seems to be available, I wish to stress that in the totality of human existence, shortages do not derive from the quantity of available resources over the long run. (Naturally ephemeral shortages and surpluses result in the adjustment process.)

Adverting to the Source of all wealth we instantly identify the problem. It is not one of restricted resources, of finite faculties for transforming these resources. The limited resource is the mind of man! And man's mind is limited only because he either prefers to deny himself the possibility of creating, of innovating, or of locating alternatives, or else he is stymied by burdensome bureaucracies that incinerate incentive, impale initiative, and incubate incompetence.

Humans are essentially lazy—and that includes possibly 98 percent of us. Few pioneers will focus their minds to penetrate the mysteries of nature and life. Whenever a rare, imaginative, and inventive three-brained being among us originates a major breakthrough in techniques, greater production with the same resources results. Many benefit.

We are concerned here only with the principles of economics and not with their multifaceted mutations. We are interested in human actions that affect our commodity trading decisions and in adapting rudimentary concepts to our own requirements.

Why People Buy

The mystery of why people buy some goods and not others is hidden in the psyche of the individual. Most economic textbooks explain that changes in demand spring from four major categories. Demand will shift in response to changes in incomes, expectations, prices of substitute and complementary goods, and habits. These factors can all affect demand. But how important are they? Look through a magazine. How many of the advertisements appeal to any of the above four categories?

Naturally, the manufacturer of a product wants the consumer to develop a habit or taste for his product. Dependence can be established through reduced prices, free samples, addiction, or repetition.

To what does the manufacturer appeal? Call it greed, if you will—that foxy gremlin, "something for nothing." Most people fail to take control of their own lives. They let others make decisions for them. They let a new

---

1. Ludwig von Mises, *Human Action: A Treatise on Economics* (New Haven: Yale University Press, 1949), p. 491.

habit creep into their mind. Subsequently they find it easier to let the bad habit rule them rather than control it. Consequently, "unwanted" habits change slowly. I understand that six to eight years are required to supplant a bad habit with a desirable one. To that, I can say "at the least."

Do you recall that I wrote in a previous chapter that 80-90 percent of the decisions of most people are made by others? "But, mother, all the girls at school are wearing them." "John, you simply must remodel our old, outdated kitchen. Besides, Mary's husband just bought a new . . ." "Smoke Fume cigarettes. All the movie stars do." And so forth.

Yes, these are habits. They are self-induced habits resulting from greed or fear or imitation. How does this relate to commodity trading? In Chapter 2, I discussed the attitude of traders. Who buys at the top of the market and sells at the bottom? Greedy and follow-the-masses-type traders! When the general public learns about an "opportunity," become a contrarian. Follow Don Rogers's advice: "Don't follow the public."[2] Take your profits and wait for a new opportunity.

People respond to all kinds of fear: fear of the future, uncertainties, worry, insecurity. The reaction is not the same as changes in expectations, but the response is identical. For example, we know that when people worry, feel insecure, or face uncertainties, they tend to eat more. I suppose one can say that a worried nation means a larger intake of food, liquids, and alcohol.

Changes in expectations, related to the above fears, somehow connote greater rationality. The prospect of war invites hoarding of storable commodities—sugar, for example. The prospect of higher prices results in purchasing now instead of later.

In a situation of hyperinflation, the object is to get out of local currency as fast as possible and into commodities or another currency, if possible. I presume you are familiar with historical instances of this sort. The prospect of deflation induces people to hoard money and postpone purchases. However, the whipsaw of depression, coupled with inflation, suggests an entirely different strategy.

We may include another one, which I will call "protest." A consumer boycott temporarily reduces demand. The 1973 meat boycott demonstrates the power of concerted effort. This action, not necessarily a permanent change in tastes or habits, does temporarily depress prices. Many speculators did not anticipate such a sharp price reaction and overstayed their positions. The meat boycott in the spring of 1973 appears to have had the unusual effect of altering habits somewhat as many consumers discovered new eating patterns. But unless new patterns are constantly reinforced, they gradually slip back into the older and more firmly established habit.

The prices of substitute and complementary goods affect the demand for a particular commodity. For example, if popcorn and peanuts are practically perfect equivalents for people who frequent circuses, zoos, and

2. Donald I. Rogers, *How NOT to Buy a Common Stock* (New Rochelle: Arlington House, 1972), p. 117.

135

movies, then a sharp increase in the price of peanuts, and no change in the price of popcorn, will result in more popcorn and fewer peanuts being eaten. In Chapter II, I will work through with you a problem on the relationship between beef and pork prices.

The price of gasoline and the demand for large and small automobiles summarize the principle of complementary goods. With a 60 percent rise in gasoline prices, consumers tend to demand more smaller cars and fewer large ones. Bacon and eggs are the example given in Chapter 7.

Changes in income require deeper analysis. Within a broad concept, higher-income people spend more in the aggregate; therefore, demand increases or shifts upwards according to the popular principle. It depends upon whose incomes are being increased, their ages, the situation in the preceding era (recession, depression, boom, war) and the near-term future prospects. (See Chapter 10 for a practical application.) Many economists tend to overlook this broader view.

Following a period of rationing or privation, consumption will shoot up rapidly for all categories. With gradually rising incomes, demand for all types of goods and services will not rise *pari passu*. Beyond a certain point, food consumption will form a decreasingly smaller proportion of the total household budget. Consumers with rising incomes may eat out more often and in more expensive restaurants, but only about 35 or 40 percent of the tab counts toward food consumption; the remainder of the bill resides in service and use of the facilities.

In Chapter 7, I employed changes in income as one of the significant variables in determining the quantity of pork bellies, or bacon, that may be consumed. This assumption is a naïve one. While disposable incomes are important, the quarter-to-quarter change is less significant. The proportion of increased incomes spent on bacon is bound to be small. Expectations of a recession or job furloughs during the first half of 1974 probably predominated some types of consumer purchases.

Model construction depends upon the reasoning process and not upon mechanical relationships. Through economic reasoning—that is, through the employment of logic—a trader will ferret out meaningful factors and discard less utilitarian variables.

Now suppose we have a situation where tastes remain static over some period. Incomes are unchanged. Price relationships are stable. Let us assume we are referring to crude oil. We still observe that smaller or larger quantities of crude oil are being purchased although none of the above factors changes.

This phenomenon depends upon the price of the product—crude oil in this case. At no time have we mentioned the price of the product in question. We talked about prices of substitute and complementary goods, of incomes, of preferences and fears, of greed and uncertainties—all of these things will cause demand to shift. Now we are speaking of the quantity of a product that will be bought at different prices.

At higher prices consumers as a whole (I'm not referring to any one or few buyers) will buy less than they will at lower prices. This is the law of demand. The line *DD* in Figure 42 is a graphic presentation of this law. Pick any point on the line. At a high price (represented by the vertical height of the graph) buyers will not purchase as large a quantity as they will at a lower price. (Quantity is represented by the horizontal distance.)

If incomes rise, or if people prefer more of the commodity for one reason or another, then the entire demand curve *(DD)* will increase, or shift to the right. If demand for the good falls, then the entire *DD* curve will shift to the left. Regardless of where we draw the demand curve, the law of demand remains valid. Consumers prefer a lower price to a higher one. Consequently, they will buy more of the good when it is cheaper.

Knowledge of demand alone does not tell us what we require. We need to know something about supply.

Why People Sell

Suppose that you own farm land and tools (or a factory). What are your alternatives? If you do nothing, you still have expenses: taxes, insurances, depreciation, interest, perhaps some employees. You may decide to rent

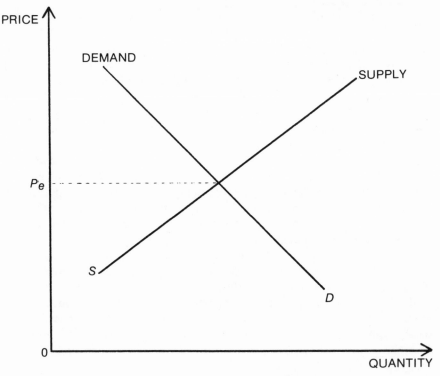

Fig. 42. Determination of equilibrium price

it. Rental income will have to be adequate to provide an appropriate return to your investment besides covering all expenses. Or you may decide to farm it yourself. (We will assume away the complications of governmental interference.)

Before you plant crops or purchase livestock, you will estimate the costs of production and feed and estimate both demand for your output and total supplies in order to arrive at an approximate future price. Then, you will calculate whether operations will cover costs of production including your salary and a return on your total investment.

If you are producing what hundreds of other farmers or ranchers are growing, then you will focus on costs. If you are in a fairly competitive industry, then your output will have practically no effect at all on price. The interaction of a *large* number of buyers and suppliers will determine price. Since you cannot affect price, you will concentrate on matters which you do affect, namely, costs of operation. Through efficiency and innovation, you will determine your present costs. Through hedging operations, to some extent, you will predetermine some of your future costs of production.

A livestock producer will observe grain prices. He will weigh the prospects of higher or lower grain costs next season. He will estimate interest charges, and all other costs he can pin down.

Farming, probably more than any other industry, is subject to the vagaries of nature. Costs of production are centroidal in the initial decision to plant or not to plant. But the question of supply at the end of the season depends upon other factors: weather (enough of it at the right time), diseases and pests, and quality of the product. Additionally, the rate of flow of product to market causes short-term price oscillations. The rate of flow may depend in part upon nature—whether the crop is premature or late—organization of the operator, availability of equipment, and transportation.

As if it were not enough to contend with weather and weevils, the operator must recognize that supplies can also be affected by governmental interference, controls, and pricing. Government meddling, of course, equally influences demand. Tariffs and quotas, the availability of marketable supplies, and even the rate of return to investment can be manipulated by government.

The rate of return to investment affects supply in the long run. High-return industries will attract capital for expansion, and bid away better-quality labor to operate the additional equipment. Naturally, the more profitable industries are high-wage industries. Profitable industries will attract newcomers, which, in turn, will increase supply. Greater supplies result in lower prices to the consumer and lower returns to the investor. In other words, capital flows from one endeavor to another as the rate of return to investment alters.

For example, if you believe that fertilizers will be more expensive and in shorter supply during the coming season, you may decide to shift production efforts from corn to soybeans. If enough producers shift, then next season's soybean crop will bring a lower price, *ceteris paribus,* with an opposite effect on the price of corn.

The question of profits should also be briefly covered. In competitive industries, profits do not accrue under normal circumstances. Profits remain after all other costs are covered. Return on investment, for example, is not profit. It is a cost of doing business, whether the capital is borrowed from the bank or mother-in-law or is owned by the operator. Wages to the owner-manager is not a profit. A manager still must be employed in the owner's absence.

Profits can be earned, nevertheless, if weather and insects destroy part of the other fellow's crops, or if war suddenly erupts and boosts demand, or if foreign products cannot be imported, or if government pays an unexpected subsidy. These situations produce profits.

An entrepreneur can augment his income through product differentiation. By different packaging, use of colors, ascribing mystical qualities to the product, or some other special talent, a higher price can be commanded. For example, few of the large numbers of actors and actresses differentiate their "product" sufficiently to command a high price for their services. Nevertheless, through special employment of their talents, entertainers like Bob Hope and John Wayne ask and receive far above average remuneration for their services.

Now if we want to draw a supply curve for a competitive industry, we can represent production with an upward sloping line. Translated into words, it states that suppliers are willing to sell more at higher prices than at lower prices. Now that is a reasonable statement, isn't it?

Figure 42 illustrates a supply curve that embodies the aforementioned properties. If the supply curve shifts downward (to the left), then weather has destroyed part of the crop, or Newcastle's disease has affected the number of laying hens, or quality of product is lower than anticipated. A shift to the right of the curve means that supplies have increased. Moving along the curve (up and down) says that whatever total supplies may be at a given point in time, sellers are willing to offer more on the market at higher prices than they are at lower prices.

How to Keep Score

"All this discussion of demand and supply is interesting, but I don't see the direct relationship with the futures markets." The interaction of demand and supply determines prices in the marketplace. Prices are a method to keep score and provide the rationing factor to allocate products among many users. Prices bring buyers and sellers together.

High prices in futures markets are really an incentive to encourage research and development. They act as an incentive to reallocate resources.

139

Capital, labor, and raw materials are drawn away from less profitable endeavors and are attracted into undertakings that hold promise for greater return on investment, and thus the process of allocation itself acts as an incentive or disincentive.

Graphically, the above-mentioned demand-and-supply curves represent various quantities that buyers will purchase and vendors are willing to sell over a schedule of prices. The curves do not mean that transactions are taking place at each of these prices. The market system is an information system, and only one price can prevail at any time.

Where these two curves intersect in Figure 42 determines equilibrium price; that is, quantities bought and sold equate at a price that both buyers and sellers can live with (P_e in the diagram). At any other price, one group or another's desires are not satisfied. The diagram illustrates a static situation of conditions necessary for achieving equilibrium price.

Of course, markets are not perfect. They make mistakes when information is inadequate or is incorrectly interpreted. Remember: I wrote previously that production and investment decisions are based on *estimates* of the future.

Prices are always fluctuating around the theoretical equilibrium. They swing back and forth like a pendulum or sometimes lash around like an alligator's tail. "Prices are often constrained into aberrant patterns by outside forces, governmental or private. For instance, wheat futures prices have displayed a seasonal bias attributable to the workings of the government loan program."[3]

Whenever conditions adjust to demand or supply, a new set of curves is graphed to represent the altered situation.

Also, we can record changes in domestic prices brought about by exports and imports. In Figure 43 exports (X) are sales. Therefore, increased sales to foreigners mean a rise in demand. The new demand curve is labeled D (domestic demand) plus X (exports or foreign demand).

Suppose that curve SS represents domestic production of wheat during a growing season. What occurs when government suddenly contracts to sell wheat to Russia, India, and China after the crop is in the ground? Futures prices rise sharply to P_x.

By the same reasoning, importation of a commodity increases domestic supply. For example, net imports of silver bullion during the second quarter of 1973 amounted to 4.6 million ounces. In the absence of imports, silver will sell at price P_e; with imports total supply is increased and domestic price falls to P_m.

The diagrams in Figures 42 and 43, drawn for those who can more readily understand the relationship in graphs than in words, condense the preceding verbal descriptions. Explaining how governmental interference distorts the market embodies the same graphic technique.

3. Roger W. Gray, "The Seasonal Patterns of Wheat Futures under the Loan Program," *Food Research Institute Studies* 3, no. 1 (February 1962): 86.

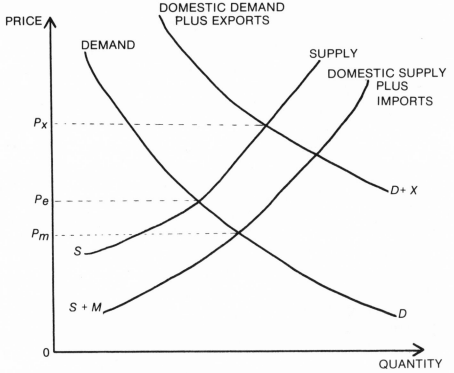

PRICE

DOMESTIC DEMAND
PLUS EXPORTS

DEMAND

SUPPLY

DOMESTIC SUPPLY
PLUS
IMPORTS

P_x

P_e

P_m

S

$S + M$

$D + X$

D

0

QUANTITY

Fig. 43. Effects of exports and imports on prices

How to Predict Effects of Price Controls

For many persons, implementation of price controls on August 15, 1971 came as a surprise. A few alert individuals, prepared for that event, expect more controls albeit in ˚different form. Not many, unfortunately, were shocked by the meaning of that step.

"In a centrally directed economy it matters little whether the means of production are under state control, or remain in private hands with the price of final output controlled. The result is the same. Not enough people recognize that the hallmark of the 'planned economy' is not planning. It is that it aims to concentrate power in the hands of the State," wrote Trygve Hoff in an editorial in the Norwegian weekly, *Farmand*.

Consumers should recognize that the directed system functions ineffectually. It causes shortages and misuse of our resources. Controlled markets are simply less efficient. "Those in the open market are forced to operate on the basis of economical use of resources since they cannot call on taxpayers to pay for their mistakes. The controlled market operates on the basis of scare headlines instead of the realities of resource availabilities and economy."[4]

4. Yale Brozen, "The Role of Open Markets in Coordinating and Directing Economic Activity," *Futures Trading Seminar*, (Madison, Wis.: Mimir Publ., 1966), 3:57.

Does economic theory predict the outcome of tinkering and meddling? Yes, quite definitely! Figure 44 demonstrates, in a simple model, anticipated results.

In an uncontrolled market, prices will fluctuate around P_e. If prices rise too far above P_e, sellers will want to supply larger amounts to the market; price will be held down. If price is depressed below P_e, people will want to buy more at the lower price than the higher price. The action of buyers will bid price up again.

Now let's say the emperor issues an edict. For example, in A.D. 301 Emperor Diocletian "promulgated an edict which fixed for the whole Roman Empire maximum prices for commodities, freight rates, and wages."[5] In Figure 44, P_c is the control price. The ceiling price is *below* the free-market price.

We already know that buyers prefer lower prices to higher ones, while sellers prefer higher prices to lower ones. The quantity of the commodity

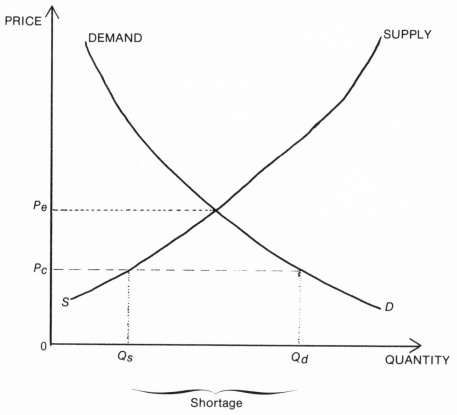

Fig. 44. How government fecundates shortages

5. H. Mitchell, "The Edict of Diocletian," *Canadian Journal of Economics and Political Science* (February 1947).

demanded ($0Q_d$ is the distance along the horizontal axis) exceeds the quantity supplied ($0Q_s$). Shortages obviously will appear. What was the 1973-74 situation? Shortages! What else does any thinking person expect to happen?

What happened in Rome with strictly enforced price controls, progressive inflation, and weakening of the military? Father Lactantius (*c.* 260-340) writes: "When by various extortions he had made all things exceedingly dear, he attempted by an ordinance to limit their prices. Then much blood was shed for the veriest trifles; men were afraid to expose anything for sale and the scarcity became more excessive."[6] Of passing interest, the price of gold, within four years, had risen from 50,000 to 120,000 denarii per pound!

This chapter has introduced some basic economic concepts that will aid you in understanding the markets. By this time, you should have an adequate grasp of what induces the market to act and react. In the process of learning, I hope, you will be able to profit from your own actions and reactions.

6. *Ibid.*

CHAPTER 10
The Importance of Fundamental Analysis

The speculator is one who observes the future and acts before it occurs.

—Bernard Baruch

"THAT MARKET'S GETTING STRONGER THAN HORSERADISH. IT KNOWS something we don't. I suspect we'd better listen to it." With that comment, the trader began systematically reviewing his open positions.

To help you understand the price relationships and demand-and-supply analysis interpreted in Chapter 9, discussion will continue with specific examples. Because most trading takes place in agricultural products, and because substantially more data, on supply especially, are available from the U.S. Department of Agriculture, the examples have been drawn heavily from this sector.

Action of Demand and Supply

Although we have been speaking of the price-determining action of the interplay of market forces, you may question whether futures transactions actually create prices. Underpinning the price of a commodity is the coming-together of buyers and sellers; that is, interaction of the forces of demand and supply and deviation from that price caused by market interference and estimating errors.

The wild action witnessed in the trading pits is essentially one of *price discovery.* Most transactions are consummated outside the exchanges, so it is unlikely that brokers can swing prices very far away from the market price and sustain it afterwards. Such action would require tremendous financial muscle. Nevertheless, I will not mislead you by writing that no hanky-panky sallies forth. *Deals* are occasionally put together, and attempts to bias futures prices do germinate. As one broker puts it, "That's the nature of the beast." But these *tours de force* do not aim to turn the trend but only manipulate it to advantage.

Some of those who criticize futures trading are the very ones who would profit if prices were kept more secret. One buyer of a certain commodity stated, "If a futures contract existed for the commodity I deal in, I'd have to pay a higher price. Now I can usually buy under the market because the grower doesn't always know what the market price should be." That sounds like a good case *for* instead of *against* the existence of futures markets.They throw a strong light on future trends.

Let us examine the hog market and speculate on the price direction according to supply and likely demand. We will focus on the easier to derive, namely, supply.

Because availability of hogs today depends, in part, on decisions made six months ago and longer (discussed in Chapter 7), we must examine the recent past. Table 6 summarizes pig production. The years 1971, 1972, and 1973 register declining pig crops comparable to the 1963-1965 era.

Conjunctive to past pig crops, current supplies depend upon how many sows are held back for breeding and also upon rate of gain in weight. Let's look at some slaughter estimates. One source, during the last quarter of 1973, forecasted 1974 slaughter as a percentage of 1973. For the first quarter, 85-95 percent, 105-115 percent for the next two quarters, and 115-130 percent for the fourth quarter of 1974, were predicted.

TABLE 6

MOST RECENT PIG CROPS

	Dec.-May	% Chg.	June-Nov.	% Chg.
1970	52,292		49,629	
1971	52,589	+ .56	45,923	-7.46
1972	48,066	-8.6	43,284	-5.7
1973	46,782[1]	-2.67	42,100[2]	-2.73

SOURCE: Saul Stone & Co., 222 South Riverside Plaza, Chicago, Ill. 60606.

[1]Preliminary government estimate.
[2]Saul Stone estimate.

Smaller pig-crop figures suggest market bullishness. Slaughter estimates are bullish for the first part of the year but bearish for the second part. In other words, if more pigs are retained for breeding during the first quarter of 1974, this decision will result in larger supply for the market during the fall and winter of 1974-75.

Rates of gain in weight relate to efficiency. An efficient farmer may be able to bring a hog to market in five months, while an inefficient one may require seven months of feeding. Rates of gain are adversely dominated by bad weather. Also, they were modulated by record-high soybean-meal prices in 1972, which caused many efficient farmers to withdraw supplemental feeding. Weight-gain time was lengthened.

The rate of gain influences kill-rate. For example, assume that two-thirds of farmers are efficient and can bring hogs to slaughter in five months, while the remainder require seven months. Therefore, average to-market time is five and one-half months. If reduction in rate of gain for efficient farmers amounts to one month, average feeding time is lengthened by three weeks. This explains falling short of slaughter estimates. On the other hand, if we expect lower grain prices for late 1974, then rates of gain and hog slaughter will rise—a bearish factor.

On the demand side, for the longer term, we examine such factors as population growth, changes in disposable income, wholesale pork prices, anticipated changes in prices of pork substitutes, per capita pork consumption, and military consumption and exports. Population growth does not enter into a short-term analysis. Within the context of hog-cycle discussion, costs of operation figure importantly.

The problems of life are not brought about so much by the known as by the unexpected. Being prepared for the implausible makes it easier to swing with the trend. For example, how would a major strike subvert commodity prices? History metes out an idea. The major automobile strike of September 7-October 30, 1967 bore upon both the cash and futures markets because demand weakened. The summary in Table 7 records the percentage decline in price during that interim.

Another example of supply and demand in action focuses on the rapid rise of beef prices during 1973, which resulted from a mixture of develop-

TABLE 7

DECLINE IN COMMODITY PRICES, SEPTEMBER-OCTOBER 1967

Commodity	Cash (%)	Futures (%)
Eggs	- 15	- 22
Hogs	- 18	- 1
Cattle	- 3	- 8
Pork Bellies	- 12	- 10

ments. Because of the shift of ocean currents, the protein-rich catch of anchovies (used to manufacture livestock feed) of Peru, Ecuador, and Chile was sharply reduced. Demand for a substitute commodity, soybeans in this case, increased (or shifted the *DD* curve to the right in Figure 43).

Inclement weather in many parts of the world induced further upward pressure on prices, and grain exports skyrocketed to record levels during 1972-73. Therefore, the cost of feeding cattle and hogs in the United States rose sharply. Reducing beef supplies were the harsh winter in the Midwest (killing large numbers of cattle) and the Food and Drug Administration's ban on the use of DES, a growth stimulant to increase beef yield.

Concurrently, due to rapid rise in disposable incomes for some age groups, consumers demanded more beef. Again, the interaction of demand and supply bore the stamp of higher prices, notwithstanding the existence of price controls. (Development of a gray market circumvented that obstacle.)

Employment of fundamental analysis combined with technical tools helps the trader to perpetuate proper perspective. But it does not imply that both sets of tools are equally solemnized. The longer-term trader tends to italicize fundamentals, while a short-term trader leans heavily on charts, volume, open interest, and other technical data. Nevertheless, balance should prevail.

Because extreme situations crop up, seek out mutable elements of demand and supply. To outmaneuver your competitors, act before the market fully discounts news.

Notes on Factors in Supply-and-Demand Analysis

Now let's attempt to isolate some supply-and-demand factors that can affect prices over the very near term (next quarter's action) and over the longer term (long enough for new production to come into the picture).

Next quarter's meat supply hinges on number and weight of animals slaughtered, seasonal and weather influences, prices of feed, number of animals on feed in the heavier weight range, disappearance rate of storage stocks, government purchases, imports, and price controls.

Over the long haul, supply of meat is determined by both present prices and expected future prices, as well as trends in feed prices coupled with the availability of growth stimulants. And never overlook the return on investment, which is reflected both in the above-mentioned price relationship and in alternative land and resources uses. Of course, the price of substitute goods bears upon demand and, subsequently, future supply projections. Naturally, disease control and greater efficiency— that is, technology—prejudice future supply constituents. The other major factor centers on trends in animal production, such as the number being fed, production of offspring, and size of cow herds or pig crops.

The immediate demand for meat products is chiefly dominated by the prices of substitute commodities, government purchase and export programs, and the profit margins of packers.

Long-range demand is determined by disposable consumer incomes, population growth and age distribution, general economic conditions and anticipated conditions, changes in consumer tastes and preferences and government economic policies.

Similarly stimulated by feed prices and seasonal supply influences, very-short-term egg output also centers upon government purchase and import programs. Two components that influence storage stocks are: disappearance rate of stored eggs (the storage cycle of shell eggs is extremely brief) and the stock of frozen eggs.

Centroidal to long-term supply, expected future prices of both eggs and feed, notwithstanding any changes in fixed costs of operation—all determine the rate of return on total investment. Too, disease control and greater production efficiency decide the size of the flock and rate of output.

Long-run return on investment for individual producers can vary substantially, based upon cost control and the extent some can make their product less homogeneous. In other words, product differentiation may allow some producers to obtain a higher price for their product. For example, Frank Perdue, who markets chickens in the Northeast, earns a higher price for his product because he feeds them to produce yellow-colored meat. Here, however, we speak of the entire industry.

While one producer may utilize such expedients to increase his own sales, total sales for all producers together can be increased only by influencing tastes—for example, so that more people eat more chicken, eggs, or hamburger.

Not only government purchase and export programs, but also breaker, hatchery, and seasonal demands sway short-term demand for eggs. Long-term demand is modified by consumer tastes, preferences, availability and prices of substitutes, incomes and population growth, governmental economic policies, and cost of complementary goods, such as bacon or ham. Grains represent inputs for meat and egg production. Their use, in part, depends upon consumption of the above.

You are already too well aware of a factor that affects short-term supply of grain; namely, government exports (or imports, too). Of course, current storage stocks—amount in storage—together with disappearance rate determine the quantity of grain immediately available until the next crop year.

Long-term supply reflects government intervention and support programs. It also pivots on anticipated costs of production (fertilizer, for example), credit availability, cost of capital investment (machinery and building, for example), carry-over of stocks (government and private), technology (yield per acre).

Similarly important is relative return on different uses of land. Should we plant corn or soybeans, raise hogs or cattle, turn the property into a trailer park or shopping center, or subdivide it?

Demand for the immediate future depends on the prices of substitute grains, government purchases, and the number of cattle, hogs, and poultry consuming grains. Naturally, the above factors, being generalities, do not apply equally to all grains.

For example, few soybeans are consumed in their natural state. Important factors to examine are the uses of soybeans; namely, to make soybean meal and soybean oil. The special trading situation of soybeans and its two products is described in Chapter 15.

Potatoes, the last food item discussed, are similarly affected. Near-term supply pivots on disappearance rate of storage stocks, government interference, weather during growing season, and seasonal supply influences.

Over the longer term, however, supply nucleates on technology, expected prices for output, and costs of production. Acres planted, weather (which tends to affect mostly the short run), government storage and incentive programs, and competing land uses also affect supply.

Demand for potatoes largely depends upon the price of substitute goods, government purchases, and seasonality in the near future. From season to season, demand hinges on the price of substitute goods, import-export programs, trends in per capita consumption, economic conditions, and (to be facetious) proliferation of fried-food restaurants.

Factors prevailing in lumber concentrate on seasonal supply potentiality and, of course, weather. Transportation costs determine market area. Government import-export programs, as well as storage inventories, should receive proportionate weight in short-run analysis.

Long-run supply of lumber depends upon availability of trees. Therefore, long run, in terms of years, is not comparable to the semiannual, annual, or biannual production cycles of some of the products mentioned in the preceding discussion.

Several factors are responsible for long-run supply: land availability (both government and private), weather cycles, expected future prices, forest technology (higher-yield trees, land-use management, and fire control, for example).

Short-run demand is tempered by the price of substitute goods (steel, aluminum, plastics, etc.). Decisions to repair, remodel, build, plus the seasonality of the building-trades industry loom important.

Over the long haul, interest rates, flow of funds, availability of suitable alternative housing, business expansion, and general economic outlook are pivotal in lumber use.

Certainly production of substitutes, trends in family size, shifts in living and business patterns, building cycles, geographic location, foreign imports, and transportation costs also rule long-term lumber use.

Metals, the last category summarized in this section, tend to be mastered by mercurial events, especially political ones. They constantly alter both short- and long-run supply, consumption, and projections.

Short-run supplies are marred by government stockpiling or sales, political eruptions and contests, socialization and confiscation of productive means, labor problems, transportation disruptions, and so forth.

Long-term supply, too, is affected by these factors. They include technological development, expected prices, wars and rumors of wars, trends toward socialization of the income and wealth of individuals, political imbroglios. Location and exploitation of new sources, bringing substitutes into production as prices of raw materials rise too much, and even environmental elements are factors, too.

Demand for metals, especially precious metals, is modified both now and later by domestic and international monetary problems, including inflation, devaluations and revaluations, payments deficits and surpluses, and price of substitute metals and substitute goods.

Other long-term factors ensphere anticipated industrial uses, government buying and selling programs, prospects of peace or war, stockpiling, and changes in laws, among other components.

Lack of space precludes discussion of all commodities traded. Neither does the above pretend to cover all the factors that may influence both supply and demand. Nor is it suggested that all factors necessarily operate simultaneously.

Nevertheless, you should be pointed in the right direction to expand your thinking and analysis and observe interrelationships that affect prices and, subsequently, your pocketbook, whether you trade or not. Remember that the price someone receives for his output represents the cost of someone else's inputs.

Prices of Inputs

While it is not necessary to become proficient in cost analysis, at least acquire some ideas on the prices of major inputs and how changes in costs dominate particular industries. Some of these relationships are well known. The hog-corn ratio, possibly best known, reflects the kinship between weight of animal and quantity of grain.

The hog-corn ratio, illustrated in Table 8, is calculated by dividing the price of one hundred pounds of live hog by the price of one bushel of corn. Lower corn prices result in a higher ratio. Higher corn prices result in a lower ratio and discourage farmers from expanding their hog business.

If a farm manager raises both corn and hogs, he faces two alternatives with respect to the use of his corn: (1) sell it now or forward, (2) feed it to the hogs. In the second case he indirectly sells corn by first funneling it through a hog. In other words, the hog-corn ratio is the exchange ratio between bushels of corn and one hundred pounds of hog.

Hog growers normally require a break-even point of 15-plus, preferably closer to 20-to-1, and a lower ratio in one year portends fewer hogs around

150

TABLE 8

Hog and Corn Equilibrium Prices

Estimated Corn Price (per Bushel)	Hog Price (per CWT)	Ratio
$3.25	$34.50	10.6
3.00	50.00	16.7
2.50	50.00	20.0
2.50	32.00	12.8
2.25	24.00	10.7
1.75	24.00	13.7

the next year. Changes in the number of sows farrowed from one year to the next mirror the correspondence between costs of production and sales of the final output (see Figure 45).

Naturally, the hog-corn ratio does not accurately specify the amount of change, but it does presage the direction of change (compare with Figure 46).

Of course, hog cycles, discussed later in the chapter, are not inspired by corn prices alone. Hog production has substantiated its own inherent

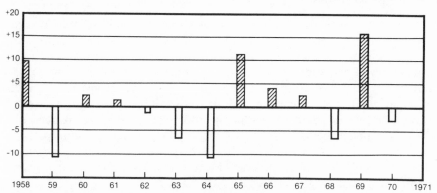

Fig. 45. Percent change in sows farrowing (Source: Livestock and Meat Situation [USDA].)

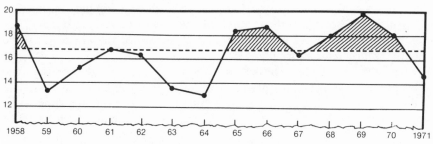

Fig. 46. Hog-corn ratio (Source: Livestock and Meat Situation [USDA].)

periodicity, although the price of feed inputs is centroidal in the decision-making process to expand or contract supplies. If the ratio is low and both corn and hog prices are historically high, the farmer may decide to sell both products and scale-down production.

The reactions of producers of broilers and fryers to the government's sixty-day price freeze in June 1973 corroborates how supplies can be sharply altered in response to projected profits or losses. The story of the Texas producer who drowned forty-two thousand five-day-old chicks to curtail losses shows that destroying them was cheaper than feeding them for two or more months to convert them into a salable product.[1] Chicken and egg growers were caught in a squeeze between rapidly rising grain prices and retail prices depressed by government control.

When costs soar, operators must quickly seek alternatives. When newly mined silver becomes too expensive, silver-recovery processes augur a cheaper source to users. When the price of cocoa spirals, manufacturers of chocolate candy economize their cocoa requirements with thinner coatings of chocolate and research cocoa substitutes. When the prices of beef and other meat products zoom too much for householders, they turn to milk products or other substitutes.

Comments on Cycles

Too, it is relevant to recognize how producers respond to price changes, which alter the supply curve. Because information and the interpretation of information are imperfect, coupled with the time lag required to adjust production either due to natural consequences or because of the impossibility of quickly reducing or increasing fixed investment, responses to information are not concurrent with price signals.

Because humans tend to repeatedly make the same types of decisions, there is a noticeable periodicity in the rhythmic flows of supply. These cycles are particularly pronounced in hog and beef-cattle production. Practically all businesses experience an inventory cycle; capital investments relate to a longer-term cycle.

These cycles are not totally mysterious. The four-year hog cycle, for example, is easily explained as a reaction to price. And price scores the result of interaction between demand and supply. When hog prices are high, they signal to the farmer that it is profitable to expand output. Because pigs are born in litters, some of the hogs can be marketed in six months, which produces an income, and a portion of the pig crop can be retained to procreate more pigs.

When this increased number of pigs is brought to the market the following year, it depresses prices. The lower price signals that it is time to diminish production. The hog cycle runs two years from low supplies to larger output, and then another two years back to smaller supplies. The

---

1. *Wall Street Journal,* June 25, 1973, p. 20.

entire cycle is completed in four years. Figure 47 registers percentage changes in production and price, which always move in opposite directions.

Most studies propound that farmers (businessmen, as well) project future prospects based on present prices. If current prices are high, they expect favorable prices to continue for a period. Consequently, production is expanded.

Contracyclical decisions by older hands, who fade current prices and speculate on continuance of the cycle, will yield larger returns on investment. Of course, there are always newcomers to any business.

Some analysts believe that with larger fixed investment, longer-range decisions will tend to flatten out presently observed cycles. Naturally, many producers, acting in unison, will still generate production cycles even if they are of different magnitude or longer periodicity.

With the cattle cycle, prolonged by nature, about two years elapse from time of conception until the beef is filleted at your favorite restaurant. The timetable cannot be compressed.

The calf spends nine months in the womb. During the next nine months it gains between five hundred and seven hundred pounds on grass (eating, not smoking it). It then spends another four to six months in a feedlot until it weighs about a thousand pounds. For all that wonderful care and delicious feed mixture of corn, soybean meal, and milo, it pays the ultimate price.

When an operator decides to build up his herd, the grim destiny of some heifers is postponed. A two-year-old heifer can be bred. Her progeny will not be table-ready for another two years.

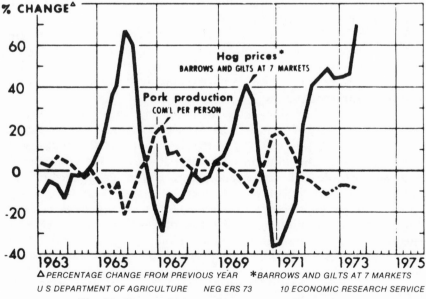

Fig. 47. Changes in hog prices and pork production

From the time the operator decides to expand until increased beef supplies reach markets, four and one-half to five years elapse. Larger marketings act as price depressants. Accordingly, farmers reduce the rate of expansion. The cycle begins anew.

In 1971, the cattle herd grew by 2 percent, another 3 percent in 1972, close to 4 percent during 1973. If the total herd is expanded at this rate during 1974 and 1975, if the rate of increase in 1976 and afterwards drops off to the rate experienced during 1965-1970, the price cycle will start to turn downward again in 1976. If, on the other hand, another 13 million people are added to the welfare rolls, it will be a different story.

Obviously government plays a major role in distorting the length of some cycles, although it has never been able to obliterate them. Because you may be speculating in lumber and plywood, awareness of the building cycle and influencing factors is à propos.

The building cycle runs its course about every eighteen years; that is, it seems to endure over a range of fifteen to twenty years. Possibly best explained as the influence of forces not fully known, there are a few apparent manifestations that retard or prolong duration of the cycle.

Because buildings exhibit variable durability, annual construction aggregates only a small proportion of the total existing stock of edifices. Speculative construction is encouraged through lower interest rates, irresponsible lending fomented by government guarantees, and availability of mortgage credit in the private markets.

One of the most important of the external factors modifying the cycle is war. Induced shortages of materials and dislocations postpone expansion. Monetary policy, through its impact upon financial markets and short-term interest rates, distorts the cycle. But these and other disturbances do not necessarily intermit at fixed intervals.

Gordon writes, "Government intervention may also be an important factor."[2] Probably the most clear-cut documentation of this fact of intervention is in the area of rent controls. The outstanding examples in Paris and New York City provide stark testimony to the debilitating effects of government meddling.

Population reproduction rates naturally contribute to demand for dwellings. The type of chateau, chalet, or shieling preferred reflects the life-style and financial condition of the dominant societal groups, which mirror type, size, and location of residential units. Land costs, possibly taxes, access to desired services and clients, and image adopted influence type, height, and site of commercial units.

Production cycles, of course, are fairly easily understood and explained; longer-term cycles result from the interplay of many factors that defy simple detection. Data on seasonal inventories, production, and demand projections for many commodities are accessible and invite interpretative analysis.

2. Robert A. Gordon, *Business Fluctuations,* 2nd ed. (New York: Harper & Bros., 1961), p. 246.

Reports on Stocks and Production

Analytical studies, forecasts, outlook reports, and data on estimated stocks and production of most agricultural products are obtainable (usually without charge) from the U.S. Department of Agriculture. All the data in this chapter, emitted by public sources, demonstrate that you can forge your own analysis and verify or supplement any reports you receive. The more you favor your own talents, the greater your chances of continuous success.

I will list only a few sources of information herein. To be placed on the mailing list, write to the Division of Information, Office of Management Services, U.S. Department of Agriculture, Washington, D.C. 20250.

Some monthly reports in which you may be interested are: *Agricultural Situation, Statistical Summary, Cattle and Calves Report, Agricultural Prices, Cold Storage, Agricultural Outlook Digest,* and *Grain Market News.* The *Crop Production Reports,* issued on the tenth of each month, state the existing supply of corn. Likewise, *Feed Situation* cites historical data and forecasts prices. Situation reports are compiled on various commodities.

Among annual reports, some of these may serve: *Field and Seed Crops— Annual Summary, Potatoes and Sweet Potatoes—Annual Summary, Livestock and Poultry Inventory, Meat Animals—Annual Summary, Cattle on Pasture, Chickens and Eggs, Commercial Broilers, Livestock-Feed Relationships.*

Quarterly reports include: *Hogs and Pigs, Demand and Price Situation, National Food Situation, Pig Crop Report.*

Some of the other major reports of which you should be aware are: *Prospective Plantings Report, Stocks in All Positions Report, Sugar Reports, Sugar Crop Production Report, Census Bureau Monthly Report on Cocoa and Chocolate, Cotton Production and Distribution Report, Cottonseed and Cottonseed Products Report, Cotton Situation Report, Wool Situation Report, Foreign Agricultural Bulletin.*

Once you decide to specialize in one or a few commodities, you will want to subscribe to one of the industrial trade periodicals. Additionally, perusual of a couple of general business periodicals is a must. The *Wall Street Journal* and the *Journal of Commerce* are published weekdays. *Barron's* is an excellent weekly for general financial information. Some of the better periodicals include: *Financial Analysts Journal, Agri Finance, Dun's Review, Forbes, Fortune,* and *Business Week.* These lists comprise only a sampling.

Also, many private newsletter and financial services are available for a price. No attempt can be made to evaluate each; it will depend upon your requirements and predilections. Many will send a free sample. The more sophisticated you become in the application of economic analysis, the greater will be your demand for more urbane services and advice.

CHAPTER 11
Further Application of Economic Concepts

If there were dreams to sell, what would you buy?

—T. L. Beddoes

"NOW I KNOW WHY THEY CALL IT THE DISMAL SCIENCE." WITH THAT flippant banality, the college sophomore abruptly exited, after one week, from his introductory economics class, never again to return. Is that how you felt a time or two a couple of chapters back? But if learning something about economics puts dollars into your pocket, isn't it worth the effort?

Use economic concepts of the marketplace to determine whether certain events are inevitable or even likely. A rapidly expanding money supply leads to inflation. A higher inflationary rate causes the international value of a currency to deteriorate, which leads to devaluation. Devaluation results in increased exports and leads to higher domestic prices. Government mismanagement, punitive taxes, and monetary manipulation, which cause shortages and surplus and an improper use of resources, lead to a depression. Then free-market forces reassert themselves to straighten out the mess.

You have already witnessed the law of demand in action; now let's mine these economic concepts for some more useful information.

Elasticities of Demand

We already know that people will buy more at lower prices than at higher prices. However, the question should be further refined. We need to discover, also, how much less they will buy if prices rise. In other words, how responsive are consumers to price changes?

If the price of a commodity is raised and consumers buy nearly the same amount as before, then demand is said to be *inelastic*. For example, a few years ago, coffee was thought to be inelastic between the prices of 40¢ and 99¢ per pound. If the price were 50¢, consumers might purchase 110,000 pounds; but if the price were raised to 60¢, consumers might buy 100,000 pounds. People still bought a smaller quantity, in accordance with the law of demand, but the reduced quantity was insufficient to precipitate less total revenue. In the example, total revenue actually mounted from $55,000 to $60,000. (Multiplying 110,000 x 50¢ = $55,000; 100,000 x 60¢ = $60,000.) Therefore, demand is inelastic and higher prices do not adversely affect total revenue to the sellers.

When coffee first exceeded $1 per pound in the 1950s, consumer resistance manifested. Further price advances caused total revenue to sellers to decline. Because people were then very responsive to price increases, demand was said to be *elastic*. Consumers reduced their coffee consumption and switched to substitute beverages. (Of course, at today's inflated prices, the above figures are no longer applicable.)

Another concept, *cross elasticity* of demand, was already furtively introduced. This device gauges the consanguinity of two commodities which are partial substitutes for each other, such as beef and pork. Normally beef retails at a premium to pork because meat-eaters prefer beef to pork if they had their "druthers." If pork prices are stable and beef prices ascend by an average nickel per pound, we know that people will tend to buy less beef. By how much will pork consumption rise?

Prior to 1972, these relationships were fairly rigid and predictable. Generally, a 1.4 percent erosion in pork production rendered a 1.0 percent increment in the price of beef. This type of kinship was fairly dependable. (Pork and beef account for roughly 95 percent of total meat intake.)

Similarly, consumers have not been very responsive to increases in the price of beef. Demand appears to have been inelastic along a broad range of prices. If prices climb by 2.1 percent, buyers reduce intake by only 1 percent.

By the second quarter, 1973, wholesale red-meat prices exceeded 1972's by approximately 40 percent. In terms of demand-and-supply analysis, what sparked meat prices to levitate so sharply? Earlier I outlined the determinants of reduced beef supply. At the same time the supply curve was shifting downward to the left, the demand curve was moving even more drastically to the right. Pressure from both sides caused the score (price) to be marked up.

157

Incomes over the preceding year gained about 10 percent. But I instructed you before to ask: Whose incomes? About 2.6 million newly employed workers received part of the increment. Remember, also, that social security payments were boosted in 1972 and again in 1973. So the elderly received a larger portion of the national pie. Between 1969 and 1973, the number of welfare recipients snowballed from 3.2 million to 13 million. Through the food-stamp programs, federal outlays about quadrupled.[1]

I suggested before that people with smaller incomes tend to spend a disproportionately larger share of their budget on food items. Three categories—newly employed workers, the retired, and welfarers—are inclined to employ initial income raises in improving their protein intake. Of course, over the long run, these higher prices, if sustained, act as an incentive for livestock producers to strengthen output.

Comprehending commodity markets draws on demand-and-supply relationships. For greater profits, a basic understanding of these rudimentary concepts will facilitate your use of these principles in your analysis. Their general treatment boosts perception of the underlying forces that reel prices along one rhumb or another. If you intrinsically fathom fundamental forces within the general framework of the economy, then efficacious application of technical tools can give you an annual return of several hundred percent on your investment.

Pressure Index

To evaluate the extent of statistical tightness between demand and supply, employ a *pressure index*. To compute it divide consumption by total supply. A short-term tool, it commands limited validity in markets evincing an appreciable time lag in adjustment of price to changing demand. The idea behind this index posits that as consumption rises, relative to available stocks, calculable upward pressure on prices develops.

Cocoa prices, an example where this technique can be demonstrated, usually lag six to nine months before sharply accommodating shifts in consumption. The model's short-coming, of course, is the very problem of time. Since many other factors also occur during such long intervals, it is presumptuous to isolate only one variable as causing those changes. Table 9 tabulates results over thirteen seasons.

A higher index implies that higher prices will follow. The extent of subsequent price moves focuses on height of the pressure index and change from the previous period. Seasonal grindings in the table measure consumption; stocks comprise total supplies consisting of initial inventories plus production.

1. See Herbert E. Meyer, "The Baffling Super-Inflation in Meat," *Fortune,* July 1973, pp. 116 ff.

TABLE 9

COCOA: SUPPLY AND DEMAND[1]
(all figures in thousand long tons)

Season (Oct.-Sept.)	Initial Stocks	Net[2] World Crop	Total Supply	Seasonal Grindings	Final Stocks	Pressure[3] Index
1960/61	346	1161	1507	993	514	65.9
1961/62	514	1113	1627	1084	543	66.6
1962/63	543	1146	1689	1135	554	67.2
1963/64	554	1204	1758	1170	588	66.6
1964/65	588	1467	2055	1282	768	62.4
1965/66	768	1193	1961	1357	604	69.2
1966/67	604	1320	1924	1367	557	71.0
1967/68	557	1320	1877	1384	493	73.7
1968/69	493	1208	1701	1349	352	79.3
1969/70	352	1404	1756	1335	421	76.0
1970/71	421	1464	1885	1396	489	74.1
1971/72	489	1533	2022	1499	563	74.1
1972/73[4]	522	1410	1932	1536	396	79.5

SOURCE: National Commodity Department, Reynolds Securities, Inc., 150 South Wacker Drive, Chicago, Ill.

[1] All figures Gill & Duffus.
[2] Derived by adjusting total world crop for one percent weight loss.
[3] Defined as $\dfrac{\text{Grindings}}{\text{Total Supply}}$.
[4] Gill & Duffus April forecast.

In Table 10, the correspondence between the computed index and the average October-September seasonal price is enumerated in order of ascending pressure indices. The relationships in this simple model—admittedly not perfect ones—indicate direction of anticipated change.

Of course, the table, related to *average* prices, tells us nothing about *range* of prices during the season. The range may be extensive. For example, the average between 20 and 60 is 40; but the average of a range between 36 and 44 is still 40.

Another difficulty: when utilizing a "world" commodity, expressed in terms of domestic prices, a price change may only reflect adjustments in relative rates of inflation or exchange rates, or the results of devaluations.

It should be kept in mind that simple models are minor subsidiary tools. Changes in expectations, creation of synthetics, and formation of buffer stocks influence prices. When the price of cocoa climbs too high, manufacturers of chocolate products research substitutes that taste and look like chocolate but are cheaper.

TABLE 10

PRESSURE INDEX VS. AVERAGE OCTOBER/SEPTEMBER PRICE (ACCRA)
(all figures in thousand long tons)

Season	Pressure Index (%)	Average Price Oct.-Sept.
1964/65	62.4	18.4
1960/61	65.9	23.6
1961/62	66.6	21.8
1963/64	66.6	24.1
1962/63	67.2	23.9
1965/66	69.2	23.3
1966/67	71.0	27.2
1967/68	73.7	30.7
1971/72	74.1	28.8
1970/71	74.1	29.4
1969/70	76.0	37.3
1968/69	79.3	45.3
1972/73*	79.5	
1973/74	85.0**	

* Based on forecasts in April Gill & Duffus Report.

** On the assumption of a net world crop of 1340 thousand tons (a 70 thousand ton decrease from the forecasted 72/73 total), and grindings of 1476 thousand tons (a decrease of 60 thousand tons from this season's projected total).

SOURCE: National Commodity Department, Reynolds Securities, Inc., 150 South Wacker Drive, Chicago, Ill.

In August 1973, the International Cocoa Organization came into existence with membership held by eight producing countries and eight consuming countries (exclusive of U.S. participation). The aim of the organization is to stabilize world market prices of cocoa. They want to ensure supplies to consumers at prices considered "fair" to producers. In the scheme of international buffer stocks, "fair" usually means higher than average prices. No cartel is formed to secure less for its members. In a competitive market, of course, prices freely respond to the interaction of buyers and sellers acting independently without collusion.

Correlation Analysis

Prices chronicle a point where buyers and sellers agree to swap goods for money so that both parties to the transaction are satisfied with the bargain. An equilibrium price signifies that the amount of commodities sold equals the quantity bought. To identify factors that influence price, simple correlation analysis pairs the elements we isolate as significant ones.

In simple correlation analysis we attempt to document, or measure, the degree of relationship between two factors. For example, you may want to correlate the relationship between extent of socialization of a national economy and number of suicides. In multiple-correlation analysis, one factor is studied in partnership with several other factors. A high degree of correlation implies an infrangible intimacy, while a low degree of correlation connotes that canvassed components do not compactly intertwine.

For example, you may wish to know the degree of correlation between the price of gold in London and monetary treason in the United States. Unfortunately, monetary muddles are difficult to pin down mathematically even though we agree on their singular importance. (One shortcoming of statistical techniques!) A series of gold prices is readily obtainable. The Gordian knot of monetary complexities in the United States may be tied to the inflation rate, international capital flows, balance-of-payments deficits, or official reserves.

Let's pick balance-of-payments (BOP) deficits as our indicator. First we will want to place data in two columns in a table: one column for gold prices and one for BOP deficits. The simplest method is to next diagram the information. On the vertical axis calibrate gold prices; on the horizontal axis mark off quarterly BOP deficits. Then transfer data from the table onto the diagram.

Find the correct gold price from your first line of data and the corresponding BOP deficit registered in, say, billions of dollars on the horizontal axis. Where these two lines intersect, place a dot. That single dot corresponds to the first line of data from the table; that is, the dot denotes both the gold price and the figure attributed to the BOP deficit. Repeat this process for the entire table. The product will be dots scattered in your diagram; each dot substitutes for a line from the table. The handiwork is known as a *scatter diagram*.

Afterwards, draw a line through the field of dots. This line symbolizes an average relationship between gold prices and BOP deficits. If all dots lay on the line, the link between the two would have been perfect. Because dots are scattered around, other factors also affect the price of gold. Too, the closer dots congregate around the line, the closer the consanguinity between the two components. If no consistent pattern flourishes, the dots will be randomly scattered far from the line.

The design of this technique, of course, is to predict price changes provided that the liaison between the chosen factors fits fairly closely together. For example, in the last chapter, we discussed the building cycle. Is there a kinship between the price of plywood and housing starts? Weekly or monthly data on housing starts are accessible. Compare them with the cash prices of plywood. Or you may want to correlate population growth rates, or rather changes in these rates, to plywood prices. In this case you will not match year-to-year data but will lag them. In other words, how many years elapse between a change in reproduction rates and its effect on residential demand? Compared data should reflect this interval.

A positive correspondence between factors will result in a line drawn upward from the graph's origin to the right; that is, the two variables tend to increase together. When two factors run in opposite directions, correlation is negative; the drawn line will descend downward to the right.

Characteristically, correlation with the moon as a variable emerges in a discussion of this topic. Not wanting to disappoint you, let me suggest an interesting relationship between phases of the moon and corn prices. One pattern indicates that corn futures bought at the time of the full moon and sold on the new moon have produced profits. There is no limit to combinations.

Effects of Subsidies and Price Supports

Before concluding this chapter, let us examine a situation where an industry pockets a subsidy; that is, its costs of production are reduced because it harvests payment from other taxpayers via the government (which extracts a "handling fee" in the process). I will relate this case to the farm-price-support program.

Diagrammatically, inheritance of a subsidy corresponds to collecting more than the equilibrium price. In Figure 48, P_e again stands for an uncontrolled price, while P_s typifies the subsidized price.

A program that induces farmers not to farm and pledges a minimum price for output fosters an inefficient use of resources and foments overproduction. Even when total acreage is reduced, more intensive cultivation of allotted acreage yields larger harvests. Among other things, this practice kindles a surplus in the first instance, higher costs to the economy in the second, and more farm votes for the politician in the third. The diagram in Figure 48 portrays the first two effects. At the higher price of P_s, only quantity $0Q_d$ of the grain is consumed, but excessive production $0Q_s$ produces the sizable surplus marked off in the diagram.

You already know the story of what befell in the 1950s. Farm surpluses mounted and had to be warehoused. So, at government expense, grain lay in public and private facilities at ever-towering costs to the taxpayer. Additionally, "rats" consumed an abnormally large quantity of the grains stowed in supposedly varmint-proof containers. This is called disappearance, loss, shrinkage, spoilage, or whatever. Now the taxpayer had his nose ringed twice. He had to pay for a misallocation of resources and subsidize the farmer to help the politician get elected, and then he paid again for storage facilities.

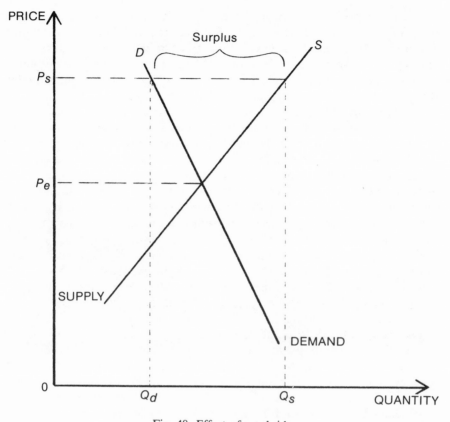

Fig. 48. Effect of a subsidy

Wouldn't you think that twice scalped is enough to ire even John Q. Milquetoast? Well, these huge surpluses were becoming an embarrassment, but vulpine politicians scored a double coup with the invention of Public Law 480. There are several sections to PL 480, but the one that provides for sales of grain to certain less developed countries, with payment in *soft currencies,* moved the largest quantity of grain.

An example of a "soft" currency is the Indian rupee. We accepted rupees in exchange for wheat. "That's great!" the public roared. "We diminish our surpluses, get paid for it, which reduces the cost of the farm-subsidy program, and it helps our balance of payments." Under the terms of PL 480 sales, we acquired rupees but pledged not to exchange them for dollars or gold or any other international medium of exchange.

Our rupees simply stayed in India. India does not have that many things to sell to the United States. Oh yes, we built a beautiful embassy, as John Kenneth Galbraith will testify. Congressmen were always taking free, all-expense-paid junkets to India. We imported thousands of Indian books and journals, which were subsequently distributed and packed away in a few key university libraries.

163

The politicians scored again! They reaped the farmers' votes and raped the public. Consumers were happy for the "reduced burden" of storage expenses. The solons even chalked up some points among anti-foreign-aiders. These were expensive votes. When the first farm-price-support program was initiated under FDR in the 1930s, 150 House members represented farm districts compared with 14 in 1974.[2]

Old John Q. paid the piper without too much protest. A few months ago I read that the U.S. government had decided not to retain ownership of the rupees it held in India and transferred them back to the Indian government. Do you understand the economics and politics of subsidies?

And to keep wheat flowing to foreign users, the U.S. government and forty-one other countries, in 1949, agreed to trade a specified quantity of wheat under the auspices of the International Wheat Agreement, which consisted of a negotiated schedule of minimum and maximum prices. Of course, "negotiated prices" were below the U.S. government support price (the guaranteed minimum price to the farmers); therefore, heavy subsidies were paid by the U.S. government to exporters. Between 1949 and September 20, 1972, the government disbursed export subsidies amounting to $4.3 billion on 10.5 billion bushels of wheat. And there is more coming on this topic!

You may wonder: With all this widespread government intervention, is it really worthwhile playing the game? You have no choice! You cannot exert a neutral attitude toward wealth. If you do, it will decline! Like everything else, to maintain wealth or make it grow, you must attend to it. Give it attention! Governments were distorting free-market forces long before you and I were around and, in spite of government, honest individuals *have* accumulated wealth. Acting with intelligence and knowledge in commodity futures markets can furnish a fast track to future security and provide means to take advantage of opportunities during the next—and probably prolonged—depression.

Before we put all this theory into practical use and develop trading techniques, one more aspect of investing must be reemphasized. There are three parties to almost every transaction. Two of them represent the general public acting, singularly or in unison, in the capacity of buyer or seller. The third force is not only unpredictable but exercises a disproportionate amount of power in the general market.

2. Juan Cameron, "A Golden Chance to Get Uncle Sam Off the Farm," *Fortune,* July 1973, pp. 112-13.

CHAPTER 12
That Unpredictable
Ingredient – Government

*The art of government consists in taking as much money as possible from
one class of citizens to give to the other.*

—Voltaire

"YOU'D BE BETTER INFORMED IF INSTEAD OF LISTENING TO WHAT WE SAY,
you watch what we do." So advised John Mitchell during his tenure as
attorney general.[1] A useful legacy, that will certainly go unheeded by
most, focuses on the attitude assumed by the successful speculator when
interpreting official manifestations.

As a rule, instruction in commodity trading centers on two aspects of
data interpretation; namely, technical analysis, covered in Chapters 4-8,
and fundamental analysis, dwelled upon in the preceding three chapters.

Reference to government as a market force is obliquely mentioned
in any description of agricultural-support programs. It focuses on price
supports, acreage allotments, agricultural loans, storage, and generally
neutral subjects. You already know the story. (There are notable exceptions, however.)

Because price supports are not relevant in times of high prices, ceilings
receive undue attention. Most people clamor for *more* government
controls to solve problems that were government-created.

1. Hobart Rowen, "Nixon Would 'Bust' Budget; Expert Says Get Going Now," *Atlanta
Journal and Constitution,* February 10, 1974, p. 2-E.

During the 1972-73 season, so many experienced traders erred in their use of technical, fundamental, seasonal, and historical data, that many concluded something unfamiliar was happening in the market—but what? Due to unparalleled situations, for which no precedent existed, some traders lost large sums of money. Others not only managed to survive but accumulated profits in the process. What did the first group do wrong? What did the second group do right?

Be a Cynic

Failing to savvy the impact of a third market force—government—an "investor" who naively believes that everyone else is looking out for his money will soon lose it. Yes, everyone is looking out for his money—to find ways to take it away from him!

Neither does it reside within the power of government to manufacture wealth. If person A bags $XX because of a "benevolent" act of government, then property from persons B, C and D is confiscated in the amount of $XXX. The extra $X pays for the middleman's services, that is, the handling fee for confiscation. No government can guarantee you peace, happiness, joy, abundance, or security. All material possessions are vulnerable to change.

> So long as government is viewed as an agency through which virtue and happiness for the individual may be attained, so long as governments are viewed as causes rather than effects, so long as individuals believe that self-responsibility may be escaped through retreat to the collective ethic, power will be rampant in our society. As the state grows more and more powerful, the individual citizen will tend to grow weaker and weaker.[2]

Throughout 1973, with probably more direct governmental interference in the commodity markets than at any time during the previous decade, unwonted situations confronted traders. Not new to either financial markets or commodities markets, government meddling through farm-price and production programs has pervaded since the mid-1930s. But they were a calculable fact. Traders knew how to contend with and figure carry-over, price supports, and all kindred calculations. What materialized most recently was unexpected.

The cynics survived. The cynic recognizes that additional rules have been introduced into the game and takes them into account. The commodity market does not differ from other markets. It happens to be one of the last ones to be brought under the destructive wing of government. Neither did changes spring up overnight. Signs were already written in the wind.

2. George C. Roche III, *Power* (Irvington-on-Hudson, N.Y.: Foundation for Economic Education, 1967), p. 50.

Watch for Changes in Policies

Survival strategy subsumes ongoing governmental interference. Let me make one point clear. Do not be frightened away from commodity futures trading because of these remarks. On the contrary, becoming aware of the truth will put more money in your pocket. All financial markets are dominated or influenced by government—either indirectly through monetary and fiscal policies or directly as a participant. As Henry Arthur points out, some of these changes occur gradually: "The agricultural control programs of the past 35 years have moved far over into the area of making government a major participant, a trader, an active influencer of price levels."[3]

Speaking some years ago about the appointment of Lester P. Condon (in 1962) as inspector general in charge of a newly established Office of Internal Audit and Inspection, USDA, Arthur said, "The reason for Mr. Condon's army of auditors, however, is not chiefly the enforcement functions of the USDA in policing markets. It is safe to say that the major reason for the auditors is the fact that Uncle Sam has moved from the role of referee to that of player in the marketplace."[4]

In other words, the tendency exists. When opportunities arise, the great bureaucracy will not hesitate to exploit advantages. The full truth is still unknown about the Russian wheat deals. Soon further information involving kickbacks on grain sales will create still another scandal.

How much did the Russians really pay for their imported wheat? During July and August 1972, the United States "sold" roughly 440 million bushels of wheat to Russia. Sales price? About $700 million! That figures out to less than $1.60 per bushel! "The sales were equivalent to 30 percent of average annual U.S. wheat production during the previous five years and more than 80 percent of the wheat used for domestic food during that period."[5] That's a lot of bread!

On August 15, 1972, the cash price of wheat was $1.51 a bushel; and May 1973 futures on the Chicago Board of Trade closed at $1.85. Why hadn't the futures markets anticipated price increases? *Russian buying intentions were not known!* But the cash price of wheat a year later, on August 15, 1973, was $4.45. An increase of 195 percent!

The Russians, of course, knew their own intentions. What would prevent them, through periodic and selective purchases on futures markets beginning in, say, June 1972, to buy contracts not only in wheat but also in other grains, for grains surely move together? Naturally, large-scale

3. Henry B. Arthur, "Impact of Government Agricultural Programs upon Market Structures and Functions," *Futures Trading Seminar* (Madison, Wis.: Mimir Publ. Co., 1966), 3:14.

4. Ibid., p. 13.

5. Clifton B. Luttrel, "The Russian Wheat Deal—Hindsight vs. Foresight," *Federal Reserve Bank of St. Louis Review* 55, no. 10 (October 1973): 2.

buying and selling moves prices around, but prudent planning yields handsome profits. After all, the price of wheat nearly tripled; it should not have been difficult to take $1.60 out of the market. Suppose the average wheat futures contract cost $1.75; an average price at the time of offset would only have to be $3.35 to wring out gross profits of $1.60 per bushel.

The fact that "sales" consisted of a series of subsidized transactions fuels the fires of indignation. The U.S. government has granted the Soviet Union $750 million in credit over a three-year period to pay for the purchase of grains.

So the Russians bought some cheap wheat (grown under government subsidies paid for by the great American sucker), with cheap credit (at the expense of the American public), and extracted huge profits from the markets (paid for by the losses suffered by hedgers). American exporters were paid subsidies too (with money extracted from the people), and still the sucker pays through higher food prices. The General Accounting Office concluded that export subsidies and sales produced a dramatic rise in wheat prices and higher consumer prices for bread and most livestock products.[6]

And if you believe that government intervention does not reoccur, even in similar forms, do you remember the 1963 wheat deal to "mellow the Soviets"? "It cost the American taxpayer at least $75 million in subsidies."[7]

If, for example, the United States government found it convenient to influence agricultural prices, do you believe the government would hesitate to invade the market?

Lester Telser ten years ago portrayed the likely sequence of events.

We may expect three major consequences of such government intervention. First, administrative decree ... replaces the price mechanism and allocates resources more or less directly. Second ... farmers, merchants, processors, etc., must spend considerable energy and intelligence learning the government regulations. Third, once government regulation and regulators come to play a large role in an economic sphere, corruption becomes a real possibility.[8]

Intervention has been largely through farm-income programs: the price-support system, supply management to keep supplies down, and direct income supplements (the most recent device). The former director of the Bureau of the Budget, Charles Schultze, estimates that "consumers pay at least $4.5 billion more a year for farm products than they would pay if there were no federal support programs."[9]

6. Comptroller General of the United States, Report to the Congress, *Russian Wheat Sales and Weaknesses in Agriculture's Management of Wheat Export Subsidy Program* (July 1973), pp. 2, 25.

7. Antony C. Sutton, *National Suicide: Military Aid to the Soviet Union* (New Rochelle: Arlington House, 1973), p. 30.

8. Lester G. Telser, "Impact of Governemnt Agricultural Programs," *Futures Trading Seminar*, 3:37.

9. Juan Cameron, "A Golden Chance to Get Uncle Sam off the Farm," *Fortune*, July 1973, p. 113.

At present the Commodity Exchange Authority only supervises agricultural products traded on commodity exchanges. "It is time to expand our control," thought the lawmakers. Creating a heavily staffed commission corresponding to the Securities and Exchange Commission has long been ideated. The excuse now? A pack of wolves are gouging farmers and consumers! "The system simply must be harnessed," says Hubert H. Humphrey.[10] The extra $4.5 billion a year that consumers pay does not even cause the senator to blush.

The current legislation also proposes to fine and jail anyone caught trying to manipulate the market. Strictly enforced that law would be an excellent one! Alas! Too few jails exist to house all the offending bureaucrats.

Prices are not made in Chicago by a handful of traders. Prices are "discovered" in Chicago (and elsewhere on other exchanges). Prices in a free market result from the interaction of hundreds of buyers and sellers throughout the country, and throughout the world in the case of internationally traded commodities. Prices in a controlled market are made in Washington.

Before embarking on another legislative spree, one would think that the senators should know something about commodity markets. The price gyrations of 1973 (which were influenced by government meddling) naturally excited them. The solution to government meddling is government control! Does it matter to the senators that they know very little about commodity trading? Senator George McGovern says, "I feel as though I just got out of kindergarten. Now I'm getting ready to go into the first grade."[11] Congressman Thomas Foley (Dem.-Washington) sums up their attitudes: "We just know we don't like the situation the way it is, so we're going to do something about it."[12]

Elsewhere I will discuss the relationship between cash and futures prices. Cash prices represent an exchange of the physical product, while futures prices are an estimate of tomorrow's prices based upon today's estimates and information. Cash prices dominate in this relationship. Do speculators cause higher prices? At one time in June 1973, July soybean futures were around $10, while the cash price was over $11. The traders were driving the futures price down—not up! Traders cannot be blamed for the senators' debacles.

Commodity futures markets are vital to the existence of an open-market system. Futures prices reflect activities in actual markets. Without futures prices, the public experiences difficulty in discovering true price relationships.

Government can more easily control the system once futures markets have been completely eliminated or prices badly distorted. And, of

10. Mitchell C. Lynch, "A New Watchdog? Congress May Bolster Efforts to Oversee Commodities Futures," *Wall Street Journal,* January 11, 1974, p. 1.

11. Ibid.
12. Ibid.

course, legislation can be expected. As Foley says, "None of us is going to get reelected or defeated because of what we do about commodities regulation."[13] Senator McGovern later admitted he might have drawn some hasty conclusions, but that was *after* he introduced a bill for stiffer market regulation. Control is the name of the game.

Observe the Trends

The long-run trend is becoming obvious even to the unsophisticated. Controls beget controls. Dr. George Roche wrote:

> If all the areas of individual creativity were preempted by the planned, collective society, our society would face extinction. As the cartoonist suggested when he depicted one Russian bureaucrat speaking to another, "When all the world is communist, where will we get wheat?"[14]

As if to update Dr. Roche's comment, in 1974 Soviet Deputy Foreign Trade Minister Vladimir S. Alkhimove remarked: "When we bought your grain, we bought it at prices in the market at that time. We bought it at the same price in other countries. Why can't we now sell to your country at the current market price?" He then quoted a proverb: "If you shall not make a profit, you shall be without trousers."[15]

Unfortunately, many shrug their shoulders and yawn, "So what! So we have more government control someday. What do I care?" And then they echo Lord Keynes's infamous dictum, "In the long run, we're all dead."

But why are we rich today? Von Mises writes, "Every single performance of this ceaseless pursuit of wealth production is based upon the saving and the preparatory work of earlier generations. We are the lucky heirs."[16] Does that mean we should spend it all within a couple of generations? Societal progress is not only a cooperative endeavor but a continuing effort of synergic action in which we become wealthier individuals but still obey the commandment "Thou shalt not steal" (which embodies the concept of private property).

Within the context of longer-term action, short-run trends are important. As a trader and speculator, you have the responsibility of not only conserving your capital but making it grow. Protection of short-term gains can be secured by stemming long-run tendencies of pervading government controls.

C. Jackson Grayson, Jr., observed that his experience as head of the price commission convinced him that "our economic system is steadily shifting from a private enterprise, free-market economy to one that is

---

13. Ibid.
14. Roche, *Power*, p. 52.
15. "Soviet Trade Minister a Profit Pragmatist," *Atlanta Journal and Constitution*, February 3, 1974, p. 7-E.
16. Ludwig von Mises, *Human Action* (New Haven: Yale University Press, 1949), p. 489.

centrally directed and under public control." He prognosticated, "Call it what you will—managed capitalism, socialism, a planned economy, a post-industrial state—the end result will be the virtual elimination of the free-market system as we now know it."[17]

Several years ago, Gruetzmacher was more cynical when he said, "I don't think we have ever seen a completely free market in the history of the world. For centuries individuals attempted to manipulate for their own benefit. Today governments are attempting to manipulate our markets."[18] And for *their* own benefit, too!

Regard the Booms and Boomlets, Busts and Bustlets (?)

The cost of government's meddling in our affairs is extremely expensive. An example of the power of misdirected monetary policy to accentuate and prolong what should have been only a brief period of adjustment, the Great Depression of the interwar period "was caused by government interference, not by the free market, free enterprise system . . . and prolonged and intensified by governmental stupidity," writes Professor Sennholz.[19]

The last half of the decade of the 1920s was one of inflationary expansion. It laid the groundwork for the inevitable. "For inflation and credit expansion always precipitate business maladjustments that must later be liquidated."[20] You will recall that the cry of the Keynesians and neo-Keynesians for a quarter of a century (and even today in some quarters) was that monetary policy is ineffective and blah, blah, blah. "They did their best but that wasn't good enough." After the publication of Professor Friedman's definitive study on monetary history, the naïve were finally convinced. During the 1929-1933 interval, the money supply was contracted by one-third.

Professor Sennholz writes, "In short, the burden of government nearly doubled during the depression, which alone would bring any economy to its knees." He adds: "He who still contends that it was economic freedom and laissez-faire that generated the Great Depression is shockingly ignorant or dishonest."[21]

Government-inspired financial panics are not a twentieth-century invention. In ancient Rome, in A.D. 33 (notice the date), a severe crisis was precipitated by irresponsible monetary action. Tiberius reduced the money supply sharply (reduction of coinage), created fiscal surpluses,

---

17. Charles E. Flinner, "Private Enterprise Eroding," *Atlanta Journal and Constitution,* February 3, 1974, p. 7-E.

18. Alfred H. Gruetzmacher, "The Philosophy of the Market Place as Seen from a Pit Speculator's Viewpoint," *Futures Trading Seminar,* 3:168.

19. Hans F. Sennholz, *The Truth about the Great Depression* (Lansing, Mich.: Constitutional Alliance, n.d.).

20. Ibid., p. 8.

21. Ibid., p. 16.

and withdrew government surplus funds from circulation. Caravan trading became unprofitable with falling demand and rising costs (especially interest costs); a prominent manufacturer bankrupted.

Further monetary contraction occurred with a run on the major banking house, Quintus Maximus. Loans were called. Bankrupt trading and manufacturing firms, it was rumored, were into the bank for rather substantial sums. Bankruptcies became rather widespread, and panic gripped Rome's Wall Street, the Via Sacra. Tiberius later reversed his policies. Acting in the capacity of a central bank, the treasury expanded the money supply through direct loans to banking institutions.[22] More than nineteen hundred years later, we still permit our lives to be governed by the whims of government.

The same sequence of events reoccurs. James Fraser writes: "From older crises and panics we see that a few criteria show up again and again. Too much currency is issued, payments are suspended. Crop failures and high prices. Capital tied up in long term ventures make loanable funds scarce."[23]

The Great Depression stands as a monument to governmental power. However, it is not always to government's advantage to create concatenary catastrophes over a decade. Our recessions since the Korean War have been produced by the stop-and-go policies of monetary authorities. Figure 49 identifies four measurable quantities. The shaded areas represent business recessions defined by the National Bureau of Economic Research. Especially compare changes in the Money Stock and the truncated growth of Real Output.

In each case, sharply expansive monetary policy precipitates a strong money demand for goods and services. Interest rates first fail when it appears that real savings have multiplied. Firms respond to more business and to lower interest costs by expanding productive capacity. Higher consumer spending and greater demand for capital goods add pressure to the economic system as it attempts to respond to the new state of affairs. Commercial-bank credit rises. Production accelerates. Job alternatives become more plentiful. This scenario approximately describes the periods: 1950-52, 1954-56, 1962-66, 1967-69.

Excessive demand brought about by money creation results in higher prices in both goods and labor services. With more money in hand, buyers bid against one another for goods. Prices are pushed up. (Back to the old demand-supply diagram again. Excess money pushes the demand curve to the right.) (See the General Price Index in Figure 49.)

Interest rates then rise in response to inflation so that new rates consist of the noninflationary rate plus an allowance for inflation. Buoyant prices constitute business costs. Because of the distortion caused by an overblown money supply, resources are misallocated.

Business costs rise. Labor productivity falls. As costs rise, expansion

22. James L. Fraser, *Crises and Panics* (Wells, Vt.: Fraser Publishing Co., 1965), pp. 2-3.
23. Ibid., p. 21.

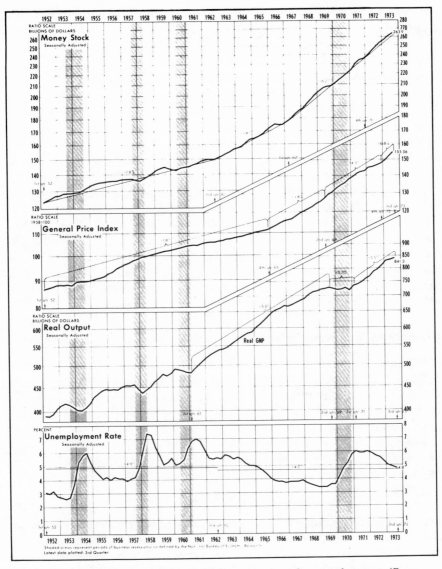

Fig. 49. Influence of money on prices, output, and unemployment (Source: Federal Reserve Bank of St. Louis.)

of capital investment slows. Inflation-induced prices eventually out-run wage increases. Demand rises at a slower rate. To prolong "prosperity," the government may continue to expand the money supply, but the prospect of higher and higher inflation rates encourages them to reverse their expansionary policies.

The sudden shift in course precipitated recessions in 1953-54, 1957-58, 1960-61, 1966-67, and 1969-70. (Notice in Figure 49 that

173

the NBER did not rate 1966-67 as a recession period.) Norman Bowsher reports:

> ... in 1966-67 and in 1969-70, vigorous efforts were made to attack the basic causes of inflation by monetary and fiscal restraint. In each period, the tempo of economic activity slowed in response to the initial withdrawal of monetary and fiscal stimulus.[24]

He is saying that the government's up-and-down policies precipitated a recession.

Neither a policy of stop-and-go nor one of progressive inflation can indefinitely stimulate the real variables of industrial output, employment, and interest rates. Inflationary build-up leads to a period of repair and despair. Ups and downs cannot continue forever. Inflation is taxation! There are ultimate limits to taxation.

Acts of government do not create wealth; they redistribute wealth. There are other real factors at work; these real factors determine the direction of growth and nongrowth. Self-correction of ordinary spending and investment decisions is thwarted by governmental policies. They exaggerate the magnitude of booms and busts. Restating Emerson's words, the government chains us to the wheel of fortune.

Consider an Inventory Cycle

When we, as speculators, study minor cycles, we need to concentrate on price-cost relationships, such as those discussed in the previous chapter, on the short-term credit market, and particularly on changes in the inventories of manufacturers and users of raw and refined materials traded on commodity markets.

Inventory cycles occur in the normal conduct of business as firms adjust to changing conditions of costs and sales. Under situations of market interference, inventory cycles appear to be less casual and more the result of stop-and-go big-brother policies.

Lloyd Metzler's explanation of inventory cycles begins with the proposition that firms maintain some relationship of inventory-to-sales. (Of course, conditions of credit availability and costs, transportation, rent, and practices of the industry alter this ratio.) Let us create a brief scenario.

Demand rises. Sales are up. At first inventories will fall in response to this lovely period of climbing sales. Firms augment their orders to not only compensate for the likelihood of continually expanding sales but also to "catch up" their stocks to maintain the preferred inventory-to-sales proportionality. Snowballing orders first translate into a rise in industrial output as excess capacities are brought into use, and later into expansion of plant and equipment, full-grown employment, and finally distended costs.

---

24. Norman A. Bowsher, "1973—A Year of Inflation," *Federal Reserve Bank of St. Louis Review* 55, no. 12 (December 1973): 10.

Then demand tumbles. Sales still may be up, but they gain by smaller and smaller amounts. Eventually sales droop slightly. Inventories build up. Now firms have larger-than-desired inventories on hand. They pare orders. New orders nose-dive faster than sales shrink in order to readjust the inventory level. Manufacturers retrench production. Working hours are cut. Finally layoffs begin.

Suppose you are speculating in copper. What are the principal uses of copper in a final form such as wiring? Which industries consume the largest amounts of products containing copper? By working backwards from final use to origin, you can posit some of your own estimates of near-term demand for copper. While copper can be stockpiled longer than agricultural products, costs, strikes, shipping, wars, monetary crises, and all other factors must be accounted for in your assessment. Nevertheless, awareness of this periodicity is a valuable tool.

If you were to study each of these concepts in depth, little time would remain for trading. Let others work out the details. You only want to read the results of their investigations. But you must know how to relate those results to the markets you follow. What is the trend? Exactly what is happening in the United States and in the world?

Read Foreign Publications

Because of a bias built into our system of news coverage, we may waste essential energy gathering the information we require and desire.

All television news is obviously slanted in one direction. One problem: national news "is filtered through and controlled by a group of producers and editors located in New York City."[25] Not only this, "but most of the news footage used to illustrate them [stories about America] are drawn from four metropolitan centers—New York, Washington, D.C., Chicago, and Los Angeles." The eastern-liberal syndrome places "a high value on sweeping reforms."[26]

The alternative is to supplement your reading diet with foreign publications. Even foreign-language publications, many of which are also available in English, may be subject to the same reformist bias. But foreign correspondents do observe and report on matters in the language of their audience and according to their own experience and education, which will provide a new slant on old matters. Enough clues can be gleaned and ideas generated to reward your efforts.

Traders who reaped substantial profits during the great price swings of 1973 fell largely into two categories. One, the younger group, was not subject to the historical prejudice of assuming there are limits on prices. To

25. Dr. Epstein, "The Bias of Network News," *Imprimis* (Hillsdale College, Mich.) 3, 1 (January 1974): 1.
26. Ibid., p. 2.

them, $6, $8, and $12 prices on soybeans were the same—always up—while old-timers restricted their horizons; previous historic highs biased their trading decisions—taking profits too soon and going short prematurely. The young traders, however, have already given back much of their gains; many have endured losses. Their gains were more a matter of luck.

Professional traders, those who consistently win and have participated in these markets for numerous years, were aware that many old rules were not operative. Something else, not the forces of demand and supply, was creating swings of extraordinary magnitude. Of course, we now know that the disturbing factor was, and continues to be, government interference.

Professional traders took cognizance of this factor, revised their estimates, and attempted to understand the extent to which this force could carry prices. They quickly learned to discount official reports and proclamations made for general public consumption and to devise alternate sources of information. Moreover, recognizing that the markets would overreact, they decided the best strategy was to ride trends and trade less frequently; that is, to trade when risks appeared reasonably low. And, likewise, they temporarily discarded some old concepts. They took a broader view of the market—in fact, an international view. In short, both minds and trading plans were sufficiently flexible to acquire profits even in unusual or adverse times.

Some recognized that dollar devaluations tend to make our products cheaper to foreigners. Fewer units of a strong currency will buy more dollars after devaluation. On the other hand, imports are now more expensive for Americans. Consequently, the added buying power of foreigners pushes demand higher. It pressures prices upward. The rest of the story is now history.

Being aware of government intervention should not keep you away from commodity markets. On the contrary, government intervention presents a strong case for investing in these markets. Knowing makes you a more intelligent and perceptive investor.

When the government interfered in the food market with price ceilings, did you stay away from the grocery store? When the government imposed quasi-controls on gasoline and speed-limit reductions, did you sell your auto and start walking? Governments license utility companies, taxicab companies, airways, etc. Have you stopped using these services because government has meddled in these markets?

And you *know* that the government affects financial markets through control of the money supply, borrowing, subsidizing, and direct participation, which alters values and *your wealth*. After a shot of government intervention, markets energetically reassert themselves.

Crises are precipitated by government action. Investors like you can suffer heavy setbacks. The extent to which you accept losses depends upon what you do. Commodity futures markets still offer a vehicle to offset government-created liabilities.

a. Telephone clerk accepting an order on the trading floor of the New York Mercantile Exchange.

b. Runners approaching the trading ring with orders to be executed.

c. Another view of the trading floor.

d. Order clerks provide a vital communication link between speculators and brokers. Both speed and accuracy are essential.

(This sequence of four photographs was taken especially for this book. Courtesy of the New York Mercantile Exchange.)

a. As required by rules and regulations of the exchange, traders must notify the world, through vocal activity, of their intentions. All offers to buy or sell must be made by public outcry.

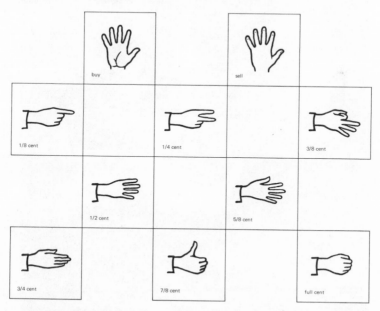

b. An efficient set of hand signals indicates whether the broker is buying or selling, the number of contracts offered, and the price desired. (Currently grains are not traded in ⅛¢ increments.)

(Courtesy of the Board of Trade of the City of Chicago.)

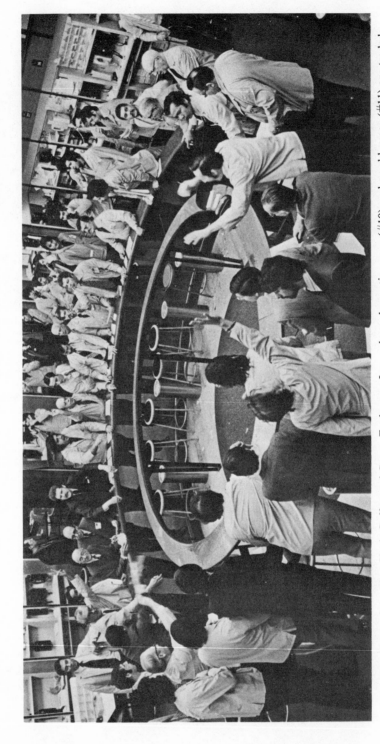

Trading floor of the New York Coffee and Sugar Exchange, Inc., where domestic sugar (#10) and world sugar (#11) are traded.

(Courtesy of the New York Coffee and Sugar Exchange, N.Y. 10005; photography by Tommy Weber.)

Cacao pod cluster on the trunk of the "chocolate tree."
(Courtesy of New York Cocoa Exchange.)

a.   Bulls make money, and . . .

b.

Bears make money, but . . .

c.

Pigs get butchered.

(a) "Lippy Leo," a 1600-pound Brahman Bull in the Western Live Cattle pit. (Courtesy of Pacific Commodities Exchange.) (b) Photography by Charles McKinley, Forest Park, Georgia. (c) Baby pigs in playpen (from Brookfield Children's Zoo) on first day trading live hog futures. (Courtesy of MidAmerica Commodity Exchange.)

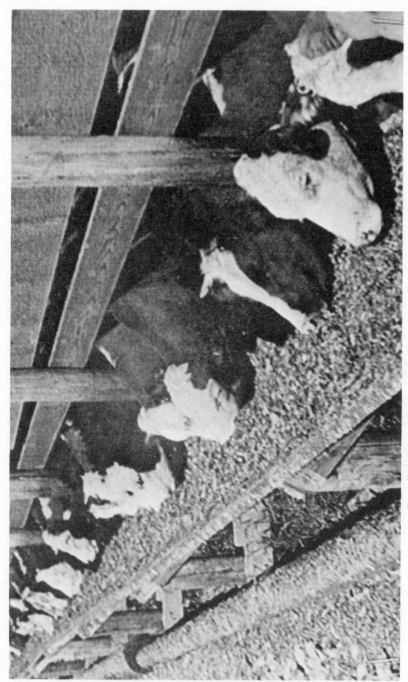

For all that good care and feeding, they pay the ultimate price.

(Courtesy of DeKalb AgResearch, DeKalb, Ill.)

Trading around the coffee ring.

(Courtesy of New York Coffee and Sugar Exchange.) (Photography by Tommy Weber, New York, N.Y.)

"Going, going . . .

Gone!"

(Trading scenes on New York Cocoa Exchange, courtesy of New York Cocoa Exchange, Inc.)

185

a. To the left of the trading pits are members' booths. The electronic board reports twenty-one commodities, eighty contracts. Closed-circuit television provides back-up reporting of market quotations. To the right of the pits are rostrums where exchange personnel supervise and report futures transactions.

b. Trading in the coconut-oil pit.

(Courtesy of Pacific Commodities Exchange, San Francisco, Calif.)

a. This new building of the Kansas City Board of Trade was erected in 1966.

b. All transactions are consummated in a single trading pit.

(Courtesy of Kansas City Board of Trade, Kansas City, Mo.)

11. CHICAGO BOARD OF TRADE

a. Topping the forty-five-story Chicago Board of Trade Building, in the heart of the "Windy City" financial district, stands a statue of Ceres, the Roman goddess of agriculture.

b. Long view of the floor where ten commodity futures are traded in the world's largest exchange, established in 1848.

(Courtesy of the Chicago Board of Trade, Chicago, Ill.)

(Courtesy of the International Monetary Market, Chicago, Ill.)

Finance (Swiss Credit Bank in Geneva)

Locations for International Organizations (Looking across Lake Geneva toward the "old" ville and the Seleve) (Photographed near Fribourg, Switzerland)

Tourism (Small village near Lucerne).

And cheese, too!

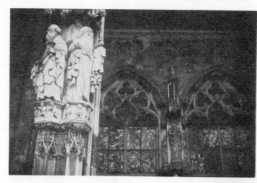

Cathedrals
(A fourteenth-century Gothic
cathedral in Ulm, Germany,
birthplace of Albert Einstein)

Castles
(Heidelberg)

Clocks
(Cologne)

Or the Porta Nigra
(The massive northern gate
to the Roman Empire in
Trier, Germany's oldest city)

191

Opening day on the IMM.

(Courtesy of the International Monetary Market.)

Shipping
(The White Cliffs of Dover)

Andy Capp
(A London pub)

Intrigue
(No. 10 Downing
Street)

Bridges
(But not the
Tower Bridge)

Antiquity
(Ruins of Herculaneum,
destroyed by Vesuvius,
A.D. 72)

Religion
(St. Peter's
Cathedral, The
Vatican)

Tourism (Venice)

Unusual Architecture (Pisa)

From Modern Steel (and pollution, too) . . . (Steel park near Monterrey, N.L.)

To Ancient Pyramids (Near San Juan Teotihuacan, Mexico.)

This swinging trio strike an antique gong to signal start of trading in Mid-America Commodity Exchange's new quarters at 175 West Jackson Boulevard in Chicago on May 28, 1974. Pictured are: J. Robert Collins (left), president; Jack Findling (center), vice-president; Leland H. Woodburn (right), assistant director of Illinois Department of Agriculture.

View of the new trading pit.

(Courtesy of R. S. Weeks & Associates, Chicago, Ill., public-relations firm for Mid-America Commodity Exchange. Photography by Plotnick & Communicators, Chicago, Ill.)

SECTION D

Putting Theory into Practice

CHAPTER 13
Plan to Win Big
and Lose Little

The best plan is to profit by the folly of others.

—Pliny

OF MANY KIND OF TYROS, TWO EXTREME CASES MAKE INTERESTING conversational topics. The overeager type, aroused by the market's excitement, studies little and ends up learning the Commodity Fox-trot. The second type, overwhelmed by the quantities of information he must absorb, never trades. He ponders and ponders.

A gentleman I know, who discovered a rather interesting system to arbitrage a couple of commodities, studied two markets carefully, followed all the steps outlined in this chapter, and concluded that his plan would produce profits. After two years he is still uncommitted. Lacking self-confidence, he wants a broker to practically guarantee him no-risk trades that will generate a 200 percent return annually on his minimum security deposit.

There are other types too. Whatever your peculiarities and eccentricities, welcome to the unusual world of commodity traders. My only advice: Don't bring your strange ways to the marketplace unless you are on an ego trip and deliberately desire to drop your dough down the drain. Enough of theory! It's time to practice!

The Commodity Fox-trot

So expensive to learn that no dance studio has ever offered instruction in these steps! If you want to dance, then you must physically wander through the steps. However, I will teach them to you for the price of this book. Drawing the steps in the book, so you can cut and paste them on the floor or wall, is the old-fashioned way. I believe you can get the idea through written instruction.

The superiority of the Commodity Fox-trot is its performance with any kind of music. To conform to the tempo, simply alter the title to Commodity Twist or Rock, Commodity Waltz or Tango, or Commodity Bunny Hop. You will always end up in the same place.

No special uniform is required but you do need an account with a commission house, one or more open positions, and to be fully margined. The steps are simple:

First, take one step forward, hesitate,

Then two steps backwards.

Take a deep breath, a long sigh.

Now sidestep once left and sprightly to the right.

Then two steps backwards.

Loudly growl, grumble, and groan.

Music stops until margin call is met.

Wire money.

Music starts again.

Vigorously bray three times.

Return to step one; repeat until bankrupt.

That wasn't so difficult, was it? The only symptoms I have ever noticed among those who have long endured this strenuous dance—after several times through the routine, a strange pain sometimes originates just south of the solar plexus and rises rapidly northward, expanding until throbbing temples pulsate with its rhythm. Other than an occasional graying of hair, no other symptom has been observed.

If you like to dance, don't waste your time reading the remainder of this book. Get with it! Donate this book and start dancing.

Your Trading Plan

The ballroom-shy may prefer to approach trading on a more sure-footed basis. Begin with a trading plan, all manuals advise. But what is a trading plan?

Essentially a trading guide prompts you to proceed as if you know what you are doing. It also induces you to formulate a set of rules you can live with. WRITE THEM DOWN. If they are good rules when you record them, stick with them. Your entire program and set of rules should match your temperament, your financial status, your objectives, and the time you can devote to homework to force yourself to think about money management.

The first step is to elect whether you intend to operate for small, quick profits, day-trade, play intermediate or long-run trends, wait for seasonal plays, trade straddles or moonbeams, or just do what naturally corresponds to your instincts.

Determine from which *group* of commodities (metals, oils, grains, red meats, currency, etc.) you will choose two or three to study. When your proficiency excels, you may resolve to diversify and digest more commodities. However, keep in mind that you are competing with specialists who not only confine their activities largely to one commodity but also to only one *option* (month) at a time. They, of course, observe action in other options, in related commodities, but they put their money on only one. Unless your particular risk-taking program allows you time to manage several situations, I urge you not to scatter your energies.

After narrowing the field, accumulate all the basic testimony you can about the commodity, its uses, and competing products. While gathering fundamental data, also obtain historical price series along with seasonal price behavior, open interest, and volume. Purchased charts afford a historical series covering several years. The annual *Commodity Yearbook*, published in New York by the Commodity Research Bureau, will subserve your quest for historical facts. Some exchanges publish *Yearbooks* that furnish important price guides, including daily high-lows.

After you have brought the commodity's price history up to date, structure your own charts from daily price quotations in your favorite newspaper (see Figure 50). Once updated, only a few minutes daily are required to construct a bar-chart entry on ordinary graph paper. Through concentrated assiduity you will begin to note trifles in the conduct of prices. Compare the price behavior of your commodity with other markets. Why does its performance conform to, or differ from, general market movement? Try to discover reasons.

After you have assembled your price data, analyze them for trends. Make note of cyclical patterns if they exist. Observe seasonal trends. Eggs have distinctly predictable seasonal waves (see Figure 51). Silver, too, sports seasonal characteristics; you will learn why in Chapter 17. Also, does the month in which you are speculating parade periodicity? Because of consumption or production arrangements, a particular option may display its own traits divergent from the general symmetry of other months of a commodity.

It would be superfluous to chart all the months traded; map two options, but observe the relationships between various ones. Which months are strongest? Which exhibit relative weakness? Trade in those months in which volume is greater. Far-out months tend to be more thinly traded and, therefore, less liquid. Superior order execution emanates from active months. If you venture in potatoes, you will interest yourself in the May option. Because of their marked seasonality, September and December, together with March options, attract more public interest in egg futures.

FUTURES TRADING LAST WEEK

Weekly range of contracts prices on major commodity exchanges. Prices through Friday's close through Thursday in Chicago, Kansas City and Minneapolis, through Friday in New York. Grains reported in thousands. Open interest as of Thursday.

CHICAGO BOARD OF TRADE

	Season's High	Low		Week's High	Low		Close Last	Prev.	Open Int.
WHEAT (5,000 bu)									
	4.36	2.49½	May	3.52	3.31		3.46	3.57	210
	5.85	2.76¼	Jul	3.56	3.33½		3.40½	3.54	41,735
	5.82	3.31	Sep	3.54½	3.38½		3.46	3.60	41,735
	5.82	3.44	Dec	3.69	3.48		3.54	3.68	23,545
	4.34	3.50	Mar	3.73	3.52		3.59½	3.72½	3,055
Sales: May 1045; Jul 85,596; Sep 37,705; Dec 22,390; Mar 1,890									
CORN (5,000 bu)									
	2.49	1.56	May	2.78	2.56¼	2.59¾	2.75¾	1,555	
	3.53	2.26	Jul	2.72¼	2.50	2.61¾	2.61¼	122,520	
	3.45	2.25	Sep	2.64½	2.44½	2.51¾	2.62	25,985	
	3.25	1.95	Dec	2.50½	2.33	2.36½	2.46¾	156,360	
	3.29	2.34	Mar	2.55	2.37½	2.40¾	2.51¾	31,960	
Sales: May 16,305; Jul 196,075; Sep 27,915; Dec 152,940; Mar 8,680.									
OATS (5,000 bu)									
	1.82¼	1.02½	May	1.48	1.41	1.41	1.48	75	
	1.85¼	1.02	Jul	1.35½	1.22¼	1.25½	1.35½	5,415	
	1.87	1.15	Sep	1.34	1.21¼	1.23¼	1.23¼	4,485	
	1.87½	1.19½	Dec	1.36½	1.24½	1.28¼	1.38	3,530	
	1.47½	1.20	Mar	1.33½	1.26	1.29	1.34½	760	
Sales: May 155; Jul 9,460; Sep 3,985; Dec 2,745; Mar 236.									
	4.54	3.68	Sep	3.82	3.72	3.73	3.91	320	
	4.53	3.70	Jul	—	—	3.68	3.86	800	
	4.56	3.81	Dec	—	—	3.79	3.98	100	
Sales: Jul —; Sep 3.80; Dec —.									
SOYBEANS (5,000 bu)									
	9.06	4.13	May	5.49	5.29	5.30	5.48½	2,390	
	9.03	5.20	Jul	5.58½	5.29½	5.54¾	5.53	89,170	
	6.94	5.17	Aug	5.74½	5.30½	5.54¾	5.55½	21,970	
	6.84	5.13	Sep	5.52	5.26½	5.46½	5.50½	5,865	
	6.66	5.06	Nov	5.44	5.19½	5.40½	5.43¼	68,490	
	6.73	5.09	Jan	5.47	5.24	5.44	5.50	23,020	
	5.81	5.11	Mar	5.52½	5.29	5.49	5.54½	6,495	
Sales: May 4,590; Jul 124,270; Aug 21,080; Sep 5,470; Nov 60,605; Jan 4,655; Mar 1,270.									
SOYBEAN OIL (60,000 lbs)									
	31.50	10.80	May	30.10	28.60	28.85	28.67	748	
	29.22	14.50	Jul	27.95	26.15	27.02	27.62	13,751	
	27.60	14.95	Aug	26.50	24.75	25.48	26.30	5,255	
	26.50	14.85	Sep	25.30	23.65	24.70	25.08	2,995	
	25.20	14.70	Oct	24.07	22.55	23.60	24.17	3,087	
	24.00	14.85	Dec	23.05	21.50	22.38	22.95	3,218	
	23.15	17.50	Jan	22.20	20.75	21.80	21.98	2,545	
	22.25	18.15	Mar	21.95	20.45	21.50	21.55	1,072	
Sales: May 1,786; Jul 17,182; Aug 4,944; Sep 2,041; Oct 804; Dec 2,337; Jan 745; Mar 431.									
SOYBEAN MEAL (100 tons)									
	283.00	102.50	May	116.00	111.00	116.00	113.70	139	
	284.00	110.50	Jul	119.40	113.50	118.70	119.50	7,611	
	203.00	114.50	Aug	122.90	117.10	121.30	122.10	4,055	
	179.10	118.50	Sep	124.50	119.50	122.90	123.80	1,857	
	192.00	121.50	Oct	127.00	122.80	125.50	126.50	3,963	
	180.00	124.00	Dec	128.70	124.50	127.50	128.70	3,758	
	172.50	126.00	Jan	131.00	127.50	130.00	131.00	1,103	
	144.80	127.50	Mar	133.00	130.00	133.00	133.50	180	
Sales: May 644; Jul 8,479; Aug 1,879; Sep 464; Oct 412; Dec 696; Jan 135; Mar 90.									
ICED BROILERS (28,000 lbs)									
	52.00	34.50	May	37.00	34.50	34.97	36.75	76	
	44.80	35.40	Jun	37.20	35.40	36.05	37.27	986	
	45.20	35.85	Jul	37.40	36.00	36.30	37.40	1,604	
	44.55	35.40	Aug	37.05	35.40	36.90	37.05	743	
	44.25	34.50	Sep	36.90	34.50	35.00	36.17	409	
	36.95	33.60	Nov	34.90	33.60	33.90	34.90	82	
	38.50	35.20	Jan	36.15	35.25	35.25	36.30	17	
Sales: May 201; Jun 624; Jul 12,317; Aug 197; Sep 152; Nov 36; Jan 3.									
SILVER (5,000 troy oz)									
	615.00	422.50	May	562.00	482.00	487.00	576.50	63	
	647.50	219.50	Jun	570.00	488.30	488.30	579.50	6,304	
	620.00	512.00	Jul	568.00	492.00	492.00	585.00	23	
	648.90	207.00	Aug	581.00	498.00	498.00	592.00	12,968	
	651.00	273.00	Oct	584.00	505.00	505.00	598.00	13,784	
	653.20	275.00	Dec	590.00	513.50	513.50	606.00	9,862	
	655.00	293.00	Feb	595.50	518.00	518.00	611.30	11,812	
	657.00	349.70	Apr	602.00	524.00	524.00	617.50	17,338	
	609.00	468.50	Jun	607.00	529.00	529.00	627.00	6,358	
	623.00	533.00	Aug	607.00	533.00	533.00	627.00	166	
Sales: May 407; Jun 5,849; Jul 78; Oct 6,691; Dec 5,318; Feb 882; Apr 1,717; Jun 884; Aug 39									
PLYWOOD (69,120 sq ft)									
	154.40	86.50	May	119.10	114.30	115.60	119.00	90	
	153.50	87.60	Jul	119.00	112.50	115.90	119.50	2,574	
	150.50	97.00	Sep	119.70	113.50	116.90	120.70	1,620	
	148.50	100.00	Nov	121.00	115.40	117.30	120.10	830	
	147.00	116.50	Jan	122.00	117.00	118.10	120.70	242	
	138.00	118.50	Mar	124.50	118.50	119.20	124.00	92	
Sales: May 225; Jul 3,358; Sep 1,612; Nov 451; Jan 126; Mar 55									
STUD LUMBER (100,000 bd ft)									
	142.50	94.00	May	122.80	120.10	120.10	121.50	11	
	141.50	94.00	Jul	119.10	117.50	118.00	119.50	40	
	136.00	101.00	Sep	119.80	117.50	118.00	119.30	22	
	133.00	104.50	Sep	—	—	116.50	118.00	11	
Sales: May 7; Jul 14; Sep 10; Nov 0									

CHICAGO MERCANTILE EXCHANGE

LIVE BEEF CATTLE (40,000 lbs)									
	61.75	38.95	Jun	42.35	38.95	38.95	42.55	6,303	
	60.62	39.35	Aug	42.50	39.35	39.35	42.60	8,487	
	56.00	37.25	Oct	40.95	37.25	37.37	41.22	5,520	
	53.90	36.30	Dec	40.05	36.30	36.42	40.32	3,003	
	49.50	35.85	Feb	39.52	35.85	36.15	40.00	1,269	
	47.90b	35.40	Apr	39.40	35.40	35.52	39.57	566	
Sales: Jun 13,571; Aug 27,124; Oct 13,088; Dec 5,690; Feb 1,535 Apr 625									
FEEDER CATTLE (42,000 lbs)									
	48.20	35.00	Aug	38.15	35.00	35.00	38.50	103	
	46.80b	34.50a	Sep	37.00	34.50a	34.50	37.40	33	
	53.00	33.10	Oct	37.25	33.10	33.10	37.50	689	
	40.00	33.30	Nov	37.00	33.30	33.30	37.02	70	
Sales: Aug 37; Sep 7; Oct 423; Nov 41									
SHELL EGGS (22,500 doz)									
	54.95	35.85	Jun	40.50	37.90	39.60	40.45	531	
	55.40	39.00	Jul	44.35	41.00	42.45	43.60	445	
	55.60	40.60	Aug	45.75	43.00	44.06	45.00	217	
	60.00	44.60	Sep	51.40	48.20	49.90	50.45	1,268	
	57.25	44.50a	Oct	49.00	47.25	48.20	50.70	97	
	59.50	46.00	Nov	53.10	50.00	51.30	52.85	169	
Sales: Jun 1,127; Jul 772; Aug 135; Sep 2,775; Oct 25; Nov 73									
LIVE HOGS (30,000 lbs)									
	58.50	27.15	Jun	30.10	27.15	27.22	29.80	2,107	
	57.25	28.60	Jul	31.40	28.60	28.90	31.22	2,007	
	55.00	27.15	Aug	30.10	27.15	27.40	30.35	2,257	
	49.10	26.20	Oct	28.85	26.20	26.67	28.70	2,801	
	50.45	27.17	Dec	30.10	27.17	27.47	30.00	780	
	48.50	29.30	Feb	32.10	29.30	29.50	32.20	253	
Sales: Jun 4,121; Jul 3,718; Aug 5,024; Oct 2,846; Dec 1,138; Feb 247									
PORK BELLIES (36,000 lbs)									
	80.25	33.80	May	37.20	33.80	34.35	35.95	11	
	81.10	34.27	Jul	37.55	34.27	34.15	36.67	3,245	
	78.40	33.25	Aug	36.30	33.25	35.10	35.95	2,021	
	65.80	38.30	Feb	41.45	38.30	39.35	41.07	1,119	
	65.25	38.10a	Mar	41.10	38.30	38.85	40.80	204	
Sales: May 189; Jul 14,617; Aug 5,837; Feb 1,659; Mar 78									

LUMBER (100,000 bd ft)

	Season's High	Low		Week's High	Low		Close Last	Prev.	Open Int.
	190.20	117.00	Jul	141.50	135.00		140.70	140.00	1,453
	177.40	117.80	Sep	133.50	131.20		137.20	136.20	532
	177.40	126.00	Nov	134.50	129.20		133.00	133.70	464
	168.10	127.00	Jan	134.00	129.10		133.00	133.60	160
	137.00	132.50	Mar	137.00	132.50		135.00	132.60	16
Sales: Jul 2,447; Sep 1,140; Nov 271; Jan 55; Mar 25									
b-Bid; a-Asked									
65.25–74 18.13edt									

N.Y. MERCANTILE EXCHANGE

MAINE POTATOES (50,000 lbs)									
	8.60	4.40	Nov	5.85	5.34	5.43	5.75	6,528	
	7.55	6.30	Jan	6.40	6.30	6.30	6.55	21	
	9.80	6.49	Mar	7.05	6.49	6.82	6.95	509	
	11.25	7.05	Apr	7.55	7.05	7.35a	7.50	274	
	11.00	7.77	May	8.49	7.77	8.22	8.40	1,047	
Sales: 7,492									
PLATINUM (50 troy oz)									
	300.00	146.80	Jul	220.00	193.10	200.70a	224.00	3,061	
	306.00	153.40	Oct	224.50	198.00	205.80a	229.00	2,513	
	314.50	166.00	Jan	230.00	204.50	210.30b	234.00	1,341	
	318.60	168.20	Apr	233.50	211.50	215.30b	237.50	461	
	325.50	218.00	Jul	235.00	218.00	221.50	242.00	285	
	253.00	220.50	Oct	234.50	220.50	225.50	242.50	6	
Sales: 3,270									
SILVER COINS ($10,000)									
	4500	1593	Jul	3908	3400	3400	3540	1782	
	4570	1731	Oct	4017	3450	3450	4065	1,847	
	4630	2125	Jan	4050	3570	3570	4125	2,119	
	4685	2200	Apr	4148	3630	3630	4206	1,614	
	4730	3200	Jul	4207	3845	3655b	4255	746	
Sales: 2,420									

N.Y. COFFEE AND SUGAR EXCHANGE

SUGAR NO. 11 ($0 tons)									
	25.60	7.05	Jul	23.35	21.10	22.50½	23.45	4,835	
	23.98	7.25	Sep	21.40	19.55	20.47½	22.13	2,850	
	22.55	7.42	Oct	20.50	18.70	19.60½	21.67	2,476	
	20.35	13.50	Jan	17.45	17.45	17.45½	19.27	101	
	19.65	7.40	Mar	18.10	16.43	17.60	18.27	2,261	
	18.35	7.80	Ma	16.80	15.30	16.35n	16.87	1,055	
	17.15	10.20	Jul	15.45	14.30	15.15n	15.43	1,201	
	15.50	10.40	Sep	14.15	13.05	12.90s	13.95	1,268	
	15.05	11.95	Oct	13.55	12.45	13.55s	13.37	712	
Sales: 13,976									
COFFEE 'C' (37,500 lbs)									
	82.95	65.45	May	71.90	70.80	70.80	70.50	11	
	85.53	66.10	Jul	73.70	71.20	72.50	73.55s	2,325	
	88.55	67.10	Sep	76.75	73.65	74.60	76.50s	1,733	
	89.75	69.90	Nov	78.25	75.15	76.25	78.35s	307	
	89.99	70.40	Dec	78.50	75.75	76.70	78.75s	516	
	85.90	77.40	Mar	79.00	77.40	78.10b	80.50	178	
Sales: 3,110									
a-Asked, b-Bid, n-Nominal, s-Split.									

N.Y. COMMODITY EXCHANGE

SILVER (10,000 troy oz)									
	644.70	208.40	May	567.00	487.50	490.50	578.00	325	
	580.00	501.90	Jun	540.00	535.80	535.80	583.00	2	
	646.90	225.00	Jul	574.00	500.50	500.50	587.00	10,005	
	649.40	231.50	Sep	582.00	509.00	509.00	597.50	8,126	
	652.10	274.80	Dec	590.00	518.30	518.30	603.90	7,406	
	653.00	276.90	Jan	592.00	520.20	520.20	605.80	6,656	
	655.30	291.50	Mar	592.00	525.70	525.70	610.89	6,753	
	657.00	342.80	May	598.00	530.50	530.50	615.30	3,116	
	659.40	466.50	Jul	605.00	535.20	535.20	619.60	1,800	
	650.10	560.50	Sep	606.00	540.00	540.00	623.40	475	
Sales: 17,436									
COPPER (25,000 lbs)									
	140.70	61.25	May			117.00	114.60	115.30	117.60	178
	137.70	66.50	Jul			115.50	106.20	110.20	115.80	3,291
	133.50	66.00	Sep			111.80	102.30	106.30	111.00	3,660
	131.00	67.40	Oct			108.20	100.30	104.60	109.00	760
	129.40	72.00	Dec			108.20	99.00	102.90	106.30	1,071
	128.20	71.70	Jan			107.50	91.00	101.80	105.80	556
	127.10	79.50	Mar			105.10	97.00	102.60	104.80	531
	126.20	96.00	May			105.20	96.00	99.20	103.40	271
Sales: 8,856									
a-Asked, b-Bid, n-Nominal, s-Split									

N.Y. COTTON EXCHANGE

WOOL (6,000 lbs)									
	267.2	158.5	Jul	170.5	161.0	170.5	161.0b	757	
	254.2	160.0	Oct	168.0	167.0	166.5b	161.5b	66	
	255.0	160.0	Dec	169.0	166.0	169.0b	163.0b	88	
	175.0	161.0	Jul	164.0	164.0	164.0b	155.5b	3	
Sales: 13									
COTTON (50,000 lbs)									
	67.00	33.20	Jul	56.60	51.60	51.70s	54.65	314,800	
	77.40	39.55	Oct	51.75	48.50	48.60	51.15	202,800	
	73.10	42.25	Dec	50.80	48.10	48.20s	50.30	690,000	
	70.20	49.50	Mar	51.80	49.50	49.60	51.65b	190,500	
	69.00	50.50	May	52.00	50.50	50.58	52.55b	11,600	
	64.00	51.85	Jul	52.97	51.85	51.48b	52.95b	11,600	
	61.60	52.00	Oct	52.30	52.00	51.40b	52.70b	3,100	
	55.50	51.75	Dec			52.75	51.75	51.40b	52.40b	10,900
Sales: 8,700									
ORANGE JUICE (15,000 lbs)									
	60.95	46.00	Jul	48.05	47.00	47.65	48.45	934	
	60.60	46.00	Sep	49.65	48.50	49.25b	49.85b	625	
	60.00	47.50	Nv	51.30	50.25	50.75b	51.60b	585	
	59.00	50.90	Jan	52.90	52.70	52.90b	53.90b	1,125	
	55.50	52.30	Mar	53.90	53.00	53.30b	53.90b	48	
Sales: 2,250									
a-Asked, b-Bid, n-Nominal, s-Split.									

N.Y. COCOA EXCHANGE

COCOA (30,000 lbs)									
	109.50	31.25	May	91.00	82.50	83.40	89.75	0	
	104.50	35.90	Jul	86.80	77.15	78.90	85.75	1,594	
	98.00	43.90	Sep	80.50	70.80	71.95	79.45	1,495	
	81.80	43.99	Dec	78.50	62.50	63.65	69.45	2,624	
	75.00	43.25	Mar	66.75	58.50	59.85	64.90	1,802	
	70.50	43.80	May	61.25	56.75	57.70	62.50	607	
	66.00	46.40	Jul	61.75	55.90	56.80	61.00	261	
	64.40	48.70	Sep	61.25	55.15	55.55	60.00	129	
Sales: 5,374									
a-Asked, b-Bid, n-Nominal, s-Split.									

KANSAS CITY BOARD OF TRADE

WHEAT 5,000 bu									
	6.10	2.39	May	5.37	3.38½		3.62	170	
	5.84	2.74	Jul	3.44	3.45	3.49	3.67½	3,390	
	5.82	3.21	Sep	3.69	3.53	3.56	3.73½	10,365	
	5.80	3.65	Dec	3.78	3.59	3.64	3.82	10,465	
	4.40	3.86	Mar	—	3.64	3.64	3.84	30	
Sales: May 755; Jul 11,710; Sep 3,985; Dec 2,330; Mar 0.									

MINNEAPOLIS GRAIN EXCHANGE

Wheat (5,000 bu)									
	5.89	3.19	Jul	3.86	3.60	3.72	3.82	6,636	
	5.81	3.20	Sep	3.77	3.56	3.62	3.72	6,725	
	5.80	3.48	Dec	3.73	3.63	3.68	3.76	880	
Sales: July 4,925; September 3,465; December 305.									

PACIFIC COMMODITIES EXCHANGE

COCONUT OIL (60,000 lbs)									
	53.00	14.50	Jul	50.63	47.50	48.10b	49.63	194	
	43.60	14.00	Sep	38.15	36.50	37.90	38.50	473	
	40.75	22.25	Nov	34.30	33.00	33.75	35.08	383	
	39.10	28.00	Dec	36.33	33.20	34.00	35.33	143	
	39.15	28.25	Jan	35.15	33.95	34.99	33.99	333	
	36.40	29.25	Mar	36.40	33.50	33.95	35.40	151	
Sales: 408									
a-Asked, b-Bid, n-Nominal, s-Split,									

Fig. 50. Futures prices

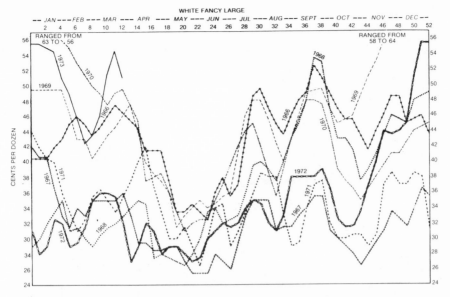

WHITE FANCY LARGE

-- JAN --- FEB --- MAR --- APR --- MAY --- JUN --- JUL --- AUG --- SEPT --- OCT --- NOV --- DEC --

Fig. 51. Cash egg chart (Source: Reed & Co., Inc., 10 South Riverside Plaza, Chicago, Ill. 60606.)

Your next step is to keep abreast of market fundamentals. If you merchant in copper, what are the prospects for demand? What are the Comex (Commodity Exchange, Inc.) and LME (London Metal Exchange) stocks of copper? On the political side, is peace or revolution anticipated in Chile, strikes in Zambia, nationalization of mines in Peru? The object is to avoid being a Harry Hindsight. A successful speculator forecasts the likely impact of information and news on *changes* in future values. "After the event, even a fool is wise." Practice, practice, practice.

Self-discipline is the purpose of formulating a trading plan. To achieve this objective, a self-created, rather than an adopted, technique is superior. Because the mind is slippery and cunningly deludes its possessor, no better system reigns than to write out each trade beforehand. No better method of self-discipline prevails than the embarrassing and unalterable testimony of errors of judgment plainly inscribed in your own handwriting. From these little notes to yourself, a success paradigm will evolve. Detect the pattern and duplicate it.

Figure 52 casts a flexible format that synthesizes the essentials but can be converted to your own requirements. Some traders have refined their written plan to a "fill-in-the-blank" system. At the beginning I do not encourage this. Filling in blanks nourishes rigidity and excludes experimentation with routine. Once you have forged a success mold that can be refined and reproduced to evoke a courted response, then you are rehearsing a self-taught model. To copy someone else's program invokes mechanicalness and ministers to lack of market sensitivity.

203

COMMODITY:

Fundamental Inputs Indicate That:

Technical Inputs Suggest That:

Related Commodities Are Bullish/Bearish.

General Market Indicators (DJ Futures Index) Are Bullish/Bearish.

Others (Letters, Brokers) Say That:

I Will Buy/Sell If Price Touches _____ .

Set Stop-Loss at _____ above/below.

Chart Action Indicates a Trailing Stop-Loss of _____ Points.

Price Objective Is _____ .

Risk Factors Are:

Odds Against Not Achieving My Objectives are _____%.

Action Taken—

   Open: Bought/Sold (Quantity) _____ (Month) _____ at (Price) _____.
   Offset: Bought/Sold (Quantity) _____ (Month) _____ at (Price) _____.

   NET   PROFIT _____. NET   LOSS _____.

I Succeeded/Failed Because:

Profits Could Have Improved If I Had:

Fig. 52. Planning inputs of data.

The written statement you educe similar to Figure 52 must answer one question. Why do you want to buy (sell) this commodity? With future prospects already forecasted, reduce your reasoning to a simple statement or two. If you cannot come up with a written expression, then your expression, then your reasoning, nebulous and unclear, needs reexamination.

Your analysis essentially encompasses the approach explicated in this book: fundamental, technical, and outside opinions. Fundamentals may embody governmental interference if it can be objectively identified;

otherwise, incorporate this probability into risk analysis. Ranking your own analysis over outside opinions, generally obtain outside opinions last and weight them least. For example, you may decide to weight fundamental analysis 50-60 percent, technical aspects 30-40 percent, and others' opinions 5-10 percent for an interpretation of an intermediate-term swing.

Essentially, however, market fundamentals underpin trend direction, while charts, volume, waves, and so forth portray market activity.

Paper Profits or Pauperism

Since one learns best by doing, isn't paper-trading little different from a game of monopoly or commodities? The argument against paper-trading states that the emotional pressure of real market action with real money is absent. The argument continues that many paper millionaires prove unsuccessful on the firing line. I have no quarrel with this statement, but the argument omits the benefits of paper-trading.

We already know that a loser is a loser whether or not he *ever* paper-trades. My belief is this: If a speculator-in-training cannot perform successfully on paper, what are his chances of success under actual conditions? If he cannot paper-trade for profits, he has *not* studied and practiced the basics well enough or is not serious about the undertaking.

So far you have written down (TO BE READ EVERY DAY) a list of rules to obey, in which, by all odds, you affirm to limit losses, not to overtrade, and other money conservation principles. You have studied a commodity and monitored it, following the proposal in Figure 52. Two additional aspects of planning appertain to types of market orders and treatment of stops.

Although any type of complicated order may be issued, rarely will it improve trading tactics. The best rule: keep it simple. The operability of commonly employed instructions leans on both market liquidity and action.

One most frequently exercised: *market* orders must be executed at the best price the floor broker can obtain. Wildly fluctuating market action may lead to an order filled far from where you intended. Alternatively, a *limit* order is specific advice to sell or buy at your designated price or better.

For example, you may direct your broker to sell four (contracts) of January '75 plywood at 139.20. A sell limit is usually localized near or above current market prices. If the market price does not rise to 139.20, then your order will not be completed.

Another example: Buy three (contracts) of April '75 platinum at 171.00 O.B. (or better). When the order is sanctioned, April platinum may be trading around 170.00. You want the order done but are not willing to pay more than 171.00. Instructed to buy at the best possible price under 171.00, the floor broker may effectuate it at 170.50.

Au pair to a limit order, a *stop* order automatically becomes a market order when a specified price is touched. Suppose that coffee charts sign-post a breakout at 70.00, and from that point prices could "run up" substantially.

Authorize your registered representative to buy two September '75 coffee contracts at 70.30 stop. The moment September coffee transacts at a price of 70.30, yours changes into a market order. The price may gallop upward and your request be filled at 70.80, or if prices backed off after touching 70.30, the order may be executed at 70.10.

Maybe you are not willing to pay 70.80. Employ a *stop limit* order (not every exchange permits every type of instruction). The "stop" part of the advice matches the above stop; the "limit" instructs the broker not to pay above a certain price. Your coffee order may read: Buy two September '75 coffee, 70.30 Stop with a limit of 70.40. As soon as the stop is activated the directive parallels buying coffee at 70.40 O.B. When the market throbs too rapidly, your request may not be consummated at all even though trades were made at interim prices. Obviously, buy orders flood in when the price charges upward, but an insufficient number of willing sellers produces a *tarantella* of prices.

One last example, the *market-if-touched* (MIT) order to buy is posted *below* market. Suppose that coffee is selling at 70.40 but you believe it may dip before resuming its upward path. Your order: Buy two September '75 coffee 69.90 MIT. Once *any* trade is transacted at 69.90, *your* order becomes a market order to buy.

Notice that a buy stop was positioned *above* the market price, while a buy MIT order is ensconced *below* into it. A sell stop is placed below the market, while an MIT order to sell is stationed above the market price.

A stop-loss order adds mechanicalness to trading, but it disciplines the speculator to accept losses. Their application does release emotional energy. Once you have resolved to accept a certain loss, the market, and not you, decides on the hour and day you are taken out. As a general rule, never place stop orders on even money. Use stops to limit losses or protect paper profits. A *trailing stop* means that it is adjusted upward (or downward) as the market price alternately dances and profits accrue.

The logical place for implanting stops, ascertained from chart action, daily price fluctuations, and the amount of capital you want to risk on the trade, is usually above or below chart congestion zones. Spotlighting massed activity 'twixt buyers and sellers, these regions of prior accumulation can shadow forth an ascendant march or typify a belt of support when prices later trail downwards. This technique of stops, no secret, equally can trap the insouciant.

Paper-trading should begin realistically. Set up a simple accounting system to keep score. Figure 53 offers a system for answering that age-old question: "How'm I doing?" You'll know when you read the bot-

DATE		COMMODITY	PRICE	COMMISSION	PROFIT or (LOSS)	NET	BALANCE		MARGIN
Buy	Sell								
April 15th		Security Deposit	—				$25,000	00	
April 29		3 - Sept Sugar	19.30						$7500
	May 14	3 - " "	21.70	192	+8054	+7862	32,862	00	
	April 30	2 - July Corn	277						4000
May 14		2 - " "	267	70	+1000	+930	33,792	00	
May 2		2 - Sept Sugar	21.10						5000
	May 14	2 - " "	21.65	128	+1232	+1104	34,896	00	
May 8		1 - Sept Sugar	22.95						2500
	May 14	1 - " "	21.75	64	(1568)	(1632)	33,264	00	
May 28		5 - July Wheat	336						2500
	June 15	5 - " "	405½	35	+3475	+3440	36,704	00	
June 5		5 - July Wheat	370½						2500
	June 20	5 - " "	443	35	+3625	+3590	40,294	00	
June 12		20 - July Wheat	380						12,000
June 14		15 - July Wheat	384½						9,000
TOTAL									

Fig. 53. How'm I Doing?

tom line. The columnar titles are self-explanatory. Begin by "opening an account" near to the amount you will actually launch your program with.

For maximum benefits try to simulate trading conditions. Believe that you have actually committed a certain sum of money. Imagine the emotion you would feel if you were winning or losing, but inaugurate the appropriate strategy beforehand. Remember: you are not playing this game for amusement or to impress a teacher; you are your own professor, and a high grade in the subject will be earned by financial successes.

The second point of self-honesty lies in order execution. You can approximate real market action by "placing" your order to be executed on opening or closing prices. You cannot fill it on the daily low or high price because these ranges cannot be ascertained in advance.

If the recorded price in the newspaper consists of opening or closing ranges, assume your order was filled unfavorably. Let us say that the closing range of June live hogs was 28.60-.75. A difference of fifteen points adds up to $45. Assume that your order was "filled" in the upper 25 percent of the range if you are buying and the lower 25 percent if you are selling. Record on your accounting form, June hogs bought at 28.72½ (transactions occur at two-and-one-half-point intervals) or sold at 28.62½.

Keep track of the petitioned security deposit. If prices edge against you, the commission house will solicit more margin money. Calculate this requisite daily to authenticate how much trading equity remains in your "account." Further, assume that initial and maintenance margins are the same. Therefore, if you debut with $5,000, retain a portion in reserve and do not overtrade. More about this important topic in the next section.

After "offsetting" a position, add the commission to gross losses, subtract the commission from gross profits, and tabulate the net figure. Information on commission rates and margin requirements can be procured from any brokerage house. You do not need to have an account to collect information from them. They are happy to court your business and willingly offer services. Minimum margins are set by various exchanges; however, the broker or brokerage firm may fix a higher requirement.

Having closed out a position, decide what you did right and where you erred. Think about this carefully. This point, the key to your future successes, forms the heart of paper ventures. Reevaluate each trade carefully, reduce your appraisal to a few short sentences, and record your sentiments in the "results" portion of the Figure 52 program.

Money Management

The other crucial success factor focuses on your management of your risk capital. Survival insurance centers on having some residual funds to sustain further speculation after consecutive losses. Not only concerned with making capital grow, money management also means deliberate conservation. Accidental successes usually turn into accidental failures; planned success denotes planning not to fail. Winning manifests both positive and negative aspects—the ying and yang of it.

The old adage, "Bulls make money, bears make money, but hogs get slaughtered," applies to money management as well. Do not try to make it all at once; only rarely will you succeed. However, if you have a bull by the horns, or a bear by the tail—even a short one—hang on. Adding to a winning position is not being piggish. It makes good sense to benefit from opportunities. Through past efforts you have created the prosperous circumstances that now confront you. Why shouldn't you take advantage of them?

If you are stopped out of a situation, do not err in the opposite direction and reverse the position. Analyze each dealing on its own merits.

Generally, the best policy after accepting a loss is to stand aside. Evaluate your situation in the manner described earlier in this chapter. Jumping in and out of the market is not graceful form even for a Commodity Foxtrotter. At least exhibit some poise.

With an account of $5,000 or more, limited diversification possibilities exist. Recent market activity suggests $10,000 minimum speculative capital. With smaller sums you must play a tighter game.

If you have committed $5,000, however, retain roughly 40 percent in reserve to finance minor fluctuations and to take pressure off. It is impossible to be right on every trade, and you should not expect price to move progressively in your favor immediately upon positioning.

Too, should you suffer a wipe-out of committed funds, at least 40 percent survives for another round. It's like tying the surfboard to your ankle—a little insurance.

Of the other 60 percent, do not pledge more than one-half to margin any one trade. On each investment, limit losses to no more than 50 percent of the latter sum.

With available risk funds of $5,000, this plan touches the limits of safety. Any heavier speculation borders on overtrading.

As your bankroll grows, gradually diminish these amounts to protect your wealth. When trading capital aggregates $50,000 or more, reduce commitment level to one-fourth of 60 percent per trade. Diversification with sums less than $5,000-$10,000 poses greater difficulty. Sound practices are even more pivotal.

For example, with risk capital of $5,000 available, try to hold back around $2,000 to keep you in the game. This leaves $3,000 to trade. For diversification, commit no more than about $1,500 (50 percent) to each position.

Let's assume that minimum security deposits equal $1,000 per contract. Overmargin by at least 50 percent, preferably more. In this example, you would add $500 to minimum requirements and commit $1,500 to finance each position.

Because only $3,000 is available, you can buy one contract of Commodity A and, say, sell one contract of Commodity B. Of your $5,000, you have committed $3,000 to two positions and are holding 40 percent of your total speculative capital in reserve for future contingencies. This $2,000 may either be held idle with the brokerage firm or placed in a savings account.

How much should you risk losing on each position? The maximum exposure should not exceed 15 percent of your total capital, or $750. Reduce this sacrifice as close to 10 percent as possible—even less as capital grows.

Stops conserve capital. Use them to limit losses. Place them in accordance with your money-management plan, chart action, and daily volatility. Shoestring financing obviously invites problems, possible losses, because it encourages overtrading. Overtrading is a major pitfall of speculators.

More broadly stated, a major pitfall is failure to develop and adhere to a money-management plan. Money management is essentially defensive. Assume the worst. Calculate what would remain should a debacle befall.

With successes, as capital grows from $5,000 or $10,000 to $50,000, trade even more conservatively. Essential to asset preservation, reduce the percentage committed to each position. Cut the amount you pledge to losses.

One speculator I know maintains $50,000 in his account. He trades $8,000, keeps the rest in reserve. He will be around a long time. Even a long series of losses will not take him out. The words *money management* should be inscribed at the top of each page of this book. Let's examine some other rules.

Some Basic Rules

During the time you are actively in the market, always keep informed, in touch with your broker. If you leave on vacation, close out your investments. For one thing, you will enjoy your trip more.

Quite a few years ago in Chicago, a trader, who frequented a brokerage firm daily and had acquired substantial wealth, opted to vacation in an isolated section of Canada. No telephones, no newspapers, no mail—only a lake plentiful with fish. And he left no instructions with his broker! The market had been quite dull. While he was away, the market livened up; the broker was faced with offsetting his client's positions. When the man returned, his fortune had been wiped out—completely annihilated!

At that time the board rooms attracted their regular audiences. This trader still visited every day with his briefcase. A briefcase filled with sandwiches from home! He sold the home-made *bonne-bouches* to other visitors until he had accumulated sufficient capital to trade once more. Never again did he take a vacation!

Nevertheless, the prudent speculator occasionally withdraws from market activity to rest—*reculer pour mieux sauter*. Being strenuous, trading can provoke the mind and tongue to become flibbertigibbety. Take time out to lick your wounds, count your profits, and reappraise the situation. Be able to sit on your cash for a while—probably one of the hardest rules for budding traders to self-enforce. In fact, anytime you are in doubt, stay out.

Do not be stubborn. Willingly consent to small losses, but also accept profits—especially large ones if the opportunities arise, and small ones when opportunities do not unfold. On the matter of losses, do not displace your protective stop-loss after it is established. In other words, do not enlarge the chance for bigger losses after planning your strategy. The exception, of course, the trailing stop-loss, is assigned to protect profits.

The subject of USDA reports springs up anew. There are major and minor reports. The trade follows these reports very closely; they substantially influence prices. To begin, you will be well advised not to carry an open position into a major report.

In practice sessions, you adopted opening and closing prices for self-discipline. As a rule, however, for at least two reasons, initiate actual trades *after* the market opens and not during opening. First, American markets open only four or five hours daily, but the forces of demand and supply are perpetual. Overnight news and price unrest in foreign markets naturally create gaps between yesterday's settlement and this morning's opening. Secondly, this brief period is requisitioned by floor brokers for evening up. Small profits achieved in opening ranges help them to restitute losses from the occasional mistakes that result from handling large numbers of transactions.

Prices during the closing session, similarly, can gyrate wildly during the last couple of minutes of trading as day traders try to even up positions and last-minute orders are being filled. As a rule, market-on-close (MOC) orders should be avoided unless there is a compelling contrary reason. For example, if you need to offset a short sale, prices during the day having not progressed much in either direction, you may elect to buy MOC if indications point toward the price dropping sharply at close.

I want to reemphasize a previously mentioned rule. Learn the causes of your successes. Developing a winning style requires persistence and discipline, but it pays. Too many people master one technique and then want to begin experimenting with others. When you have found a winning style, stick with it.

Westward Ho!

Before returning to risk analysis, let me point out that the range of trading opportunities is not only broad but expanding. Commodity transactions are not confined to New York and Chicago and do not stop with wheat in Kansas City. San Francisco, too, boasts its own exchange.

The somewhat unique Pacific Coast Exchange, the only regulated exchange on the West Coast and the only publicly held commodity exchange in the world, actually was the first *regulated* (by the USDA, Commodity Exchange Authority) exchange to open in the United States since the Chicago Mercantile Exchange was inaugurated in 1919.

Being a publicly held corporation, membership is by owning (two) shares rather than purchasing a "seat." And PCE stock trades over-the-counter for around $3,000 per share. Additionally, the PCE does not set minimum commissions. Therefore, commissions are negotiated. However, the exchange does charge $5 per contract bought or sold.

Its contracts are unique to the West Coast. Crude coconut oil, largely imported via the West Coast from the Philippines, began trading on October 31, 1972. Western shell eggs, begun in February 1973, parallel nest egg futures initiated on the Chicago Mercantile Exchange on July 1, 1974, only in parts of the specification contract. Delivery is effectuated strictly west of the Rockies. Western live cattle was launched on October 31, 1973. By June 1974, the PCE had drafted a proposal on a silver contract.

Although there are differences between the live cattle contracts of the Chicago Mercantile Exchange and the Pacific Commodity Exchange, the possibility of arbitrage exists. The similar situation prevailing between crude coconut oil and soybean oil is explored in Chapter 22. Both Chapters 15 and 18 survey straddles and arbitrage. The potential is only mentioned here.

For example, the chart in Figure 54 depicts price differences (through

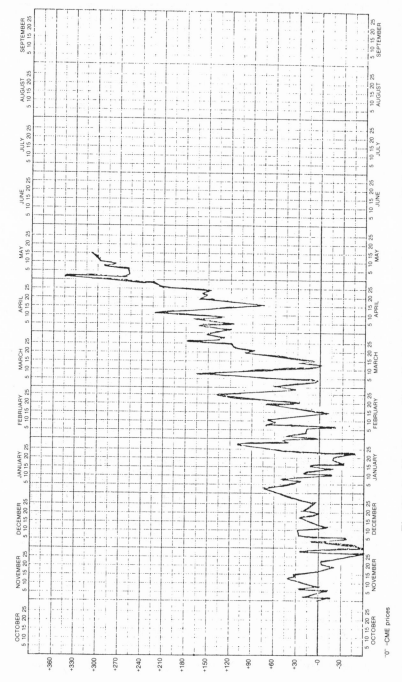

Fig. 54. Pacific Commodities Exchange August cattle contract. Daily price spread of PCE August cattle contract plotted against daily prices of CME cattle (Source: Courtesy of Pacific Commodities Exchange, 315 Montgomery Street, San Francisco, Calif. 94126.)

May 15, 1974) of August '74 live cattle contracts traded in Chicago and San Francisco. Prices equal each other on the "zero" line. The chart demonstrates independence between Western and Midwestern prices. Interesting possibilities of straddling emerge from the largely seasonal price differentials. However, before studying straddles, let's once again return to risk analysis.

CHAPTER 14
Select the Degree of Risk

Any activity directed to change involves uncertainty as to its results and is inherently a gamble.

—Frank H. Knight

DECISION-MAKING SPECIFIES WEIGHING OF ALTERNATIVES IN TERMS OF objectives, age, personality, financial and emotional status, and degree of estimated risk you must assume to achieve your goal. Steps adumbrated in this book are:

1. Identification of commodities you are willing to study.
2. Arrogation of required inputs—data, information.
3. Evaluation of information.
4. Selection of alternative strategies.
5. Evaluation of perceived risk (and chances of surprise risk) for each alternative.
6. Selection of strategy.
7. Actual commitment to the position.

In various ways we have taken counsel on the above steps; however, the subject of risk perpetually obsesses us. The term *risk* arises incessantly in commodity more than in other financial literature. Certainly, speculators (really gamblers) take high-flyers on questionable stock; investors do purchase equities in firms whose product or management they know little about; government bonds are possible prey of debt repudiation; and assets like time deposits, savings accounts, insurance, and fixed-income annuities, owned by conservation-minded investors, are vulnerable to erosion at a rate of 5, 10, 15, 50 (?) percent a year by the simple act of inflationary monetary policy. Nevertheless, risk *is* a valid topic; ergo, an entire chapter is devoted to step no. 5 above. First examining risk in general terms, we will proceed to practical applications.

Likelihood

Wealth accumulation really boils down to the question of time preference. When you receive, generate, or earn income, you must choose whether to spend all of it, part of it, or none of it. If you spend everything now, future expenditures depend on variability of future income. If you do not spend all your present income, part of it has been saved. Since $1,000 is worth more to you today than receiving the same $1,000 several years hence, the saving act involves some sacrifice; therefore, you expect to be rewarded for sacrifice. Savings transformed into investments produce future income—a rate of return—in sufficient amounts to induce you to save.

People save, or forgo present pleasures, in order to have more later. Other than saving for major purchases—automobile, house, yacht, vacation—most of us have a long-term wealth-accumulation plan primarily for two reasons: financial security during our less productive years, and to pass something on to our heirs.

Some degree of risk inheres in the act of saving. Saving means purchasing a financial asset, whether foreign or domestic currency, debt instruments, or equities. There is no complete certainty that in some future period your savings will be worth more than, or even as much as, they are worth today. So the question of risk returns.

Risk is stated in two different ways: (1) an intuitive approach (often just a good or wild guess), and (2) in probabilistic terms, "There is a 60 percent chance of showers today." (Be sure to carry 100 percent of your raincoat.) Stating price objective is largely the first approach. Neither highest nor lowest price objectives represent a reasonable estimate of expectations.

The "scientific" method is a probability distribution similar to the histogram in Figure 55. The diagram conveys a 30 percent chance that the price of a commodity will climb only 40 percent, a 40 percent chance that price will rise by only 50 percent, a likelihood of 65 percent that the price will peak out at 80 percent higher, a 35 percent chance of doubling, and only a 5 percent likelihood that ultimate price will exceed 100 percent, and so forth.

In the last chapter, in discussing money management, I urged you to risk small amounts on each trade—preferably as close to 10 percent of your trading capital as possible, and certainly never more than 15 percent. Why?

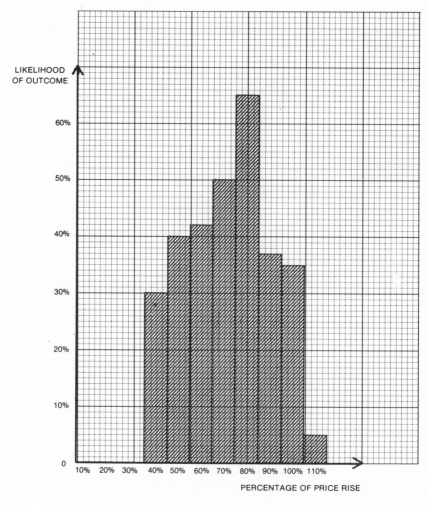

PERCENTAGE OF PRICE RISE

Fig. 55. Likelihood of outcome

A brief example on expectations will demonstrate that risking around 15 percent per transaction will evict you from the game after six consecutive losses, while risking less, of course, will keep you operative longer.

Abstractly, if p is the probability of winning m dollars, expectation can be defined as mp. What is the expectation of a person who will receive $400 if he can throw three coins that all land heads up? Every time he shoots, there are eight possible alternatives: HHH (a winner), TTT, TTH, THT, HTT, HHT, HTH, THH.

To calculate p (the probability of obtaining three heads to win), the following equation applies, where s represents number of successes (in this

216

case only one success or winning combination is possible with each toss) and f signifies number of possible failures. In other words, $s + f$ equals eight possible outcomes each time you toss the three coins, but only one combination wins and with any of the other possible results you will forfeit your dough. You have one chance to win, the house seven.

$$p = \frac{s}{s + f} = \frac{1}{1 + 7} = \frac{1}{8}$$

Therefore, the probability of winning is one-eighth, and the likelihood of losses is seven out of eight possible combinations. The expectation to win, mp, is $400 x $\frac{1}{8}$ = $50. A player's expectation (mp) is the fair price to pay for the privilege of playing.

If, each time, he risks losing more than $50 per turn—that is, he pays an amount exceeding $50 to play—he will lose his trading capital if he plays long enough. On the other hand, paying less than $50, he is certain to win over some long period of time.

Do you see the analogy to proper money management? How many consecutive times can you afford to lose before you win the apple? A trader can sustain several small losses and still win if large-enough profits occasionally accrue to offset them. But it all pivots on your style.

Some odds, of course, are easily measured. In flipping a balanced coin, there is a fifty-fifty chance that it will land tails-side-up. In commodity transactions the odds can be improved to exceed fifty-fifty. Where human action is a variable, a guesstimate really replaces precise calculations. There is no perfect method, even if you are acquainted with all the market participants. The market is a faceless, impersonal, unprejudiced organism. There is no accurate system for judging the composite characteristics of all traders or even predicting how each personality will react to a set of data. Multiply the number of market participants by the number of possible different circumstances and you will appreciate the magnitude of the problem.

About all you can say is that the average speculator is forty-five years old, earns $25,000 a year, trades contracts in twos and threes, and more than likely resides in California, Illinois, New York, Texas, Iowa, or Ohio. Roughly two-thirds of speculators are college graduates, mostly male; nearly one-third are professional persons; while 15 percent represent farmers, feeders and processors. Does that tell you much? Of course not. What do we know about speculators?

Cognition

An investor's probability estimate of various alternative situations depends a great deal on his personality and age. The cautious individual assigns a higher probability to failure. The investor who acts without sufficient information, thinking, and deliberation, and responds with uncontrolled impulses, is more likely to be a big risk-taker.

On the other hand, extended deliberation and large quantities of information do not portend greater profits. Quite the contrary; in most cases a speculator can acquire as much information as he can absorb. The more information he is able to accumulate, the more likely it is known to larger numbers of people—that is, it begins to appear eventually in popular media—and the more information he requests before rendering a trading decision, the lower the potential profit from a correct decision. Generally the investor's goal should be to achieve a workable approximation of truthfulness.

The difficulty is not only in obtaining, deciphering, and analyzing information. Many analysts do well here, and information from an independent firm can be purchased for a price. The problem centers on the trader's thinking processes, which are sometimes colored and dominated by motivational factors that may have their roots in childhood experiences. Through self-analysis, a good trader will discover the nutritive source of these adversaries and tear them out mercilessly by their roots.

Another common obstacle in rational risk assessment is the postdecisional process. Starting with the premise that decisions have consequences, what relates selection of trading strategies to monetary results? When results are positive, the goal has been achieved. When consequences are negative, will past decisions affect subsequent ones? It should not if emotions are under control.

The anxious and defensive trader will be pushed into further high-risk situations after a series of losses. Failure among these single-minded risk-takers makes them adhere more to the riskiest of positions; shooters are not inclined to employ capital-conservation policies. The excessive risk-taker either enjoys the excitement of the game more than the goal of winning or is frustrated from inability to win.

I am not condemning plunging if that is your style. There have been a few successful gentlemen of fortune. High-flying is a "trading plan" to accumulate large sums quickly. Some plungers living around the world find it inconvenient to return to the United States.

We should not exclude mention of the ladies. Possibly only 5 percent of players are women; that is, aside from instances of joint ownership, very few accounts are retained in the name of women. How do they trade?

They seem to prefer extremes: either excessive risk-taking or over-conservatism. Females appear less risk-sensitive in judging individual trades. But those who do adopt middle-of-the-road policies tend toward overall successes. In judging individual cases, winning traders emerge in every category.

Disagreement

It is an interesting fact that among any given group of people who possess identical information, all will not concur on the direction of prices.

Each trader, operating in his own world, acts on predictions based upon his (or someone else's) interpretation of informational inputs. The individual trader's predictions of future trends reflect his expected return on investment, perceived risk, most recent series of profits or losses, remaining capital, and open commitments.

We have covered each point already. Expected rate of return is frequently expressed as potential extent of price movement versus possibility of failure and losses rather than as an annual rate of return for any given trade.

Referring to the postdecisional process, results of recent trades will not only tend to color present decisions but also determine available capital.

Open commitments, the "portfolio" of positions, determine overall risk, time over which results are expected, and likely "return." If present positions are low-risk, intermediate-term objectives (more than one week but less than three months), then you may consider a short-term, high-risk situation if sufficient capital remains.

All traders do not agree on the likely outcome of future events. There are buyers and sellers—some net long, others net short. Differences of opinion provide market liquidity. Because no special set of rules exists for short sales—just as easily executed as purchases—commodity markets are excellent vehicles to operate in during any economic conditions. Boom or bust, it does not matter; both furnish opportunities to garner profits.

Every sale, except those where a physical commodity is delivered, consists of a buy order and a sell order, at different times, for the same trader. Every position must be offset.

Assessing risk on short sales parallels determination on the long side. As long as sales price exceeds purchase price, profit (less transaction costs) accrues. It matters not which side of the transaction is initiated first.

Suppose that you anticipate a housing recession in six months. Contractors are now fully employed. But you have talked with architects and engineers. They have indicated a slow-down in orders.

Interest rates climb; loanable funds appear scarce. Officials jawbone about tighter monetary policy.

Population growth has approached zero over several years. Vacancy rates mount in apartment and office buildings. New property listings overflow. You seize an opportunity to sell plywood short.

Impending an encounter with an owl or raven to augur a turnaround in the present uptrend, chart a seasonally weak month. When you sell short you have an open position. It must be offset before expiration of the contract. Or be prepared to deliver against it.

We actually "go short" more frequently than realized on many ordinary daily transactions. Credit purchases mean you are short cash, long merchandise. Once we understand that either side of the transaction may be originated first, we open ourselves to many profitable opportunities. For the flexible-thinking enterpriser, recessions, and depressions too, offer as many, or more, opportunities to scoop up profits.

Remember that not everyone agrees. More profits are earned by those who can accept the emotional risk of going against universal opinion. The hoi polloi are not always right—and are usually wrong!

Odds

In hazarding odds, examination of historical data sometimes provides a clue to future action. The historical player asserts that in similar cases, tomorrow will be almost exactly like yesterday. Charting and moving-average techniques are essentially historical approaches. Charting information, of course, graphically reanimates the past for as far as desirable. Through employment of continuation charts, or cash charts, very-long-run trends may interest the enterpriser. However, in risk analysis, the purpose is to calculate chances that the future will (or will not) be like the most recent past. Good risk analysis is, in part, an intuitive exercise for which no appropriate substitute exists.

In the praiseworthy instance of crops and their derivatives—grains, oil-seed, fibers, foods—there is a distinction between old and new crops. The first new crop contract for corn is December, November for soybeans. Too, the soybean crop may arrive early with good weather, and September prices will partly reflect new supplies. If shortages emerge toward the end of the crop year, then near-term prices may considerably outrank later options.

In a normal, *carrying-charge market,* later months of storable products will sell at a premium to near-term options or cash markets. Theoretically, a contract scheduled for delivery three months hence should reflect a higher price that includes storage costs, insurance, and interest charges. Cash prices should slightly trail the nearest futures option.

Present high demand, resulting from heavy exports, may lead to later options selling at a discount to near-term ones so that normal price relationships are *inverted.* Prices effectively allocate product to users in most urgent need of it.

Prices also marry the commodity to its products. Soybeans provide the best example of this. In their natural state, soybeans have limited sales, their two products—soybean meal and soybean oil—are traded in the futures markets. The value of soybeans depends mostly upon the prices of these two products, and, of course, the prices of these products are affected by fish meal and oil substitutes. In the next chapter, specific instructions will apprise you how to trade in soybeans and soybean products.

Because of the consanguinity of cash and future prices (see Chapter 15) brandished by some commodities, one historical approach commences by charting (or tabulating, if you prefer) periodic (weekly or monthly) cash prices. Figure 51 exemplifies a seasonal cash egg chart. Grains really accommodate well to this sort of exercise. Profitability studies typify buying and selling dates founded on historical performance, but investment

220

opportunities cannot be ferreted out with such mechanicalness; nevertheless, such information may spare you some losses.

Well-known seasonal archetypes predominate spot commodity prices. For example, wheat and oats flaunt high prices in January and May and low ones in August-September. Both of these grains (as well as soybeans) commonly react sharply in February—the "February break"—preluding a substantial rally. One "never-fail" technique posits to buy wheat on February 22 and sell it on May 10.

Recurrently more subject to deviation from "normal" seasonal patterns, coffee peaks in January-February but lays bare its double bottom in April and November; while sugar usually reaches its apogee in September and its perigee in March.

As an exercise, tabulate the monthly average cash prices of wheat for the twenty-five-year interval 1950-1975. Do any patterns emerge? In how many years did wheat rise in price from August to May? Over twenty-five years, how many times did cash wheat exhibit a higher price in June than in April? In the cash market, do the historical odds favor a long or short position between August and May? Or to be long or short over the April-to-June period?

Now let us perform a similar exorcism on oats. Tabulate, as before, the monthly average cash prices of oats over several years. You may more readily identify seasonal mutualities if the information is plotted on graph paper. Once more let us say you are examining the April-June quarter. In how many years did cash oats sell at a higher price in June than April? From your data you have now cognized the expected trend of prices for this period according to the frequency of parallel relationships.

Because not every year exhibits analogous behavior, next determine whether the current year displays characteristics akin to any, or several, tabulated years. The purpose is to probe for repetitive price patterns preferably by prospecting the most recent months and pairing them with previous periods. For those who comfortably identify with mechanical devices, odds can be calculated by using this historical system; that is, the likely occurrence of a similar event may be stated according to the number of repetitions out of, say, the past twenty-five years—eight out of twenty-five? Fourteen out of twenty-five? Nineteen out of twenty-five? And so forth.

However, you are transacting in tomorrows, not in the cash product; ergo, you want to calculate odds on a specific option—say, July oats. Through information found in the Chicago Board of Trade *Yearbook,* construct two tables, or graphs, first by tabulating monthly highs for July oats, then by tabulating monthly lows for July oats. Assume interest centers on the April-June period. Determine how many times during the past ten or twenty-five years (or whatever span) the price of July oats rose (or fell) from April 1 to June 1.

Your computations from the *Yearbook* will expose the highest and lowest prices reached by July oats for the months and years recorded. How many times during the last twenty-five years did the price of July oats drop from April to June? This relationship, or odds, will indicate the chances of the same event occurring again this year.

Preferably select those years which best echo the present year's action. You can do this by examining similar patterns and fitting them in the current year's prospects for an encore. Additionally, fundamental analysis, also in order, determines which year's conditions approximate this year's. You may discover sister-ships in weather conditions, surpluses or deficits of other grains, livestock population, or you may learn that this year is rather unique since no historical homogeneity turns up.

Here is one trade you may have been tempted to try. A recent historical study reveals that July pork bellies' prices tend to rise from March 1 to sometime before the March 22 *Pig Crop Report*. Table 11 demonstrates that profits could have materialized if you had purchased contracts approximating the settlement price of the first trading day in March and were lucky enough to pick the top price at some point during the first three weeks of the month. Historical experience suggests placing a stop-loss 100 points down; it does not predict potential losses-to-profits. The historical study supplements what you have already discerned, but it is not a sinecure.

It would not have worked in 1974. Between March 1 and March 22, the highest price was 56.85 on March 1. Prices steadily deteriorated to 45.50 on March 19, and recovered slightly to close at 47.10 on March 21.

Better to have them in your favor than against you, playing odds is far from scientific. Figuring them may provide only a well-researched guess. If the market has already discounted price (your competition is competent!), efforts will not yield a profit. On the other hand, your account may luxuriate with pelf and wealth.

Reduction

Searching for a mechanical technique to subjugate risk propounds no simple task. The first step in risk reduction is prior knowledge of risks by calculating odds as best as possible and to thoroughly acquaint yourself with each commodity.

Because an adverse price run can dissipate minimum margin deposit so quickly, an appearance of riskiness is conveyed all out of proportion to the hazards in other financial markets. Still many investors, in oblivion, will sit through a 20 percent decline of their favorite stock. Because they have paid 50, or 75, or 100 percent of the stock's purchase price, they are loath to sense the risk of loss.

You do not have to play the commodities game with only the minimum required margin of 5 or 10 percent. Do you really need all that leverage? As *International Moneyline* suggests, "But why not play commodities on

TABLE 11

SEASONAL TRADE IN FROZEN PORK BELLIES

Calendar Year	Close First Trading Day of March	Prior to March Pig Crop Report High Price	Prior to March Pig Crop Report Low Price	Maximum Gain Prior to March Pig Crop Report ¢ per lb.	Maximum Gain Prior to March Pig Crop Report $ per contract
1967	35.25	36.60	34.30	1.35	405.00
1968	33.32	35.20	33.30	1.87	561.00
1969	36.35	39.40	36.10	3.05	915.00
1970	44.75	46.90	44.35	2.15	774.00
1971	27.40	28.97	26.70	1.57	565.20
1972	36.62	40.70	36.25	4.07	1465.20
1973	54.22	58.50	53.65	4.27	1537.20
1974	55.55	56.85	45.50	Loss	—

SOURCE: Seasonal recommendation prepared by Lincolnwood, Inc., 141 West Jackson Blvd., Chicago, Ill. 60604. The 1974 figures are updates by the author.

50 percent margin, just like you now can do in the stock market? Then you can avoid the intermediate washouts and take advantage of the long range inflationary trends."[1] By employing maximum leverage, you can increase risk assumptions; by employing less leverage, you decrease chances of a wipeout with a small price fluctuation.

Diversification, another technique to reduce risk, requires a great deal more calculation than it implies. Buying a couple of contracts of live hogs, a couple of live cattle, and a couple of pork bellies, certainly portfolio variegation, does not necessarily diminish risk, and perhaps adds to it. The entire meat complex tends to drift together so that if you commit a *faux pas* with one you will probably incur losses in all positions, but not exactly at the same rate.

Diversification, by owning contracts in different categories—grain, meat, and oilseeds, for example—does not always underlie risk minimization. Certainly these commodities are related in their final uses. Random selection may or may not generate the coveted consequence. Calculation of separate odds and investigation of each commodity may disclose that you have augmented total portfolio risk.

Diversification may scale down total risk. Selecting the most fortuitous trades out of several possibilities may also extract the least profitable opportunities. Diversification should reinforce total risk control to permit hazarding a portion of capital in higher-risk, higher-profit situations.

1. *International Moneyline* 1, no. 7 (January 22, 1974): 4. (Published by Cambronne Financière, S.A., 43 rue Goethe, Luxembourg.)

Trading is not an exercise in finding the least chancy situations; its objectives center upon achieving balance in your total campaign to reach your end-of-the-year goal of having more rather than less wealth.

The *hypothetical* open positions in Table 12 represent an imaginary speculator's *attempt* to achieve balance in ventured funds, to pare risk. Investing in some commodities with less consanguinity, being both short and long, promotes diversification. On balance, of course, this trader is net short.

While this type of analysis pinpoints capital deployment, this particular "portfolio" presents several hazards. Following six commodities in distinct areas necessitates considerable research time. We can only assume that the investor either has time to pursue these activities or has purchased research from reputable services. He has plunged nearly one-third of his venture capital on two commodities—sugar and cocoa—which offer greater chances of *not* reaching anticipated price objectives than does corn. However, nothing has been mentioned on the time horizon. Possibly corn is a three-months investment, while he expects cocoa and sugar to precipitate the solicited results within a few days.

Of course, at the time of opening positions, risk assessment may have been entirely different from the July 15 picture in Table 12. New facts and subsequent reassessment may have altered his outlook. He is interested in *present* forecasts of already-held positions before pioneering new ones. Considering the overall risk, his uncommitted reserve (30 percent of his trading capital) looks low. Naturally, he will offset his live cattle position shortly, which will release funds, along with any accrued profits.

Performing a mental exercise in which you assess present positions relative to *future* prospects allows for greater rationality in deciding upon new stakes. The imaginary investor in Table 12 may have retained

TABLE 12

An Imaginary Speculator's Open Positions (July 15)

Commodity	Option	Number of Contracts	Position	Proportion of Total Funds Committed (%)	Projected Price Increase (%)	Likelihood of Not Reaching Target Price (%)
Iced broilers	Nov.	2	short	12	90	40
Live cattle	Aug.	3	short	13	140	20
Sugar (World)	Sept.	3	long	18	80	50
Cocoa	Sept.	2	short	12	80	50
Platinum	Oct.	1	long	5	40	45
Corn	Sept.	2	long	10	100	33
Uncommitted funds		—	—	30	—	—

cocoa contracts for some time, the market has been dull, he has a small loss, and it now appears even less likely that cocoa prices will drop. He may do well to offset his cocoa contracts, accept the small loss, and devote some released funds to a better situation—say, selling March iced broilers short. Trading of iced broilers in different months provides some diversification; funds are engaged in lower-risk but equally high-return investment.

Two rules grow out of this approach. First, never get married to a position; divorce is the norm. Second, in rearranging your investments, you improve your position if you obtain the same anticipated rate of return with lower estimated risks, or if you achieve a higher rate of return with the same amount of risk. Shifting from cocoa to iced broilers accomplishes both: higher return and lower risk. (Review the diagram in Figure 1.)

Another method of limiting risk—buying and selling the same commodity simultaneously—usually offers less action but is a legitimate trading scheme.

CHAPTER 15
Try Straddles, Spreads, Stretches, or Racks

Every stick always has two ends.

—Gurdjieff

BECAUSE NOT ALL PRICES MOVE EQUALLY TOGETHER, TRADING ON PRICE differentials is another attractive method of profiting from certain types of speculative activity. Correspondence between cash and futures prices, an important guideline, merits further discussion as a prelude to this chapter. As delivery time nears, cash and futures prices converge.

Additionally, price differences among various futures options may offer profitable opportunities and, in some cases, risk reduction. Buying one option and selling another simultaneously in the same commodity is a *straddle*. The price divergence between the two contracts is the *spread*. In common parlance, however, these two terms are employed interchangeably. Putting on or taking off, *unwinding,* a spread or straddle means the same, although the term *spread* is most commonly used. *Stretches* and *racks*, my terms, describe certain variations of straddles.

Besides intramarket straddles, intermarket *arbitrage* (that is, buying in one market and selling in another) is employed between related commodities, such as selling Kansas wheat and buying Chicago wheat against it, or between silver coins and silver bullion (discussed in Chapter 18). Or you may prefer to straddle live cattle and hogs (substitutable commodities), plywood and lumber, or among the commodity and its products—soybeans, soybean oil, and soybean meal.

Spot and Futures Prices

Many traders give little thought to the affinity between cash market and futures prices. The exchange of physical commodities for money takes place in the cash market. Futures represent estimated projected cash prices based upon today's circumstances, plus anticipated demand-and-supply factors several weeks or months forward.

As the future month arrives, the dissimilarity between spot and futures prices will narrow. If the futures market has correctly anticipated tomorrow's spot price, cash price will rise (or fall) to meet the futures price. If facts become altered, the futures market will adjust to the cash market's higher or lower price.

Undoubtedly, many projections are predicated on present prospects. Humans—and therefore the market—fall far short of perfection. In grains and meat markets, where cash prices are determined under fairly competitive conditions, recording and plotting spot prices provides an additional guide, another tool, in determining near-term direction of futures. Not perfectly correlated, it is only a signpost.

Comparability of cash and futures prices is especially important to hedging operations—producers, processors, others who hold inventories. If the futures price is low relative to the cash market, it is profitable to buy futures, take delivery of the commodity, and redeliver on the cash market.

Commercial traders have an advantage over public speculators. They know channels for disposing of the product; they possess the necessary storage facilities. Although a speculator should observe and record cash price changes, spreads and straddles should be confined to futures markets.

Bull Spread or Bear Spread

Erroneously thought to automatically reduce risk, straddles and spreads require the same close attention applied to all trades. Simultaneous buying and selling of the same commodity in different months suggests that as price goes up, gains in the contract you bought cancel losses in the contract you sold. Naturally, this is true; but profits are earned through changes in the spread, or price difference, provided the commodity was correctly straddled.

As a general rule, if you expect the front months of a commodity to rise in price more rapidly than the back months, then you will buy, say, September eggs and sell December eggs—a *bull spread.* Although both September and December egg options advance, profits depend upon the relative rate of climb. If September eggs boil up from 45¢ to 55¢, while December eggs scramble from 53¢ to 58¢, a 10¢ gain on September eggs is cracked by a 5¢ loss on Decembers. (You are long September, short December.)

On the other hand, let us assume that February and June Chicago silver prices were at less than full carrying charges. Carrying charges represent cost of storage, insurance, and interest on invested capital. In this example, we can assume that carrying charges equal 2½¢ per month, but that the current spread amounts to 1½¢ per month per ounce. Sell February and buy June silver—a *bear spread*—anticipating that the relationship will correct itself to the carrying charge differential. If prices strengthen, June silver must rise faster than February to restore a 2½¢ dispersion. If prices abate, February silver will drop more rapidly than June. Being short February and long June, you profit whether prices of *all* silver contracts rise or fall.

In straddling, you do not speculate on the direction of prices so much as on price differences. Of course, basic fundamental analysis cannot be compromised. Study will reveal why you expect these changes to occur. And if prices move sharply higher, these linkages must adjust to reflect higher interest costs and probably higher insurance costs. Fluctuating short-term interest rates will alter carrying charges. In an inflationary spiral, price deviations tend to be biased upward. Price distortion primarily results from shifts in buying pressures in which monetary phenomena—inflation and devaluation—play a contributing role.

Although price disparities may be readily compiled in tabular form, transfigure data onto a line chart for the life of contract. Determine price dispersion by subtracting the later from earlier month. Negative figures result when the later month sells at a price higher than the earlier one. But when the earlier month's prices exceed those of the later, the difference will be positive.

With a little practice, spread charting becomes a fun chore. On graph paper, draw a horizontal line; label it zero. If price differences are mostly negative, draw the zero line high on the paper, but draw it toward the middle if results are mixed. On the vertical axis record prices—expressed in points—plus above zero, minus below it, according to preferred graduations. Measure time horizontally. It is not necessary to mark every day on the chart. Certain key points provide adequate reference to check for errors. You may want to note the first of each month, or on each *dark* line of the graph paper write the corresponding day.

Figure 56 exemplifies all the negative numbers for February-June Chicago silver. Notice that spread relationships vary. During the last few months of the year and the first month or two of the new year in Figure 56 *a,* tax straddles increase silver activity. (Also see Chapter 20.) February-June 1975 Chicago silver in Figure 56 *b* illustrates silver-price links during part of the year's second quarter.

Slow-moving spreads are unattractive to traders who like action every day. Spread-trading, not suited to everyone, benefits from much lower margin requirements—roughly 20-25 percent of the normal security deposit on net positions. Properly executed, risk may be substantially reduced. Disadvantages include lower profits per trade, less action, sometimes difficulty in calculating risks.

On the other hand, comparison of profit-to-margin ratio unsheathes a more attractive picture. Let us say that the required security deposit—that

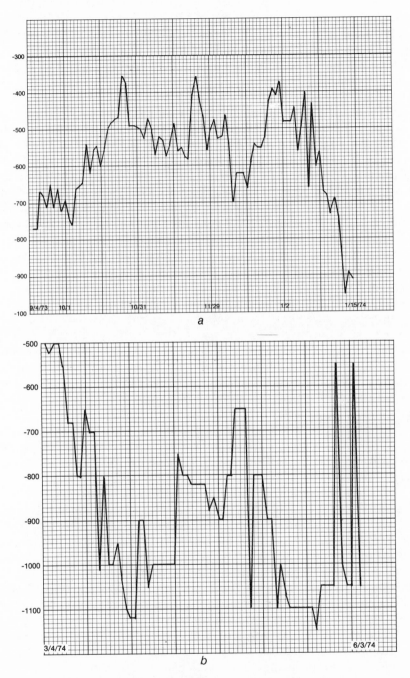

Fig. 56. Silver-spread charts: *a*, February over June 1974 Chicago Board of Trade silver; *b*, February over June 1975 Chicago Board of Trade silver

is, margin—for live cattle is $1,600 per contract, and that during the week price changes by 1¢—a gross profit of $400, or 25 percent of your margin.

The same sum finances four cattle straddles. If the spread moves only ¼¢ in your favor, four contracts still yield $400 gross profit with substantially less risk. Transaction costs, of course, are over four times greater in the second situation.

Minimum commissions on straddles, considerably less than on two contracts, are generally only slightly above transaction costs on one. The minimum commission charge on a single contract of cattle, eggs, or lumber is $40, but only $43 on completed straddle operations in spite of two contracts being bought and sold.[1] For corn, oats, soybeans, and wheat, commissions are $30 and $36 respectively; they are $30 and $32 for Chicago silver and Maine potatoes. Commissions for New York silver are $45 and $64 for spreads. For Idaho potatoes $20 and $33, but for sugar and platinum, spread commission equals round-turn commission on a single contract.

Commission charges are small when a substantial move occurs, such as January-March lumber in Figure 57. With a $200 margin requirement, profit within a month amounted to six times this amount. If the spread had been reversed, profits could have been earned in both directions.

In Figure 57, with January 1974 lumber selling at a premium over March lumber, price differences are recorded on the plus side, above zero. When November lumber went *off the board* (trading ceased in this contract), buying pressure shifted to the January contract, which outdistanced March by 1,230 points (= $1,230). Once it became apparent that the top had been reached, profits already encashed, you could have switched from a bull spread to a bear spread; that is, in a bear spread sell January, buy March, for possible retracement of this precipitous movement.

The bear-spread risk is greater. Nevertheless, with newly earned profits, a riskier position may be assumed. One strategy might be to put on bear spreads at a 1,000-point difference with a stop at 1,250 points for one-half as many positions.

You may have originally held ten bull spreads and earned an average $1,100 profit each. By reducing your new commitment to five bear spreads, risking around $250 per contract, you conserve about 85 percent of previously earned profits. This particular trade, however, would have produced even better results.

In spread-charting the same interpretive rules apply. A single chart may contain more than one spread to determine relative strengths and weaknesses (see live hog charts, Figure 58). Trend lines can be drawn, support areas ascertained, general technical analysis applied.

While examining the hog charts in Figure 58, observe that price relationships fluctuate rather sharply. As long as February hogs sell at a premium to April or June hogs, plus figures are charted. But price dif-

---

1. Commissions are being increased; check for latest information. Note also that not all brokerage firms charge the same rate.

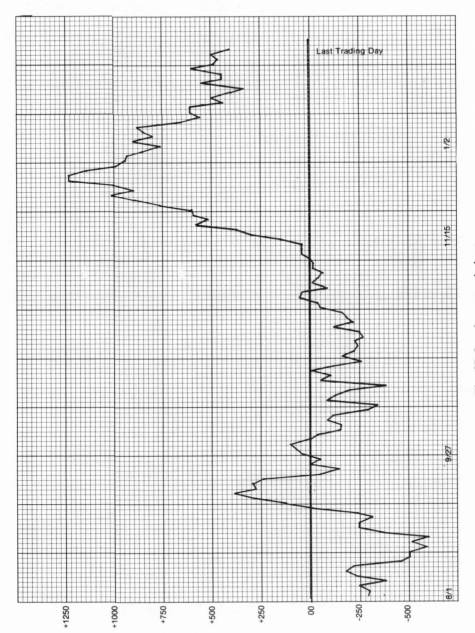

Fig. 57. Lumber spread chart

231

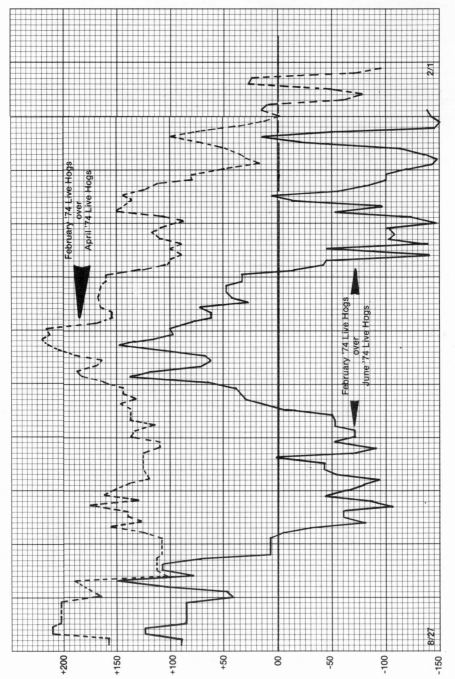

Fig. 58. Hog spread charts

232

ferentials diverged so widely that, at times, February hogs sold substantially under April prices (falling below the zero line).

Spreads may increase total risk. Obviously, by inverting one, loss can be substantially greater than an outright net position. Spread trading, therefore, does not dislodge study, research, and cogitation.

Analysis should embody consideration of the length of time between the option months selected. Short-term demand-and-supply factors may apply to the near-term month, while long-term demand-and-supply factors may cause the later month's prices to move quite independently. Especially with perishable commodities, such as hogs, eggs, and cattle, spread trading can be riskier than holding net positions, but it can be very profitable.

Stretches and Racks

Some traders who claim to be "spreaders" actually employ a combination technique of day-trades plus straddles. They will *leg* into a spread by positioning one side first then waiting for a small price movement to "leg into" the other half of the spread. The purpose is to *lock in* a profit larger than would accrue if both sides of the spread had been put on simultaneously.

Successfully executed, such a system provides a profit *cushion* to withstand any temporarily adverse reaction. To qualify for reduced spread commissions in most markets, both sides need only be executed during the same trading session. For a period, the trader who legs is either net short or net long. Initially he should treat the market from the day-trader's same short-term outlook.

Before completing the straddle operation, a trader will sometimes err; price edges against him. Before the trading session ends he faces two choices: either complete the straddle, lock in a loss, or close out the transaction for a day-trade setback and pay a reduced commission. To postpone accepting bereavement, hoping to improve his position through subsequent day-trades, the "spreader" will "lock in a loss." My term for this situation is a *stretch*.

Unless a little milk is spilled, the only chance of improving his position is through subsequent trades, always working under the pressure of a loss-in-hand. The preferable solution, to accept the original day-trade decrement, is try again the 'morrow. A known sacrifice can weigh heavily on the mind. Starting with a clean slate, with the irretrievable already behind, enhances trading attitude.

The second sin is even more hopeless to resolve. A trader may have shuffled the cards too soon or too late; price has moved substantially against him. Let us say that he buys two contracts of corn; price dips by 10¢ ($1,000 loss). After the fact, he essentially has two alternatives: either sell out and accept nonrecovery, or hold in the belief that his original assessment was correct, that corn prices will bump sharply.

He may, however, undertake a third alternative—to sell a distant corn option against his long position; in other words, because he is either over-trading and short of funds, uncertain and in need of time to think, or psychologically unable to accept the loss, he decides to "spread" and lock in at least a $1,000 loss.

I've tagged this state of affairs a *rack*; it is not truly a spread. Definitionally, a rack is a violent stretch. And if you are familiar with medieval torture devices, you will understand the mental anguish I am trying to convey.

All the texts abhor this technique. It is widely practiced. Is there any justification for a rack? In the first place, it is *not* a technique. I have never heard of anyone who planned in advance to get racked. Neither is it a substitute for sound money management. A loss is a loss! Being frail humans, we do get into difficult situations; a textbook scolding at that point is of no comfort.

People can, do, and will overtrade. When a loss has been incurred, get it out of the way, preferably while it is still a small one. On the other hand, there may be a rare occasion when "spreading up" is justifiable. To prevent panic and allow you a brief time to sleep on the problem, a rack can furnish a breathing spell. It is unlikely that you can turn the loss into profit. But you may figure a way to reduce your losses. If a rack calms you to leg out of it and reduce losses even slightly, then it is justifiable. Remember, nevertheless, that a rack involves two commissions; it is not a legitimate spread and does not entitle you to a reduced commission.

If you are on margin call and do not have additional funds in reserve, a rack, or stretch, may get you off call long enough to formulate your next move. It does relieve pressure. Your next move may well be to accept the full loss. At least you have had the opportunity to think through the alternatives. As a general rule, however, stretches and racks are *not* trading techniques and should never be among the alternatives considered in normal trading.

Bacon and Eggs

But trading in two markets simultaneously is a legitimate straddle when a distinct correspondence between them exists. Although a kinship may exist among sugar, cocoa, and corn, a "sugar-coated, chocolate-covered corn-puff" straddle does not involve major uses of the products.

Commodities may be partial substitutes for each other—hogs and cattle, for example. Other things being equal, consumers prefer beef to pork; but, of course, other things can cause this intimacy to diverge, as was pointed out in an earlier chapter, and 1973 was an especially unfortunate year for this straddle. Because a 1¢ move equals $400 in cattle but only

$300 in hogs, this straddle cannot be placed on a one-to-one basis unless a bias toward cattle is desired. The proper method is three cattle contracts against four of hogs.

Another example is corn and milo because they are substitutes for each other in feeding. The same thing is true between oats and corn or wheat and corn. A seasonal straddle that has worked well and was especially lucrative in 1974 was corn and wheat: in late January, buy corn and sell wheat. Because wheat prices have exhibited more weakness than corn, the combination has been profitable. A straddle is also possible between Idaho and Maine potatoes.

One commodity may be a raw material and the other a product derived from it. Live hogs and pork bellies, feeder cattle and fat cattle, are two examples of another type of intercommodity spread. Because a certain economic comparability does exist, price fluctuations are entwined with these common supply-and-demand factors. Lumber and plywood, also mentioned as a straddle, are used by a few speculators; the difference in contract size again obliges a two-to-three ratio. In this last example, these two commodities are traded on different exchanges and experienced handling is necessary.

Another situation is where certain commodities are derivatives of another commodity: for example, soybean meal and soybean oil are products of soybeans.

Doing the BOM

Other than buying them in a health-food store to eat, whether salted or unsalted, toasted or roasted, soybeans have only minor economic uses until they are processed. The processor buys soybeans, crushes them, and sells the resulting products.

The ratio of product to raw material is fairly constant; a sixty-pound bushel of soybeans yields about eleven pounds of soybean oil and forty-eight pounds of soybean meal. All three commodity futures are traded on the same exchange—the Chicago Board of Trade. Naturally processors employ these markets to hedge and to assure themselves of profits. Exporters use futures markets, too.

When a processor has put on the *crush*, he is long soybean futures and short product futures. When he orders these positions, he has fixed the *board spread* between the price he will receive for output and the cost of raw material. If the spread narrows, he will recover in the futures market what he may have lost in the cash market.

When a processor puts on a *reverse crush*, he is short soybean futures, long the two products. When product values are low relative to the price of soybeans, poor profitability will tend to diminish crushing operations, which, in turn, will reduce demand for soybeans. Weakened demand will cause soybean prices to decline. Because the tendency exists that poor margins will not continue indefinitely, the crush margin should eventually widen.

The soybean crush margins in Table 13 are based upon Chicago futures settlement prices for soybeans, soybean meal, and soybean oil. Since each of these contracts is traded with different specifications—cents per bushel for soybeans, dollars per ton for meal, and cents per pound for oil—they must all be expressed in some common value for comparison. The ordinary way is to express each product in terms of soybeans, that is, in cents per bushel.

In a contract of soybean meal there are one hundred tons; a bushel (sixty pounds) of soybeans yields roughly forty-eight pounds of meal. Meal futures must be converted to cents per pound, then value per bushel. This two-step operation can be accomplished by multiplying by a factor of 2.4. In Table 13, multiply the price of January meal, quoted at $171.70 per ton, by 2.4. Rounding, equivalent meal value amounts to 412¢ per bushel of soybeans.

In a contract of soybean oil there are sixty thousand pounds; a bushel of soybeans yields roughly eleven pounds of oil. To convert oil futures to an equivalent per bushel value, multiply 26.35¢ (above) per pound by 11; rounding the result will give oil value 290¢ per bushel of soybeans.

Adding together oil and meal values equals 702¢. Compared with the price of soybeans per bushel, 620¢, the "board margin" of 82 emerges. In this case, where product values exceed bean price, margin is plus; otherwise, score it with a negative sign.

Some traders will put on the BOM spread at a 1:1:1 proportion. Based on varying contract size, oil would be understated by nearly 10 percent and meal overstated around 20 percent with this unitary ratio.

TABLE 13

Soybean Crush Margins

	Soybeans	Soymeal	Soyoil	Meal Value	Oil Value	Board Margin	Change
JAN.	620	17170	2635	412	290	82	UP 8½
MAR.	629½	17320	2405	416	265	51½	UP 3½
MAY	635½	17320	2270	416	250	30½	UP 4
JULY	639½	17370	2175	417	239	16½	UP 1¾
AUG.	638½	17450	2150	419	237	17½	UP 6
SEPT.	636	17550	2120	421	233	18	UP 2

Source: Commodity News Service, January 17, 1974.

To eliminate bias, the proper method is fifty thousand bushels (ten contracts) of soybeans, nine contracts of oil, and twelve contracts of meal. Security deposit amounts to the normal margin required on ten contracts of soybeans; if the margin deposit is $1,000 per soybean contract of five thousand bushels, then the entire straddle of 10:9:12 can be placed for around $10,000.

Commission charges are reduced: $62 per straddle on a 1:1:1 basis. In the above example, the special commission rate of $62 applies to nine contracts and normal commission charges for five thousand bushels of soybeans and three contracts of soybean oil, the excess above nine contracts.

The factors that underlie these relationships must be thoroughly studied before mechanically accepting a spread recommendation. For example: What is the soybean supply situation and projected domestic and export demand? What are prospective supplies of protein meals? What are competing oilseed supplies? Is there excess crushing capacity or is the industry operating near capacity? And don't forget government meddling and possible labor difficulties.

Getting It Done

Placing spread orders is not difficult, but do summon a bit of caution and understanding. As a first step, be certain that your own broker understands both the mechanics and the rationale behind spreads and straddles. All of them will say they do; some of them don't possess adequate expertise.

Straddling the same commodity, same market, in actively traded months is easiest to achieve. Rarely should you place "market" orders; they are seldom filled to your satisfaction. Employ "limit" orders.

In the lumber spread, for example, let us assume that you decide to buy January and sell March lumber with a 100-point premium (+100) on the January. Even if January trades at less than +100, there is no guarantee that the order will be filled.

March lumber may not be trading very actively; it is not possible for the pit broker to execute both sides of the trade nearly at once. Remember that you have shifted risk onto the broker. If he can only get one side of the spread done, he personally holds a net position he may not want.

Watching intraday prices alone may be deceptive if one of the options is fairly inactive. Although you are calculating spreads determined on closing, or settlement, prices, you may complain that the order was not filled even though the closing difference was below 100. Trading is more hectic during closing minutes; spread orders are usually not executed. Too, in a closing range, trades do not necessarily take place at every price; settlement prices create a false impression.

Suppose you decided to place a bear spread in a very active egg market—short September and long December eggs. Prices are wildly gyrating but your order is not filled. Why? Each option trades in different parts of the pit. The broker must execute the buy and sell sides of the spread with two different pit brokers. When the market is *fast*, your broker cannot be expected to assume the chance that the entire spread cannot be filled. If one price moves quickly away from him, he may have "to eat" the mistake. The risk is his, not yours. In the egg market, for example, you will usually have to give away quite a few points as an incentive to the broker; otherwise your order will never be filled.

Where there are pit brokers specializing in straddles, you can request the "spread price" at which he will do it. Let's say that February silver has traded in the range of 800-820 under June; your order for +800 on the June has not been filled. The spread broker may quote you a price of +780 on the June even though you have seen prices farther apart. If you are eager, it can be done at 780 difference.

Dealing in more than one market usually means the risk is on your shoulders. If you are engaged in arbitrage between London and New York silver, or New York and Chicago silver, or Kansas City and Chicago wheat, you will have to be fleet-footed. These trades will come much later when you have practiced the easier ones for a period. (Wheat is traded on both the Kansas City and Chicago Boards of Trade; see Plates 10 and 11.)

With the BOM, these three commodities are traded in different pits but at least within the same exchange. However, trading activity varies among them. Because of the difficulty sometimes encountered in executing orders in three separate pits, brokers cannot be held responsible for not filling orders. Limit orders may be entered in cents per pounds:

Buy 9 July soybean oil
Buy 12 July soybean meal
Sell 50M July soybeans
Products 16¢ over beans

The disadvantage for narrowly moving straddles is the transaction expense. Always consider commission charges relative to potential profit rather than to total contract value. Commissions reflect the cost of doing business. Of course, the many people who perform this service for you must be paid. (Review "Trailing a Trade" in Chapter 3.) Nevertheless, from your point of view commissions and losses occupy the same side of the ledger; both similarly affect the bottom line.

So far we have mostly confined our examples to food products—either raw or processed—and to commodities occurring in nature that have been transformed—lumber, plywood, copper, for example—with occasional mention of precious metals—platinum and silver. One of the newest investment media—foreign currencies—is attracting an increasingly larger number of sophisticated traders who have taken the time to learn about these fascinating markets. Within the next two years, investors who are vitally concerned with conserving wealth and earning an income in an inflationary-recessionary economy will turn in larger numbers to these markets.

SECTION E

The International Monetary Market

CHAPTER 16
From Francs to Yen
and Coins Again

Gold is not made by man but by God. Man only makes the stamp. All things come from God. Not a grain of corn or wheat, or a dollar, is made by man.
—Paramahansa Yogananda

THE VALUE OF MONEY, WHICH SOME CALL THE ULTIMATE COMMODITY, IS determined no differently than the value of coffee or cotton. The same factors prevail: demand, supply, governmental policies, news, world conditions. The mystique of money confuses many—professionals and novices alike—because of its dual role as medium of exchange and financial asset.

This dual role offers an advantage to the money commodity that its brethren, crude oil, soybean oil, and coconut oil, do not possess. Money (so far, at least!) is the ultimate in liquidity. It can readily be exchanged for other commodities or other currencies. Currency markets provide an opportunity for international savants to protect their other assets and furnish flexibility to programs of wealth accumulation.

Although foreign-currency markets primarily serve commercial hedgers and international investors, the speculator provides breadth, depth, and resiliency to these markets. Transactions can be achieved through banks (domestic or foreign), but the futures contract is easily available, settlement is immediate (same day), the mechanics are simple, the market is flexible, and it is not too costly.

The International Monetary Market

Developed during 1972 as an offspring of the Chicago Mercantile Exchange, the International Monetary Market (IMM) transacts principally in major foreign currencies with limited activity in U.S. and Canadian silver coins. Forward contracts in foreign exchange are not new, but the IMM has developed uniform contract sizes and has promoted their use not only by the speculating public, who have been wise enough to avail themselves of these facilities, but also by exporters and importers, multinational firms, and anyone else who transacts in foreign exchange.

Filling an order on the IMM proceeds along the same route as any other commodity. Quotation of foreign currencies is in dollars. The only confusion that may arise is that some foreign currencies are worth more than the dollar—the British pound and the Canadian dollar—while some units—Italian lire and Japanese yen—are valued at only a fraction of a penny.

The number of digits to the right of the decimal point is not uniform for all contracts, but one point means a change in the digit farthest to the right. For the British pound (BP) there are four digits to the right; for example 1 BP = $2.1840. For the Canadian dollar (CD), West German Deutschemark (DM), Mexican peso (MP), Swiss franc (SF), and Dutch guilder (DG), there are five digits to the right; for example, 1 CD = $1.04200, 1 DM = $0.42748, 1 MP = $0.07895, 1 SF = $0.36252, 1 DG = $0.41120. For Italian lira (IL) and Japanese yen (JY), there are seven digits to the right; for example, 1 IL = $0.0016908, and 1 JY = $0.0034620. (See Figure 59).

But do not let small changes in value mislead you. Contracts are large enough in size. There are 25 million Italian lire in a contract;[1] minimum fluctuation of four points equals $10, a small change from 0.0016908 to 0.0017178 equals 270 points, or $675. Before getting into analysis, however, let us briefly review various currencies now being traded on the IMM.

Swiss Francs

One of the most important currencies for haven-seekers, the Swiss franc (ticker symbol SF) enjoys active trading on the IMM. A contract consists of 250,000 units of currency, which carries a value, in terms of dollars, of around $90,000, depending upon the applicable rate of exchange. Minimum fluctuations are five points, or $12.50, per contract.

Switzerland is about three times the size (nearly sixteen thousand square miles) of Connecticut, and its 6 million inhabitants survive largely from outside trade. Roughly one-third of the gross national product originates with exports; nevertheless, in recent years the country has experienced

1. Contract specifications effective June 1, 1973, for all currencies mentioned in this chapter. Copper and gold futures have also been added on the IMM since the writing of this book.

	OPEN	HIGH	LOW	SETT. PRICE	POINT CHANGE	$ VAL. CHANGE	VOL.	OPEN INTEREST	--YR.AGO-- SETT.PRICE
BRITISH POUND-									
Sep	2.3270	2.3350	2.3090	2.3150	-190	- $475	34	284 + 25	2.5620
Dec	2.2900	2.2950	2.2850	2.2850	-265	-$662.50	10	173 - 23adj	2.5552
Mar	----	----	2.2690A	2.2690	-340	- $850	----	113 unch	2.5420
Jne	----	----	----	2.2600	unch	unch	----	5 unch	----
				Total British Pound:			44	575 + 2	
CANADIAN DOLLAR-									
Sep	1.02700	1.02860B	1.02700	1.02860	-250	- $250	5	98 unch	1.00780
Dec	1.02650	1.02770	1.02650	1.02770	-180	- $180	2	85 unch	1.00910
Mar	1.02400	1.02400	1.02400	1.02400	-580	- $580	1	13 unch	1.00960
Jne	----	----	----	1.03120	unch	unch	----	150 unch	1.00960
Sep75	----	----	----	1.03100	unch	unch	----	150 unch	----
				Total Canadian Dollar:			8	496 unch	
DEUTSCHEMARK-									
Sep	.39200	.39200	.39150	.39150	-500	-$1250	4	351 + 2	.39340
Dec	.39500	.39500	.39300	.39300	-500	-$1250	12	439 + 3	.39580
Mar	.39350	.39350	.39350	.39350	-500	-$1250	1	498 + 1	.39780
Jne	.39450	.39450	.39450	.39450	-500	-$1250	130	267 unch	.39700
				Total Deutschemark:			147	1555 + 6	
DUTCH GUILDER-									
Sep	----	----	.37600A	.37600	-200	- $250	----	9 unch	.37220
Dec	.37700	.37700	.37700	.37700	unch	unch	1	31 + 1	.37560
Mar	.37620	.37620	.37500	.37500	-320	- $400	3	70 - 1	.38104
Jne	----	----	.37600A	.37600	-200	- $250	----	62 unch	.38320
				Total Dutch Guilder:			4	172 unch	
JAPANESE YEN-									
Sep	.0035050	.0035050	.0034860	+.0034880	-220	- $275	13	455 + 11	.0038312
Dec	.0035000	.0035080	.0034900	.0035000	-380	- $475	16	124 + 12	.0038800
Mar	----	----	----	.0035000	unch	unch	----	102 unch	.0039120
				Total Japanese Yen:			29	681 + 23	
MEXICAN PESO-									
Sep	----	----	----	.07965	unch	unch ++	1	646 + 4adj	.07975
Dec	.07924	.07924	.07914	.07914	- 2	- $ 20	3	527 unch	.07950
Mar	.07866	.07876	.07866	.07876	+ 1	+ $ 10	176	2684 + 74	.07920
Jne	.07826	.07828B	.07826	.07828	- 4	- $ 40	200	3112 +200	.07900
Sep75	----	----	----	.07787	unch	unch	----	1108 unch	.07870
Dec75	----	----	----	.07800	unch	unch	----	1 unch	----
				Total Mexican Peso:			380	8078 +278	
SWISS FRANC-									
Sep	.33120	.33120	.32900	.32900	-340	- $850	19	162 - 6	.33180
Dec	.33250	.33250	.32990	.33020	-345	-$862.50	98	636 + 15	.33560
Mar	.33250	.33340	.33050	.33100	-340	- $850	30	367 + 4	.33880
Jne	.33400	.33400	.33180A	.33180	-350	- $875	3	72 - 2	.34384
Sep75	.33600	.33600	.33250	.33250	-500	-$1250	4	6 unch	----
				Total Swiss Franc:			154	1243 + 11	
U. S. COINS-									
Jne	----	----	----	----	----	----	----	2 unch	----
Sep	3350	3350	3260	3260	-150	- $750	43	79 + 10	----
Dec	3450	3450	3360	3360	-150	- $750	14	227 + 8	----
Mar	3498	3498	3440	3440	-150	- $750	3	379 + 1	----
Jne75	----	----	3514A	3560	- 40	- $200	----	202 unch	----
				Total U. S. Coins:			60	889 + 19	
CANADIAN COINS-									
Sep	----	----	----	2850	unch	unch	----	1 unch	----
Dec	----	----	----	3000	unch	unch	----	19 unch	----
Jne	----	----	----	2960	unch	unch	----	15 unch	----
				Total Canadian Coins:			----	35 unch	
				Total Monday, June 24:			826	13724 +339	

Source: International Monetary Market.

Fig. 59. IMM daily information bulletin

trade deficits. Most of its goods are imported from the European Economic Community (EEC), principally West Germany, plus the United States.

Approximately 40 percent of Swiss exports consist of metallurgical and engineering goods, chemicals, watches, and textiles. Tourism and investment income have contributed to reducing the trade deficit; these two areas form an important segment of the economy.

Through a system of strict immigration laws, sound fiscal and monetary policies (until recent years), and strong demand for its products and services, Switzerland has not suffered the unemployment problems typical of its neighbors. At a European ministers' meeting a couple of years ago, each minister was grumbling about the unemployment problem. One mentioned that his country's unemployment rate was around 5 percent, another was slightly above 4 percent, a third believed his country's rate was closer to 6 or 7 percent. Finally the Swiss minister spoke, "Well, I believe at last count ours was down to two. And the last I heard just before I left Berne, both of them had found jobs."

Several interesting books on the market describe various aspects of Switzerland. If you have not read it, you may want to examine Harry Schultz's *What the Prudent Investor Should Know about Switzerland and Other Foreign Money Havens* (New Rochelle: Arlington House Publishers).

Deutschemarks

Also of considerable commercial importance, the Deutschemark trades in units of DM 250,000 on the IMM with a minimum fluctuation of five points, $12.50 per contract. The dollar value of a contract, based on recent prices, oscillates around $105,000—again, of course, depending on changes in the values of both the DM and the dollar. Ticker symbol is DM.

West Germany is six times the size of Switzerland. Its ninety-six thousand square miles would cover all of Ohio, Pennsylvania, and New Jersey plus about half the state of Delaware with Washington, D.C., thrown in for good measure (probably not a bad idea!).

The "miracle" of German postwar recovery, effected as a result of the intellectual influence of Wilhelm Röpke on economic policy, was less of a miracle for those who understand the creative energy of free-market forces that have not been stifled by excessive government intervention—policies no longer promoted in West Germany. Over the past decade-and-a-half the D-mark strengthened, resulting from an aggressive export sector (contributing more than one-fifth to GNP) and the accumulation of international reserves; the German government was "forced" to revalue it upward on several occasions.

The DM was revalued 9.3 percent in 1969 and 13.6 percent in 1971. In June 1973, Finance Minister Helmut Schmidt announced a 5.5 percent revaluation of the mark to maintain the currency relationship with its joint-float partners—France, Scandinavia, and the Benelux countries. During the 1969-1973 period, the Deutschemark rose 55 percent in value over the U.S. dollar as a result of American devaluations and German upward revaluations.

In spite of the fact that the German government *denied* any intention of revaluing right up to the time it finally took action in 1973, informed traders expected revaluation. Uninformed ones, if they read the papers at all, apparently believed Schmidt's statement that an upward revaluation was "unnecessary and unjustified." They were short on the IMM. Obviously the smart money did not believe Schmidt. They tried to make last-minute purchases of D-marks.

If your timing had been fortunate, two December 1973 D-mark contracts purchased on June 26 and sold on July 3 for a 3,300-point gain *each* would have yielded about $16,500 profit on the two. Happy Fourth of July! Of course, devaluations and revaluations do not occur that often, but when they do a good student of the market will be prepared for them. They can be quite profitable!

Guilders

Although the value of the Dutch guilder has closely approximated the D-mark's exchange rate, contract size measures only 125,000 guilders. (DG is the ticker symbol.) In terms of dollars, a contract is worth $50,000-$55,000. Minimum fluctuation is four points, $5 per contract.

The thirteen-thousand-square-mile area of the Netherlands, the size of Maryland and Delaware together, holds about 13 million people. Contrary to popular opinion, only 7-8 percent of national income derives from agricultural activities. The country is strongly dependent upon world trade, with close to 40 percent of its GNP made up of exports. The principal trading partner of the Netherlands, and of Switzerland as well, is West Germany, which purchases about one-third of the Netherlands' exports and sells a nearly equal amount to the Netherlands. The country's trade deficits have been financed by capital inflows.

The Dutch guilder, too, was revalued upwards by 5 percent in September 1973 in spite of a 71 percent rise in consumer prices between 1963 and 1973. Again, another opportunity for perceptive traders! Along with the D-mark, the guilder has been revalued upwards on several occasions during the last fifteen years.

Possibly most traders will not think of the DG as an investment vehicle. Perhaps the tulip-bulb mania of the far past is still recalled by some. More recently, the revolutionary behavior of its liberal priests, developing welfarism, and monetary intervention have caused others to shy away from this currency. Nevertheless, among twenty-six major currencies, the gold content of the DG is exceeded only by the Lebanese pound; the DG slightly exceeds the gold backing of the Swiss franc. In his recent book, Harry Browne has calculated a possible premium the guilder could command over the dollar if major currencies are returned to a full gold standard.[2] What are the future prospects of the Dutch guilder?

2. Harry Browne, *You Can Profit from a Monetary Crisis* (New York: Macmillan, 1974), cf., especially, chap. 24.

British Pounds

Crossing on an overnight ferry from Rotterdam to the white cliffs of Dover and "Merrie Old England," we find it not so merry these days, what with labor problems, inflation, the declining international value of the pound, and all the other problems brought on by welfarism. The British pound (ticker symbol BP) trades on the IMM in units of 25,000 BP, a contract worth roughly $60,000-$65,000 (and perhaps considerably less by the time you read this). Minimum fluctuations are five points, $12.50 per contract.

Nearly equal in size and population (55 million) to West Germany, the United Kingdom is considerably more dependent on foreign trade for its survival. Nearly all of its oil, 50 percent of its wool, other fibers, plus chemicals, iron ore, and tobacco all are imported. Sources of income include insurance, finance, and shipping, plus the export of machinery, vehicles, textiles, jet aircraft, and whiskey, among other items.

The most important single participant in the economy is the government sector. Like West Germany, too, taxation is extremely high. Among IMM currencies traded, taxation, highest in the U.K., is closely followed by West Germany. In spite of burdensome taxes, the British federal budget continues to operate on a deficit, which has been financed through monetary expansion. The high rate of inflation is accelerating.

Formal entry into the European Economic Community occurred in January 1973. Access to a larger market area, however, has not been without costs to consumers and dislocation of resources.

For British residents exchange controls have long existed. They are not allowed to own gold bullion (in one of the world's leading gold markets) and cannot purchase more than a limited sum of foreign exchange (in one of the world's leading financial centers) for foreign travel. The paradoxical popularity of the pound sterling as an international money for business transactions and key reserve currency results from the dual system of controlling citizens' rights and permitting convertibility to foreigners.

The pound sterling was devalued from $2.80 to $2.40 (14.3 percent) in November 1967, then was revalued 8.3 percent to $2.60 in December 1971, and it has since "floated" downward toward its true worth.

Italian Lire

Before departing from the Continent, travel southward to another remnant of the medieval age still struggling with its past and examine the Italian currency. The fascination of the lira is in its big numbers. I once purchased a small auto in Milan for the "astronomical price" of nearly 2 million lira. (I always drop the zeroes; it simplifies the mental arithmetic.)

Earlier in the chapter I mentioned there are 25 million IL in a contract; the minimum fluctuation of four points equals $10. The contract value has been fluctuating closer to the lower end of the $40,000-$45,000 range.

To entertain you with more geographical data, the Italian territory of 116,000+ square miles exceeds the political area of any of the other countries mentioned and would occupy the area covered by Maine, New Hampshire, Vermont, Massachussets, Rhode Island, Connecticut, and New York, plus we'll have to throw in Washington, D.C., again. In European terms it's about the size of Germany plus one and one-quarter Switzerlands and supports a population (not counting those who travel to Austria, Germany, and Switzerland to work) roughly equivalent to that of the United Kingdom.

An interesting aspect of the Italian is his ability to survive by circumventing the government's many controls. Lugano does a lively business. Why else would so many banks have branches there? There is an interesting story of an Italian businessman who was driving across the frontier into Switzerland. The Italian customs agent asked to search the auto. The first ransacking yielded nothing. Much to the consternation of the businessman, he was ordered to drive the automobile onto a rack. The usual inspection—of the underside, pulling wheels and spare tire, and draining the gas tank—yielded no results.

By this time, raging with a flair that only a Milanese can muster, the businessman threatened to report the officer to every imaginable bureaucrat and politician. Still, the officer was determined that the auto contained contraband and he renewed his probe. Door paneling was removed, upholstered portions of the vehicle were expunged with long needles, bumpers and other chromed parts were scraped, tubes and hoses were disconnected, finally the engine itself was dismantled. The results: negative. No gold was found!

No group of adjectives can describe the fuming businessman's tirade when, after a nearly nine-hour search, he was allowed to leave for Switzerland. Of course, the officer was fearful of losing his position; yet he seemed reluctant to admit error. For one thing he had received an anonymous report that a man fitting the businessman's description, in a similar car, was attempting to smuggle gold.

The sequel to this event occurred a week later. The same businessman managed to pass the frontier at a time when the same officer was on duty. In his best tone of sarcasm, the businessman asked, "Do you want to search my auto again? "Nooo sir," was the quick reply. "Continue."

If the customs agent had bothered to lift up an old blanket on the rear floor, he would have discovered a rather sizable quantity of gold. The businessman had correctly gambled that by anonymously reporting himself the previous week, he would precipitate such a scene that the officer would not risk making another error again so soon.

Japanese Yen

Halfway around the world, another economy, like the United Kingdom, lacks sufficient natural resources for industrial survival and depends heavily on imports. On the IMM the Japanese yen trades in contract units of 12,500,000 JY, equivalent to $40,000-$45,000. Ticker symbol is JY. Minimum fluctuation is ten points, or $12.50, per contract.

About the size of Italy, Switzerland, and the Netherlands together—or Ohio, Pennsylvania, New York and three-quarters of New Jersey—Japan's 143,000 square miles are occupied by 106 million inhabitants. Japan has developed its industries through a combination of restrictive exchange controls, government participation, unique cooperation between labor and management—which helps to hold wages down, and the Japanese habit of a high savings rate. During the 1966-1971 period, GNP achieved an annual growth rate approaching 20 percent a year, partly accounted for by inflation. Since 1971, however, there has been a substantial slowing in the growth rate—a fact the Japanese have not been too happy about. Naturally the "capitalistic" system has received a large share of the blame.

During the decade of the 1960s, the yen's par value was maintained at $0.0027778. A new par of $0.0032467 was established in December 1971, an upward valuation of 16.88 percent. After mid-1973 the yen floated downward with a subsequent devaluation in the early part of the fourth quarter, 1973. (Notice the precipitous drop in the chart, Figure 60.

An interesting sidelight on Japan is that the first modern futures market appeared there in 1697. At first, the system was the sale of a type of warehouse receipt, by absentee landowners who needed money in the big city, to users of rice (wholesalers, for example) anticipating their future requirements. This trading developed into the formal Dojima Rice Market in Osaka, complete with regulations, open bid, clearing house, and other major features of a futures market. Formal development of forward contracts did not appear in the U.S. until the mid-1800s, although private contracts certainly prevailed prior to that time.

Mexican Pesos

Completing our world tour in North America, we'll stop first in Mexico and then in Canada. The Mexican peso (ticker symbol MP) is traded in 1 million MP units with current values ranging on either side of $75,000. Minimum fluctuations of one point equal $10.

Mexico's 52 million inhabitants occupy territory equivalent to six and one-half West Germanies, or very roughly one-fourth the land area of the continental United States. About 25 percent of its foreign exchange earnings derive from tourists, chiefly Americans and Canadians. Mexico's rapid economic growth can be attributed to political stability, a certain amount of fiscal conservatism earlier in the 1960s, and most importantly, its propinquity to the United States and attraction of direct foreign investment.

In his inaugural address in 1970, President Echeverría expressed a negative attitude toward foreign investment which transcended the intent of the

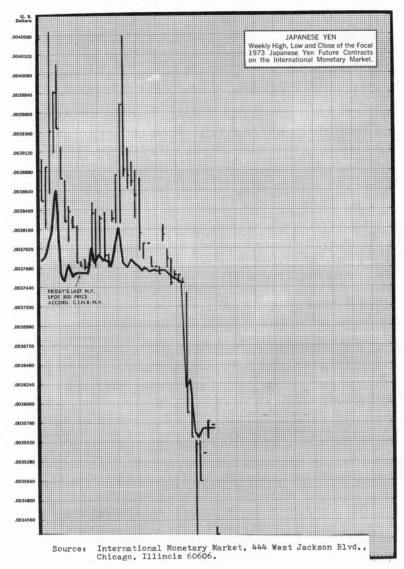

Source: International Monetary Market, 444 West Jackson Blvd., Chicago, Illinois 60606.

Fig. 60. Japanese yen

Mexicanization program. A private talk by Dr. Victor Urquidi in Geneva in 1972 further supported the more critical attitude toward direct foreign investment. And with subsequent passage of the new foreign-investment law, Mexico has dried up this important source of financing trade deficits.

The money supply has been increased at a substantial rate for several years, but with a fairly long lag this policy has resulted in higher prices only fairly recently. The turning point was coincident with the Olympic games in Mexico. There had been price controls on basic foodstuffs, cheap public transportation in the capital, and royalty payment controls on imported foreign entertainment, which was politically advantageous to the monolithic Institutional Revolutionary Party (PRI).

High rates of inflation coupled with recent labor difficulties have diminished the competitive advantage of Mexico over other tourist spas. As a result of these problems, the future value of the peso has recently been substantially discounted from the par value of 12½ to $1 established in 1954. An alert trader may discover speculative opportunities in this currency.

Canadian Dollars

The currency of the last country on our world tour, the Canadian dollar (ticker symbol CD), trades in units of 100,000 CD, which were roughly equal in value to the U.S. dollar through the first quarter of 1974. With steadily rising value, the contract's worth now fluctuates around $105,000. Minimum fluctuations is ten points, or $10 per contract.

Geographically larger than the United States, but mostly empty, Canada has 22 million residents, the majority of whom inhabit the narrow strip from Quebec to Windsor. Because of its proximity, coupled with heavy U.S. direct investment, the U.S. market absorbs about 70 percent of Canada's exports and sells a comparable amount of goods to Canada.

Canada has had protective tariffs since 1879 to foment industrial development and political independence. More recently, however, the nationalistic tide has dampened the extension of U.S. industrial dominance.

Canada's inflation rate, although erratic, has been significantly less than the rate in the United States. The Canadian dollar was maintained at a par value of $0.92507 from May 1962 until June 1970. Afterwards it was floated and has since risen in value. Currently the Canadian dollar sells at a premium to the U.S. dollar.

Silver Coins

In addition to the above foreign currencies, both Canadian and U.S. silver coins are traded on the IMM. But U.S. silver coins are not traded exclusively on the IMM. They are also traded on the New York Mercantile Exchange and the MidAmerica Commodity Exchange. On the New York Mercantile Exchange, contract size is ten bags of $1,000 face value each.

On the IMM, trading in silver coins began October 1, 1973, in contract sizes of five canvas money bags ($5,000 face amount) of pre-1965 dimes, quarters, or half-dollars. Minimum price fluctuation is $10 per contract, and maximum is $500 per contract except on the last trading day, when the limit is raised to $750 per contract. In a subsequent chapter I will discuss various trading techniques in silver coins.

Less actively traded, pre-1967 Canadian silver coins are also available for speculation in five-bag units ($5,000 face value) consisting of Canadian dimes, quarters, and half-dollars. At present silver bullion prices, the contract value of coins centers largely on potential silver content of coins. Because the amount of silver contained in Canadian coins is less than the quantity of silver in U.S. coins, Canadian coins tend to sell below the latter at existing exchange rates.

The fascinating world of money and foreign-currency futures should tend to attract a growing number of speculators and hedgers who are striving to preserve their wealth and perhaps increase it in the process. But what are some of the factors that determine the direction of values in foreign exchange?

CHAPTER 17
Interpreting the International Scene

If a man will begin with certainties, he shall end in doubts; but if he will be content to begin with doubts, he shall end in certainties.

—Francis Bacon

TRADING SWISS FRANCS AND JAPANESE YEN CERTAINLY SEEMS A MORE romantic pursuit than purchasing futures contracts of pork bellies or propane. A small investor can now speculate on the rise and fall of international currencies. Should you become a swinger in this circle?

The prospect of dealing in large sums of $40,000 to $110,000 certainly stirs the embers. Perhaps this market will be your alpha and omega! Of course, analysis precedes profit-making.

Chart history on IMM currencies will embrace a limited span. Point-and-figure techniques serve as well as line charts. Due to relative market thinness, reversal charts bear far less graphic detail. These tools are useful, but speculators tend to follow fundamentals.

Fundamental analysis is complicated. Overlapping factors separate causes and eventual results. Official information may be incomplete, falsified, or withheld. A whole range of tactics drawn from the official bag of tricks can postpone adjustments of exchange rates in fixed or rigid systems of rates.

Nevertheless, focusing on a few key indicators will promote development of market sensitivity. Preferably, acquire expertise in only a couple of the more actively traded currencies.

Cognizing the Incogitants

One of two indicators on which to keep a wary eye is government— governments anywhere and everywhere. With a stroke of the pen, one man— bureaucrat or politician—can vagariously recast your present life-style. Your next-door neighbor may try to discourage you from importing a new XJ 6, but his words—envious or encouraging— fail to carry the force of coercion.

But that same person, dispensing foreign exchange, can obstruct your exchanging dollars for pounds sterling. As an official he is supported by the brute force of government. He wields vast police powers. He can turn you into a criminal if you should decide to exercise your freedom and procure pounds sterling illegally. Of course, we can purchase foreign exchange and still invest in foreign financial assets with certain restrictions.

Government interference is a powerful factor in the market. It is always best to assume the worst. This attitude has nothing to do with patriotism or love of homeland or the other side. We are talking about investment survival, not about ideologies.

Every day I ask myself this question: What can the government do today that will (or could) cause me to lose in the markets? Prepared for adversity, you can turn it into an opportunity. While not always successful in these markets, when you do win, win big. Go home with more money in your pockets than you came with to the game. Play to win! Be a cynic!

How can government adulterate the dollar's international value? I cannot foretell the exact course, but I predict they will surely do something.

Naturally, monetary and fiscal policies, trade decisions and treaties, and other longer-range policy issues of government must be included in your analysis. But wars, "temporary" taxes, political scandals, currency swaps, balance-of-payments window dressing, investment controls, and private arrangements between governments present only some possibilities of permuting values.

For example, I was planning a residency of several months in Switzerland beginning late 1971. Early in the year my interpretation of events suggested that some type of exchange restraints might be imposed by mid- or late summer. To protect my plans I arranged to purchase Swiss francs during the spring. While I was mistaken about the exact nature of the constraints, the gigantic step toward socialization of the U.S. economy by means of price rules did transpire on August 15,[1] along with formal recognition of the de facto suspension of gold payments in official international settlements of accounts.

1. Although these specific regulations were lifted in 1974 after costing Americans billions, a liberal Congress can capriciously reinstitute them. Moreover, government still remains in the business of price manipulations through less obvious devices.

Because of my prior purchase of Swiss francs, I predetermined my expenses in terms of dollars. Had I exchanged dollars for francs only as needed, I would have been caught in subsequent devaluations and would not have known, in advance, the exact toll of my sojourn due to the continual decline of the dollar vis-à-vis Swiss francs.

Suppose you require a large sum of Canadian dollars in six months and anticipate U.S. dollar depreciation in the meantime. Furthermore, assume that you lack funds to prepurchase needed CDs. You can hedge against the added costs of changes in value by buying a futures contract six months forward. In the next chapter I will help you to calculate possible protection in a similar example.

Political elections should be carefully weighed. Changes in policy, in keeping with the ideology of the opposing party, alter international values. If you are unfamiliar with parties or candidates in another country, study the speeches, writings, and published documents of the individuals involved *before* they became major political candidates. Valuable clues on the tendencies and potential programs of the leading candidate may become evident. Is he anti-foreign-investment? To which group of voters does he appeal? Does he favor controls or a free-enterprise system?

Regard the little things occurring over long periods because they lead to big events. It pays to observe. Nothing just happens overnight. Devaluations, for example, mirror symptoms of a long era of maladies.

Take cognizance of mounting restrictions or nonrestrictions: Investment tax on foreign assets or tax credits? Tourist import-duty exemptions based on retail or wholesale values? Reporting or nonreporting of assets owned outside the country? Proposed legislation to tighten or loosen controls on the international flow of goods and money? Are you beginning to get the picture?

There are two very important aspects of government intervention to analyze. The first encapsulates both minor and broad-scale direct intervention. The second is inflation.

Cruelest of Taxes

The American public has become increasingly sophisticated in its knowledge of the degenerative effects of inflation. This lesson, like all instruction, wrings out a price, but it has been only partially assimilated; the full price will yet be paid.

The consumer understands how inflation bears upon his grocery bill, but beyond that stage his awareness dims. Unfortunately, many economists, too, fail to accurately comprehend this cancer. Recognize inflation for what it is.

Inflation is theft! Inflation is fraudulent conversion by the government of real purchasing power from your pocket. It is a tax! Unlike an income tax, the inflation bane has no limits! You and I cannot determine how much of our hard-earned wealth will be mulcted away in this form.

But the speculator in international currencies employs this tool as an indicator of a currency's relative weakness. By transacting in foreign currency and switching the nationality of his assets, he strives to preserve wealth. All the countries of the world are inflating. Here I refer to relative rates of inflation, not to an absolute rise in price level. Let's employ a simple example.

Suppose that England inflates its currency at an average annual rate of 20 percent, while Germany inflates at 9 percent. With prices rising faster in England than in Germany, an Italian importer prefers German over English products; they are cheaper.

When the Italian buys English goods, he converts his lire into pounds because the Englishman pays his obligations in pounds and not in Italian currency. In other words, demand, first of all, exists for pounds sterling. Once the Italian switches his preference from English to German goods, claims on pounds will fall; claims on D-marks will rise.

In the final analysis, a currency's value depends upon demand for it and supply of it. If demand for pounds sterling declines while the English central bank, the Old Lady of Threadneedle Street, increases the supply of currency, the "price" of English pounds will fall. The pound will be worth less in comparison to other currencies.

If exchange rates are permitted to adjust smoothly and freely, a system of freely floating rates, then the exchange value, or "price," of the pound will drop because the English central bank has been increasing the supply of its currency at too high a rate, while demand for it has diminished. The inflation rate indicates how rapidly government has "printed" money.

The root of *all* inflations dwells in the supply of money. All the talk about cost-push, demand-shift inflation sidetracks the real issue. These are symptoms of maladjustments that occur in the economy after too much money has been injected into it.

Let me repeat it so that this truth is traced into your memory. The cause of all inflations rests with irresponsible actions of government and monetary authorities. Inflation arises when money is "printed" too rapidly (in whatever form money is created)!

If exchange rates are fixed by agreement or decree so that they do not freely fluctuate, then a continued high rate of inflation will cause that currency to be overvalued in the international markets. The day of reckoning may be postponed a long time through tricks, controls, swaps, borrowing, and delaying tactics if the rate of inflation is not too high. But an adjustment must eventuate. Sooner or later the exchange ratio must conform to the worth of other currencies.

If you anticipate devaluation, you can considerably enhance your financial position by purchasing futures contracts in a suitable currency at an appropriate time. I will equip you with concrete examples in the next chapter when we review the steps in trading. Watch relative rates of inflation. They will reveal secrets to the careful observer.

Of course, you will also be mindful of fiscal budgets—surpluses or deficits. Deficits are essentially financed by inflating the money stock. A deficit budget is inflationary and, therefore, bearish for a particular currency. Budget surpluses tend to be bullish. Since we are primarily interested in the international economic activities of a country, we scour balance-of-payments statements to obtain a broader picture of the flow of goods, services, and capital.

International Balance

The statement on balance of payments may be examined in three parts: the current account, the capital account, and changes in international reserves. Because we are dealing with very complex matters here, it is necessary to oversimplify the mechanical aspects.

The balance of trade links exports and imports of goods. A "favorable," or surplus, trade balance means that the value of exports has exceeded the value of imports. The current account includes not only goods but also services (freight and insurance, for example) plus interest received and paid out on foreign investments.

Obviously, if we buy (import) more than we sell (export), the difference must be compensated for somewhere. If we can convince our trading partners to grant us credit, then we can buy and buy. One day, however, we will have to pay the piper. But there are other ways of "paying" bills.

If foreigners accumulate dollars, they can invest these dollars in our financial markets. We then exchange notes and equity participation for dollars held by foreigners. This is a flow of money capital.

Besides paying for imports with exports, IOUs, or financial exchanges, another method of settlement is to reduce international reserves. In earlier times we exchanged gold for dollars. The U.S. government now refuses to settle debts in this fashion. Creation of special drawing rights (SDRs) pipes in a source of "international reserves." Up to certain levels, countries may exchange surplus currencies for SDRs.

In the private sector we are basically concerned with two movements: the flow of goods and services, and the flow of short- and long-term investment capital. These flows, along with what the government spends abroad, comprise the essential elements of the balance-of-payments (BOP) statement.

A BOP deficit suggests that other countries are accumulating dollars. If they are willing to hold dollars, or exchange them for international reserves (or other assets), no immediate problem exists. Difficulty arises with cumulative deficits and foreign saturation of dollars.

With cumulative deficits a country's currency becomes less desirable.

Eventually sufficient pressure exerted on foreign-exchange markets sparks off adjustment in exchange rates—a devaluation. Or the surplus country will be "forced" to revalue (upwards) its currency. Either way, the resulting alteration in exchange rates ministers to changes in the prices of goods and services traded internationally.

Within the balance of payments, movement of short-term capital frequently affords an excellent indicator of coming adjustments in exchange rates. Actually, short-term capital responds essentially to two stimuli: interest-rate differentials among countries, and expectations.

Higher interest rates in one country will tend to attract short-term investments; capital will flow from one country to another in response to interest-rate changes. Because an international investor wants to protect himself against possible devaluation, he will hedge his short-term investment in the forward market by buying dollars in the future. Whether or not any capital movement occurs will depend upon both interest rates and forward rate. This process is known as *interest-rate arbitrage*.

However, we are more interested here to take advantage of any possible devaluation or revaluation of a currency. When expectations of possible revaluation prevail, statistics indicate substantial movement of short-term funds *into* that country. For example, during the early part of 1971, billions of dollars flowed into West Germany in anticipation of the Deutschemark's being revalued upwards in terms of other currencies.

When dollars are presented to the German central bank, dollars are exchanged for D-marks. Strong demand for D-marks pressures its price upwards.

Finally, in 1971, the German central bank allowed the mark to float by refusing to buy any more dollars. The exchange rate was then established by interaction of the forces of demand and supply. In other words, the exchange rate was determined in the free market rather than by government interference in the foreign-exchange market. Revaluation became a fact. Afterwards, the dollar bought fewer D-marks.

Deutschemarks were then worth more in terms of dollars. Investors who correctly anticipated revaluation protected their assets and, in fact, earned profits in terms of dollars. The dollar profit does not materialize until funds are converted back into dollars.

Dirty Floats

These fundamentals affect both spot and forward exchange rates; however, there is a close and complex correlation between spot and futures prices. Because central banks primarily intervene in spot markets, forward rates are more sensitive to market forces. Because bankers hedge transactions between forward and spot markets, spot rates shift in the same direction as forward rates. A freely floating rate signifies that exchange rates result from forces of demand and supply freely interacting to determine the value, or price, of foreign currencies. Because central banks (in the United States, the Federal Reserve System) do intervene and influence the international values of currencies, this meddling is termed *dirty floats*.

Recall the big fuss in August 1973. By that time the value of the dollar had stopped declining; some European (including Swiss) bankers proclaimed the undervaluation of the dollar; the turnaround appeared imminent; the value of the dollar actually did rise in August 1973, not due to strengthening of the U.S. economy but as the result of official intervention in foreign-exchange markets.

Both the United States and West German central banks poked their fingers into the pie. The Federal Reserve Bank borrowed $273 million in foreign currencies. Such arrangements are nicknamed *swaps*; as the term designates, a swap, or loan, has to be reciprocated or repaid. The German central bank purchased $300 million in the market. Naturally, reducing the supply of dollars makes the dollar scarcer; therefore, worth more compared to other currencies. Exchanging D-marks for dollars increases the availability of D-marks and, therefore, tends to drive its price, or value, downwards. (Review demand and supply relationships again in Chapter 9 if you need to.)

Since bankers and brokers buy, or sell, forward to service their customers, they may hedge a forward sale with a simultaneous purchase in the spot market. Thus, forward market activity affects the cash market. (For comparison of spot and forward rates, refer to Table 14.)

Exchange rates also reflect seasonal fluctuations, for reasons which similarly affect many other commodities already discussed. Seasonal buying of imports (Christmas purchases, for example), tourism, production of new models—all influence demand for currencies. If the United States imports, it supplies currency to purchase foreign exchange and weakens the dollar's worth. Exporting countries experience increased demand for their currencies (in order to pay for goods and services purchased in the foreign country) and their currency values strengthen. In the absence of overriding factors, seasonality can be predicted from long-term charting. Of course, for major countries, following the big war after the depression, spot rates did not always float and were not adjusted frequently but remained fixed for long periods.

International Conspiracy

The original intent of the International Monetary Fund (IMF), when it was formed in 1944, was to maintain a system of rigid exchange rates as opposed to a system of floating rates. In the 1971 example, Germany was supposed to buy dollars and sell its own currency. The development of the IMF system promoted the importance of central bankers and decreased chances that control of monetary systems could be wrested away from governments and returned to the people.

TABLE 14

New York Spot and Forward Prices

New York Spot Prices (Bid) . . . June 21, 1974

	High	Low	Last	Point Change	$/Point	$ Value of Change (One IMM Contract)
BP	2.3830	2.3720	2.3745	-118	2.50	-$295.00
CD	1.03130	1.02860	1.03100	-120	1.00	-$120.00
DG	.37510	.37430	.37490	-110	1.25	-$137.50
DM	.39360	.39290	.39330	-190	2.50	-$475.00
JY	.0035320	.0035300	.0035300	- 50	1.25	-$ 62.50
MP	.08002	.08002	.08002	unch	10.00	unch
SF	.33230	.33120	.33190	-110	2.50	-$275.00

New York Forward Prices (Bid/Offer) . . . June 21, 1974

	Bid/Offer	1 MO.	2 MO.	3 MO.	6 MO.	12 MO.
BP	2.3755/	2.3670/	.23545/	2.3430/	2.3070/	2.2410/
	2.3765	2.3690	2.3565	2.3450	2.3090	2.2440
CD	1.03080/	1.03170/	1.03220/	1.03280/	1.03310/	1.03150/
	1.03100	1.03210	1.03280	1.03320	1.03350	1.03250
DG	.37480/	.37530/	—	.37630/	—	—
	.37500	.37570	—	.37670	—	—
DM	.39340/	.39440/	.39530/	.39620/	.39820/	.39880/
	.39360	.39480	.39570	.39660	.39870	.39940
JY	.0035310/	.0035285/	—	.0035335/	.0035260/	—
	.0035350	.0035362	—	.0035362	.0035350	—
SF	.33190/	.33210/	.33250/	.33310/	.33430/	.33510/
	.33220	.33260	.33300	.33360	.33490	.33590

Source: International Monetary Market.

Exchange-rate adjustment was permitted under IMF rules only when there was a "fundamental disequilibrium" in the balance of payments. The term *fundamental disequilibrium* was never adequately defined.

As became apparent during the late sixties, the IMF was losing its hold on the system. Additionally, there were greater flows of short-term capital from one country that was overinflating its money supply to countries that seemed more stable at the time.

This international mobility made it more difficult for governments to control investors. As a major step toward international coordination and control of the world's money supplies, a new international reserve was fecundated—the special drawing right.

Special drawing rights (SDRs) are simply bookkeeping entries intended to eventually replace gold as an international reserve. Gold can still be bought or sold on the free market. However, SDRs strictly represent the pen power of a supranational central bank. The public cannot get its hands on SDRs even if it wanted to. Available only to the elite—the governments of the world—distribution of SDRs has taken place only on a modest scale until a new world order is molded for the benefit of few.

Of course, halfway into the 1970s, the original IMF system of rigid exchange rates is no longer viable. The major countries have temporarily moved toward quasi-floating rates whereby price of foreign exchange is largely determined by free-market forces, although central-bank intervention is not precluded under the present interim system.

The September 1973 meeting of the IMF in Nairobi was generally unproductive. As usual in the absence of agreement, a committee was formed. Action was subsequently postponed to hammer out a new international agreement.

The ultimate objective is to demonetize gold. The United States, especially, would like to see gold demonetized and simultaneously legalize private gold consumption.

Not that the U.S. government has suddenly become benevolent. The government *hopes* that allowing private citizens to own gold bullion will accomplish at least two things: (1) Citizens will lose interest in gold once it has been demonetized, and the price of gold will fall in the free market. (2) Owning gold may tend to draw attention away from the real purpose of the SDR system. Once the state monopolizes foreign-exchange markets and imposes controls on capital flows, it will not be easy to determine the real value of a currency.[2]

Creation of SDRs represents a worldwide inflationary system. Governments can more easily coordinate their inflationary programs so that no "safe" currency is readily available to the public. It is a cooperative effort by the governments of the world to tax, to financially squeeze citizens on an international level so that no one can escape the cruelest of taxes.

Will the price of gold decline? Whether it does or not several years from now is not significant to us. We are interested in trading foreign currencies now. The price of gold today bears watching.

Historically, gold has had a very close relationship with exchange rates. When the price of gold rises, it means that investors are switching from money and other investment forms to gold.

Gold, of course, produces no income. To own gold is actually an ex-

2. For example, the official rate of the Russian ruble is about $1.35. On the free market in Switzerland, it is worth approximately 25¢.

pense (interest plus storage charges). But if the price of gold rises faster than cost of owning it, then gold doubles as a source of potential gain and a means of protection.

Besides preserving one's assets, gold is demanded for industrial transformation. Therefore, gold partly reflects foreign-exchange activities. A rapidly rising gold price suggests anticipated monetary uncertainties.

Discussion of everhanging problems paralyzes some people. If you have missed the point of this last chapter, or even of the book as a whole, you may visualize excessive dangers in trading commodity, currency, or coin futures. Realize that you have lived with government interference all your life—and this canker-worm feeds on our budding enterprises and consumes the foliage of our historic production. But futures markets are relatively free of regulation, offer wealth opportunities for the equipped pioneer, yield quick cash to the profit-making investor. Being aware of pervasive governmental manipulations should not turn an *individual*—someone who controls his own life—into an ostrich. The astute speculator will combine all these factors in his analysis before transacting in foreign currencies.

CHAPTER 18
Trading in Foreign Currencies and Coins

Money is like sex in one respect: most people understand it, but not too well.
—Anthony M. Reinach

ALTHOUGH THE MECHANICS OF TRADING IN FOREIGN CURRENCIES DOES not differ significantly from trading in other commodities, the dual role of currency futures as both medium of exchange and asset may tend to confuse some readers. Therefore, the present chapter discusses situations that will introduce the potential speculator, investor with foreign assets, international businessman, and arbitrageur to these markets.

The previous chapter emphasized trading on fundamentals. Essential areas to study include a country's entire balance sheet, especially balance-of-trade figures, political situations (with stress on elections), relative rates of inflation, short-term interest rates, and expectations. These indicators, not a formula, only point out the basic elements of fundamental analysis.

Technical analysis proceeds from an examination of spot and forward rates and premium or discount of various futures options to the cash market. For some currencies, seasonality may be significant. At times, gold prices provide some clue or guideline on the direction of dollar prices, but recently, with distrust of all currencies prevailing, the price of gold has been divorced from currency values. Currency futures speculation, not focusing on destined gold or silver prices or any single money, hangs on changes of foreign-currency values relative to the U.S. dollar, or the reverse, changes of dollar values relative to francs, yen, pesos, and so on.

How to Speculate in Foreign Currencies

Speculating in foreign currencies, as well as other commodities, begins with market analysis, employing the concepts previously discussed. Your time horizon will determine the weight attached to each variable. A short-term speculator is handicapped compared with traders in meats or grains due to a dearth of information. Data on day-to-day price deviations are usually not available, and interpretation of information requires considerably more sophistication.

What are some key indicators for short-term traders? Possibly most significant for an immediate—maybe only a flash-in-the-pan—impact are news and announcements of political and social changes. For example, a crippling nationwide strike in the United Kingdom will immediately debase the pound sterling. Riots in Tokyo or Mexico City will pressure the international price of the yen or Mexican peso. Any new governmental policy that can modify output, costs, investment, money supply, or exchange controls, for example, will have an immediate consequence on foreign-exchange values.

Lacking daily indicators, watch major statistics, such as balance-of-trade figures and changes in international reserves. The composition of international reserves is not identical for every country. Try to estimate total intervention by central banks in the spot market. This is purely a guesstimate since daily figures are not available.

Because intervention takes place in the spot market, the forward market rate may indicate the probable direction of a currency's value; it is an estimate by dealers in foreign exchange of future outlook discounted back to today's prices. Too, do not fail to observe daily exchange rates quoted in major financial centers.

Interest rates to watch include central-bank rates, the price of credit to their own domestic financial institutions. These rates are more significant in some countries than others. Two free-market rates to record: rates paid on Eurocurrency deposits and loans; rates on Eurobonds. Similarly, commercial-paper rates measure current credit situation for short-term commercial borrowers.

Other indicators already mentioned comprise changes in money supply plus comparison of current changes with monetary growth over the previous twelve months together with the past four or five years, to gather some idea of the course and rate of inflation. Naturally, government attitude toward inflation is important. The party labels of "conservative" and "liberal" provide absolutely no guideline. The so-called conservative factions in both American and British politics have outliberaled the "liberals" since World War II. Political stability and governmental agreements (such as trade treaties) have already been mentioned.

On the other hand, demand factors for a currency must not be over-looked. Demand for a country's currency is tied to demand for its resources and production. A strong demand for a country's resources results in strong demand for its currency. Because domestic commodities are paid for in local currency, local currency must be purchased first. Exporting and importing ensphere two transactions: one for goods, the other in the foreign-exchange market.

The financial demand for a currency depends on relative interest rates. This situation is especially true where two countries' markets are closely interrelated, such as Canada and the United States. International firms will tend to borrow in the market where interest costs are lower and place temporary surplus funds where short-term rates are highest as long as gains are not offset by exchange-rate differentials (discussed later in the chapter). If a currency is bullish (or bearish), find out why. Which factors bolster increased (or decreased) demand?

The security deposit for currency transactions is substantially higher than for most other commodities—currently ranging from $2,000 to $4,000. However, my personal recommendation to speculators has always been $10,000 for the first contract and $5,000 for each subsequent one. (Less for hedgers, of course!) Especially during a period of frequent devaluations, revaluations, and exchange-rate adjustments, until the trader develops a feel, an expertise, for the currency market, this more conservative approach allows for a substantial margin of error and still leaves funds for continued trading in the event of losses.

The most expensive method for meeting margin requirements is to transfer cash to the broker. A less expensive method: pledge Treasury bills or listed securities (usually accepted at the rate of 70 percent of face value). Another method is to deposit a letter of credit; the bank charges a small fee for this service.

You can also participate in this market through straddles, which require substantially less margin money—probably ranging from $500 to $1,500, depending upon the volatility and anticipated weakness of the currency. Again I suggest depositing more than the minimum by upping limits from $1,000 to $2,000.

Commission costs on straddles are $50, compared to $45 on regular transactions. In general, for the speculator, leverage in these markets differs from other commodity markets, margins are higher, and information less well developed. The latter may contain certain advantages, considering the quality of some reports emitted from Washington in these times.

Values move sufficiently to furnish ample opportunity for substantial profits. It is not an in-and-out market except in special cases of devaluations or revaluations where you have exercised excellent timing. In these situations big money is made quickly, provided that *not everyone* has come to the same conclusion. Sometimes it becomes so obvious that devaluation is in the official making, that all traders are already short. Those who want to sell cannot find anyone to take the opposite side of the trade.

A devaluation comes under the broader heading of "expectations." Economic analysis will reveal whether a currency is overvalued, but politics dictates precisely *when* the new rate becomes the official one. For years many economists and market students were aware that the U.S. dollar was overvalued; this was glaringly obvious over a decade of exchange controls, swaps, and window dressing before devaluation became actual fact.

Franz Pick and Harry Schultz, among many others, advertised their views and anticipated that an explicit breakdown in the international monetary system would occur earlier than it publicly manifested. Even at a late date, Harry Browne's now famous book met a spate of disbelievers. Correct timing is sometimes a matter of luck. More than likely it is a question of substantial investment in research, purchasing quality service, and having sufficient capital to support your convictions.

Be aware, nevertheless, that foolishly getting locked in on the wrong side of a devaluation or revaluation can be extremely costly. When currencies are traded at limit prices over several days, the daily limit widens until a no-limit day is reached. Even a 2 percent change can quickly wipe out a minimum security deposit; you will then be required *immediately* (usually by wire transfer or hand delivery) to pay the debit in your account. Being overmargined compensates for that contingency.

How to Take Delivery of a Foreign Currency

For the few readers who may want to take delivery of a currency, I suggest that you write to the International Monetary Market, 444 West Jackson Boulevard, Chicago, Ill. 60606, for its free booklets.

If you intend to take delivery of a contract of Swiss francs (SF 250,000), notify your broker, who will, in turn, notify the clearing house, and file a "Buyer's Delivery Commitment" like the one in Figure 61. By the last trading day, sufficient funds must be deposited with your broker or wire-transferred to the Continental Illinois National Bank and Trust Company of Chicago, official IMM depository bank. Actual transfer of funds is negotiated through banks here and abroad.

The buyer selects the bank where he would like to receive currency. The seller names the bank he wants to effect transfer. The Continental Illinois Bank monitors the process. It holds U.S. funds until transfer has been effectuated. For example, you may designate Crédit Suisse in Geneva to receive funds. The seller may select the Schweizerischer Bankverein in Zurich to effect transfer. Obviously, if discretion is preferred this method may not be suitable, and there is the added inconvenience of the current U.S. requirement to report "export" of any sum equivalent to $5,000 or more.

However, using the IMM need not be confined to either pure speculation

ANSWERS TO THIS FORM MUST BE TYPEWRITTEN

BUYER'S DELIVERY COMMITMENT

_____
(Name of Clearing Member)

DESIGNATION

☐ House   ☐ Customer Account No. _____

We will accept delivery of _____ on _____
                          (Amount & Currency)   (Value Date)

for the account of _____ at _____
                                                        (Bank)

in _____
            (City, Country)

We will remit U.S. $ equivalent not later than 1:00 p.m. by:

        ☐ Check to the IMM Clearing House

        ☐ Wire Transfer to Continental Illinois National Bank and Trust

        Company of Chicago from _____
                                    (Bank & Address)

        _____   _____
        Authorized Signature   Telephone

        _____   _____
        Authorized Signature   Telephone

— —

FOR IMM USE

Transaction Completed _____
                                    Day-Time
Signed _____

FORM IMM 100

Fig. 61. Buyer's delivery commitment (Source: International Monetary Market.)

or taking delivery. It may also be utilized to protect short-term investments in foreign paper.

How to Invest in Foreign Short-term Instruments

Suppose that interest rates on one-year certificates of deposit are higher in Canada than in the United States. The arbitrageur who seeks out the highest interest rates will hedge, or *cover*, associated exchange risk. Using an example, let's assume a hypothetical situation where one-year certificates yield 7.0 percent in Toronto and 6.0 percent in New York; you desire to invest 93,500 Canadian dollars (CD), but do not want to risk unfavorable shifts in the exchange rate between Canadian and U.S. dollars.

On December 18, 1973, you purchase CD 93,500 at the spot rate of 1.00000, paying $93,500. Then exchange CD 93,500 for a time deposit, due in one year, paying an interest rate of 7 percent.

Because you do not know what the exchange rate will be in one year, you simultaneously sell a December 1974 futures contract for CD 100,000 on the IMM at a price of 0.99800.

On December 18, 1974, you collect your principal, CD 93,500, plus CD 6,500 (actually 6,545—the extra 45 pays the IMM commission) in interest, and deliver CD 100,000 against your futures contract. The futures contract grosses $99,800. Gross profits on the entire transaction equal $6,300, compared to the net amount of $5,610 you would have received by investing the original $93,500 at 6 percent in the United States. Table 15 summarizes the entire transaction employing covered interest arbitrage.

TABLE 15

INTEREST ARBITRAGE

Spot	*Forward*

18 XII 1973

Buy CD 93,500 @ 1.00000 = $93,500	Sell 1 Dec. '74 futures contract @ 0.99800 = $99,800
Invest CD 93,500 in Canadian time deposit @ 7% interest (about CD 6,500)	

18 XII 1974

Collect principal (CD 93,500) plus interest (CD 6,500) on Canadian investment.	Deliver CD 100,000 against futures contract

Original cost	$93,500
Gross profit on transaction	$ 6,300

If you had employed funds in the United States in a comparable investment, return would have been $93,500 × 6% = $5,610. With a nearly riskless investment, surplus funds can take advantage of higher interest rates over similar-type U.S. investments. The example could just as well have applied to Treasury bills or Eurodollar deposits.

This simple explanation of a complex matter opens channels for smaller investors to initiate ways to preserve and accumulate wealth. The investor must remember there are two rates with which he must concern himself; price of credit (interest rate), and price of foreign exchange in the future.

It is entirely possible to invest in a country where the interest rate is *lower* than at home if the futures rate of the currency is selling at a large enough *premium*. On the other side of the coin, the forward rate of the currency of the country with a *higher* interest rate will tend to sell at *discount*. Arbitrageurs watch for these opportunities. The objective is to earn a greater yield on investments than could have been earned in the absence of international transactions.

How to Protect Your Assets

Interest arbitrage may not appeal to you, or may seem too complicated for your needs. Nevertheless, as long as you own foreign assets, or anticipate owning them, you should seriously consider employing the futures market, or forward market in the interbank system, to hedge foreign assets, anticipated foreign expenditures, and reported or unreported income.

Suppose that you own Swiss francs accounts abroad but temporarily require use of your funds at home in dollars. You can borrow, possibly, leaving your Swiss franc accounts undisturbed. However, let us assume that you decide to convert SF 250,000 into U.S. dollars for a year, after which time you intend to reconvert them back into Swiss francs.

In this example, during the year you are holding dollars, your foreign-exchange risk increases, especially if you anticipate further depreciation of the dollar vis-à-vis the Swiss franc. If the dollar does depreciate, your dollars at the end of the year will buy fewer Swiss francs. On the other hand, if the value of the Swiss franc depreciates, your dollars will buy more Swiss francs; you will have profited. If you are not interested in speculating either way, a *buying hedge* will tend to proffer at least limited protection against foreign-exchange risks.

Let us begin this hypothetical example by assuming you have requested your bank to convert SF 250,000 into dollars and wire transfer funds to your American depository. The transfer rate on May 24, 1974, day of purchase of dollars, is 0.34180, equal to $85,450.[1] To protect your purchase

1. Multiplying SF 250,000 × 0.34180 = $85,450; all other calculations may be done the same way. To state the value of $1 in terms of Swiss francs, use the reciprocal: 1/.34180 = 2.93 Swiss francs to the U.S. dollar.

against unfavorable changes in the exchange rate, simultaneously buy one June 1975 futures contract in Swiss francs at 0.34840, equivalent to $87,100.

By the end of February you no longer need these funds; on February 28, 1975, you repurchase Swiss francs. To complete the operation two transactions are necessary: one in the spot market, the other in the futures market.

In the spot market buy SF 250,000 at 0.36000, at a cost of $90,000. Offset the futures contract at 0.36470. Because the franc's price has risen during the interim, Swiss francs cost more; in the cash market you lose $4,550. Because you have hedged the transaction, losses are reduced by $4,075 with profits earned in the futures market. Loss amounts to $475 plus transaction costs. Table 16 summarizes the Swiss franc hedge.

The buying hedge shown in Table 16 illustrates, in this example, how exchange risks can be shifted to others who are willing to take a position opposite to yours in the futures market. The cost of protection? Around $500 versus a potential loss of $4,500.

In another example, suppose that you have contracted to buy a cooperative apartment near Lugano or perhaps a chalet in Gstaad. It is under construction; you have signed a contract to pay the balance of SF 250,000 in nine months—just in time to enjoy the winter season.

You already know the balance due on your vacation home but not the "price" of Swiss francs, that is, the exchange rate nine months from now. You can lock in the current cost of Swiss francs by purchasing a futures contract for delivery of SF 250,000 nine months hence. The foreign-exchange exposure is hedged; cost of property in terms of U.S. dollars is locked in. Whatever happens to the dollar-Swiss franc exchange ratio—up or down—the eventual price of Swiss francs has been predetermined.

TABLE 16

THE SWISS FRANC HEDGE

Spot			Futures		
		24 V 1974			
Sell SF 250,000 @ 0.34180	=	$85,450	Buy 1 SF June '75 futures contract @ 0.34840 =		$87,100
		28 II 1975			
Buy SF 250,000 @ 0.36000	=	$90,000	Sell June '75 futures contract @ 0.36470 =		$91,175
Loss	-	($4,550)	Gain	+	$4,075

The steps in this situation are similar to the buying hedge example in Table 16. First purchase a futures contract (nine months away), which will require a security deposit. You may not have funds available now to pay the balance on the chalet, or it may be advantageous to hold funds in dollars during the interim. Second, when payment on the chalet becomes due in nine months, close out the futures position by selling a contract. Third, buy needed Swiss francs in the cash market. By purchasing a futures contract, speculative risks have been shifted to others via the futures market. Practice with a few examples to get the feel of hedging.

Before examining the scourge of mankind—taxes—and how to reduce or postpone them—the last section of this chapter will introduce the budding arbitrageur to an interesting relationship between the price of U.S. silver coins and silver bullion.

How to Arbitrage Coins and Bullion

Because there are so many trading opportunities other than outright net long or short positions in a few commodities, I feel obligated to at least introduce you to a few situations where you can acquire expertise for profits and excitement. One such situation is the price relationship between U.S. silver coins and silver bullion.

The examples here assume trading coins on the IMM and bullion on the Chicago Board of Trade. Nevertheless, the same operation can be accomplished on New York markets where both contracts are twice as large: U.S. silver coins on the New York Mercantile Exchange and bullion on the Commodity Exchange.[2]

Before Johnson's copper-clad coins beginning in 1965, a bag of silver dimes, quarters, and halves—face value of $1,000—would melt down to very roughly 715 ounces of silver. If silver bullion were priced at $1.40 per ounce, the value of the silver content in a bag of coins would slightly exceed the face value of $1,000. As the price of silver rises, the value of coins exceeds their exchange value as purely a medium of exchange for goods and services.

Therefore, when silver prices were resurrected at $2 per ounce in the dark ages of early 1973, the silver value per bag of coins was $1,430. When silver reached that first important psychological goal of $4 in January 1974, a bag of silver coins should have commanded close to $2,860; a $6 per ounce silver price means that a bag of coins should theoretically sell for around $4,300. However, prices of each have not ascended or descended *pari passu* and have presented potential profit opportunities for the alert arbitrageur.

Until the rapid ascent in silver prices, coins normally sold at a slight

2. At the time of writing, serious proposals were being entertained at the Commodity Exchange to reduce its silver contract by one-half, to five thousand ounces, equal to the Board of Trade's.

premium to silver for no other reason than their high degree of liquidity. The face value of coins creates a floor, or minimum price, of the commodity. However, U.S. coins are largely an American phenomenon, while silver is traded worldwide. Strong European demand on the London Metal Exchange in times of monetary uncertainty tends to wipe out differences because U.S. coins are not widely traded in Europe.

When silver bullion sells for $5 an ounce, the value of the silver in a bag of coins equates to about $3,575. Suppose, however, that coins sell for $3,700 a bag. Either silver bullion is undervalued or coins overvalued. The arbitrageur will buy silver bullion, sell coins, and reap a profit when prices approach each other. Arbitrage is buying a contract of one commodity and simultaneously selling a contract of another commodity.

To research price behavior these relationships should be recorded over some period to estimate ranges within which price differences fluctuate, and to determine entry points that minimize risks and maximize profit potentials. These data may be kept in tabular form; I prefer to transfer them to a spread chart for quicker understanding.

To convert price per bag of U.S. coins into an approximate bullion price equivalent, multiply by factor 0.14. This process shifts all prices to a common denominator, that is, everything is expressed in the per-ounce price of silver.

Prepare a spread chart of the variety found in Chapter 15. If the closing price of coins is at a premium to silver bullion, record it above the zero line in the + section of the chart. If bullion is trading at a premium to coins, the computed result is a minus figure.

Figure 62 presents an example of IMM June '74 U.S. coins vs. Chicago June '74 bullion. Notice the wide swings, which provide ample opportunities for the arbitrageur. If you are in a position to record intraday swings —say, once an hour—the same erratic oscillations will appear.

To reduce bias, the position should be balanced with five silver bullion contracts against seven U.S. coins. In five bullion contracts there are 25,000 ounces of silver. In each five-bag coin contract, there are approximately 3,570-3,580 ounces and seven contracts (or thirty-five bags) equal 25,000 ounces of silver.

Another possible combination is three coin contracts vs. two bullion contracts, but it is not a near-perfect hedge. If you buy coins and sell bullion, the unstraddled portion of the position will make you net long by 700 or more ounces, which is satisfactory only if prices are rising. Another alternative, trade on the MidAmerica Commodity Exchange, where silver is sold in contract sizes of 1,000 ounces each. The proper combination would be seven mini-contracts (=7,000 ounces) and two coin contracts (=7,150 ounces).

Because of high transaction costs, the first combination has performed best; that is, seven coins against five bullion. On Chicago markets, commission is $30 per contract (check for latest commissions), or $360 per strad-

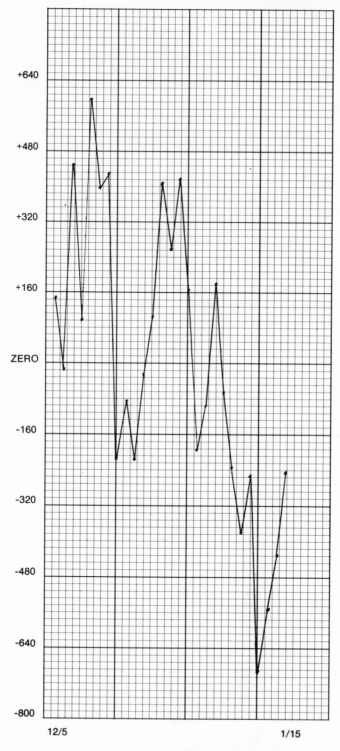

Fig. 62. IMM June '74 silver coins over Chicago June silver bullion

272

dle. Obviously, the spread must widen or narrow sufficiently to cover these costs. The trader must exhibit sufficient patience for profits to materialize. Security deposit should be no greater than seven coin contracts; some brokerage houses may do even better, but not likely. Few are acquainted with positions of this type. You will have to shop around considerably to find both a registered representative and a brokerage house capable of consummating the transaction for you. Now that you have generated all those profits, a silent partner who has shared *none* of the risks but may want as much as *one-half of the profits*—and I'm not referring to the mafiosi either—cannot be ignored.

SECTION F

The
Financial Aspects

CHAPTER 19
Straddling for
Tax Advantages, Gains,
and Postponement

Patience, and Shuffle the cards.

—Don Quixote, II, 23

THE PROBLEM OF TAXES USUALLY DOESN'T ENTER THE MIND OF A PART-TIME speculator until the tax year ends or even *after* it has terminated. By that time, of course, it is unlikely that manipulations can be accomplished in the market to reduce, postpone, or eliminate taxes. Profits must be planned for in advance, and appropriate action taken if tax delays or reduction is your bag. If you are not concerned with taxes, then skip this chapter.

What about investors who have year-end losses? Most profits and losses in commodity or currency trading are short-term, that is, less than six months. If your only alternative is to offset short-term losses against ordinary income, then you are handicapped.

Another discriminatory feature of present tax laws only allows deductions of $1,000 in losses annually against ordinary income—a long time to work off a $10,000 loss in this manner. Even this situation can be turned to your advantage. And your losses, or profits, do not necessarily have to result from futures market activities.

Finally, this chapter does not proffer tax advice. See your accountant, attorney, brother-in-law, or whomever you talk to in these matters. After you have decided whether you require short- or long-term profits or losses, income postponement or protection, fit the ideas presented in this chapter to your own special requirements.

How to Delay Taxes Due on Gains and Accumulate Losses

Because tax laws change frequently, because each individual's tax problems are unique on the more complicated level, the techniques suggested here are for general cases. Before applying any of them, I would advise consultation with your tax man on exactly what you require to reduce or postpone taxes. I do not advise, however, that you discuss trading mechanics; if he does not understand them, he may only confuse you.

After you have acquired the necessary information from him, obtain the services of a broker who is well acquainted with tax straddles, who is able to execute your trades without enlarging your risks. Not every registered representative adequately understands these techniques! A surprisingly large number lack any knowledge of mechanics and application of income manipulation.

Let us begin with a simple case where you have made $30,000, short-term gains, in the commodity markets during the current year. Because of other incomes, profits, dividends, and so forth, minus expenses and losses, you estimate that receiving income next year will be more advantageous than reporting it this year. There can be many reasons. You may anticipate larger expenses next year or lower income from other sources. Possibly forthcoming tax legislation will favor postponement of income. Or you may be retiring, expect to take a leave of absence, or for some other reason prefer not reporting $30,000 extra this year. What can be done?

Traditionally the silver market has been employed for this manipulation. Silver brokers are very accommodating. There tends to be less fluctuation in the spread, or price difference, between months; over time, the difference usually returns to full carrying charges. Silver prices oscillate sufficiently to accumulate quick losses or profits. Especially during the last two or three months of the year and the first month or two of the following year, open interest in silver changes sharply. Many floor brokers are familiar with tax advantages.

By early November, let's say, you know your requirements and request your broker to put on several tax straddles. Most silver bullion is traded in Chicago or New York. For these examples, I will assume using the 10,000-ounce contract on the Commodity Exchange in New York.[1] Assume that silver prices ought to move at least 30¢ before year's end. You put on ten silver straddles—buying ten March and selling ten July contracts.

Silver prices rise by 30¢ within three weeks; buy in ten July silver. You have now established a $30,000 loss plus $450 in commission (also a tax-deductible expense). For tax purposes you have offset a short-term credit of $30,000 with a $30,000 short-term debit in November.

1. Occasionally exchanges alter contract sizes for marketability; however, such changes do not affect the principles discussed in this book.

At this point you are net long ten March silver with $30,000 in paper profits. However, January 2 is still a month away. You may risk losing $30,000 in accrued profits, or silver prices may climb before reacting. Accumulated winnings could mount; you decide not to speculate. Profits are protected by selling ten May silver against the outstanding ten March contracts.

In January unwind the straddle. Profits earned the following tax year: $30,000 minus commissions. Your short-term gains have been successfully shifted forward. Now your only problem is to worry about these acquisitions in the new tax year. Obviously you can renew this process every year and indefinitely postpone payment of taxes.

There are two costs associated with this service: one certain, one possible. Certain costs are commissions. Naturally, the larger the potential price moves, the fewer contracts you will require, and the lower transaction expenses will be. The other cost is the possibility of a price-widening or narrowing between the months. Studying markets, spread charting, and the services of a good broker will minimize that risk. It may be beneficial to switch from a bull spread to a bear spread. Initially you may have bought ten May and sold ten July; if price differences varied, you may then find it necessary to have bought ten March after offsetting the ten July. There are a couple of ways of eliminating this risk.

One method is a *butterfly* straddle. In the same situation as above, go long ten May silver and short five January and short five September silver. Again assume price rises to desired objectives by the end of November. Offset five short January and five short September contracts to establish your losses. Since you are still net long ten May silvers, protect profits by selling five March and five July contracts against them. At current levels, the cost per straddle is $45.50 on the first positions offset and $64 round-turn commission on straddles. Additional cost is income forgone on the $4,000 or $5,000 tied up in security deposit.

The second method, more popular in the currency market, requires a partner you can trust. You may want to pair off with a friend, or possibly with a pit broker with whom you have established rapport. The straddle operation is identical except that your partner has taken the opposite side of the trade in, say, Mexican pesos. If the spread changes, then one partner gains while the other loses; but these losses and profits are adjusted in a personal exchange, and cost of operation narrows to commission charges.

But you may be saying: "My problem is losses, not gains. Now I know how to trade better; from now on I'll be successful; but what about all these short-term losses I've accumulated from past errors? I haven't been able to acquire enough gains to use up these losses, and I can offset only $1,000 a year against my ordinary income. Is there something I can do?"

Of course, this section of the tax code is extremely unfair. Carrying losses forward means offsetting them against inflationary income and paying a higher tax rate. Too, both tax laws and tax rates do change, perhaps not in your favor, so that additional costs add to these setbacks.

Immediately, you can simply reverse the straddles recommended above by lifting the winning leg of the straddle. This step establishes short-term gains this year to match your previous short-term losses. Also, your commission costs will be deductible now. However, you still have a short-term loss locked into the straddle, which will materialize next year. If you generate speculative profits next year under more favorable tax conditions, then postponing the loss with the tax straddle operation is rewarding; otherwise your only benefit may by psychological.

In the next section of this chapter I will demonstrate how to turn the above situation into a definite advantage. Also, I should caution you again to check on current tax laws; for example, you will want to know whether short sales qualify as long-term gains, or only as short-term gains regardless of length of time held. Know what you require. Then apply these money-saving techniques.

How to Convert Short-term Gains into Long-term Profits

It may have occurred to you that earnings could theoretically be postponed indefinitely, or at least spread out over years of lower incomes or after retirement. This is not only theoretically but actually possible, although not practical for a long period; the hooker is commission costs. Planned carefully so that you perform the operation once annually for a substantial sum, the procedure may be worthwhile. The technique is more viable with a shorter time horizon. The key is holding the jackpot for six months and a day.

Using the example given in the previous section, begin with the following butterfly spread: long ten September 1975 silver, short five May 1975 and five December 1975 silver. Assume that you put on the straddle on October 22 with the objective of creating $30,000 in short-term losses, and that you lifted the losing leg of the straddle on December 19 after having achieved your aim. We will suppose that the price of silver rose during this interim, debits accumulate on the short side of the transaction.

You now have a $30,000 loss for this year and a paper profit in ten long September 1975 silver. To protect the bankroll, again sell against it, five July 1975 and five January 1976 silver. Instead of unwinding this straddle in January, if it is to your tax advantage to have long-term gains, wait until after the end of May before converting your position into actual cash. Through alchemy your short-term winnings of one year were first canceled out with short-term losses, then transmuted into long-term capital gains this year.

Depending upon your individual tax situation, the saving can be substantial. Of course, operation of this example depends upon the price of silver rising. Suppose that the price of silver had retraced by 50 percent after the first of the year. Profits are still protected. The difference now is that about one-half of your benefits are long-term rewards originating from ten long

September silver, while the other part of the gain occurs from the short side of the straddle. Short sales are treated as short-term gains.

In the example of the individual with deficits, by reversing the above sequence, a portion of this year's short-term losses are offset by short-term gains. Next year, however, these short-term debits are transmuted into mostly long-term losses and some short-term losses for more favorable tax treatment. Even in the case of adversity there are methods for lessening the harshness of the experience.

How to Hedge Assets and Income

Suppose that you have lucre and losses from purchase and sale of assets and investments other than commodities. Gains are gains, losses are losses; in the final accounting all are lumped together.

Therefore, if you have earnings from transactions in equities, real estate, debt instruments, foreign exchange, or any other source, the same procedure of obtaining an improved tax advantage can be acquired through transactions in commodities markets.

In the above examples, profits and losses, assumed to have originated in commodity trading, are not required. Gains in stock transactions may be offset by losses in commodities markets.

Diversification of assets is not always insurance against failures. Your investment portfolio must be constantly monitored. Through your Swiss banker you may have purchased stock in an English firm. Its market value not only fluctuates according to profitability and return on investment, but also on the international markets, according to value of the British pound. If you are an American, more than likely your final calculations are figured in dollar terms. Even if you calculate your wealth on a base of Swiss francs, you are still using a common denominator to measure the value of *all* your assets.

In the above example, the international value of the British pound may fall vis-à-vis U.S. dollars and Swiss francs. Rather than sell out your equity in the English firm, you can selectively hedge the investment by selling short British pounds. If your investment is $50,000, for example, sell one contract of pounds sterling on the IMM.

Naturally, foreign-exchange transactions can be consummated through either your American banker or a foreign banker. But for such a small transaction, the IMM will probably be cheapest (commission charges $45) and most convenient. Depreciation of value in stock will be compensated for through gains in the short sale of pounds sterling.

On the other hand, you may own a large interest in an American firm with substantial unhedged foreign assets. If you don't believe foreign-exchange losses do occur, look at recent statements of F. W. Woolworth, American Broadcasting Co., Procter and Gamble, Chesebrough-Pond, Deere and Company, to name a few. Even banks err. The story of the branch manager of one of the larger American banks in a Benelux country has been retold.

He was on the wrong side of the market in D-marks and incurred a whopping big loss for his bank. A couple of years ago I heard he is still living in Europe—working as a gardener.

Let's say that you own a large interest in an American firm that manufactures locomotives. The firm carries substantial receivables on its books in Mexican pesos originating from sales to the Mexican government.

Recognizing the risk of unprotected receivables, you can hedge your investment in this firm against exchange risk by selling Mexican pesos short, should you believe the value of the peso will depreciate further. In other words, though the firm has left itself exposed to losses, not every investor is obliged to accept the reckless decisions of management.

Another applicable case: you may wish to hedge future income against dollar depreciation. Twelve months from now you anticipate receiving, say, $40,000. Buy a futures contract in Dutch guilders one year forward. If, in fact, the dollar falls against the guilder, you have hedged the loss with offsetting gains in the DG. Cost of insurance—$45, the round-turn commission.

In this example, you are *overhedged*, if the value of the guilder contract is $50,000, against receivables of $40,000. About 80 percent is hedge and 20 percent speculative because of the difficulty of matching assets and contract sizes precisely. Even being *underhedged* is better than no hedge at all.

The next situation is an interesting possibility for short-term considerations. Suppose that you own a Swiss franc account. During July 1973, action of the September futures contract suggests some retracement from recent highs (see Figure 63 for chart action). Swiss francs are worth more, in dollars, in June or July, and you want to protect profits derived from the appreciated value of the SF.

To protect a SF 300,000 account, sell one March 1974 futures contract against it at 0.36000. In this example, you are underhedged—but better than no hedge. Since you have anticipated correctly, profits lost in Switzerland were partly compensated for on the IMM. You may have closed out your position in November at 0.31500 (short-term gains taxable this year) or risked waiting until the following year to encash.

On the other hand, if you had anticipated incorrectly, a tax deductible loss would have been sustained in the futures transaction in the United States. Across the sea, appreciation in value of Swiss francs does not really become profits until converted into dollars—on one hand, tax deductible losses, transaction costs; on the other, untaxed gains. Check this one out!

Now let us return to the example where you have purchased Dutch guilders. Suppose that a sharp price runup occurs after a couple of months; you want to protect the quickly accrued profit. By selling a distant month against the open position (actually a reverse "stretch"), accrued profits are safeguarded; however, no further accumulation of profits is likely. Holding

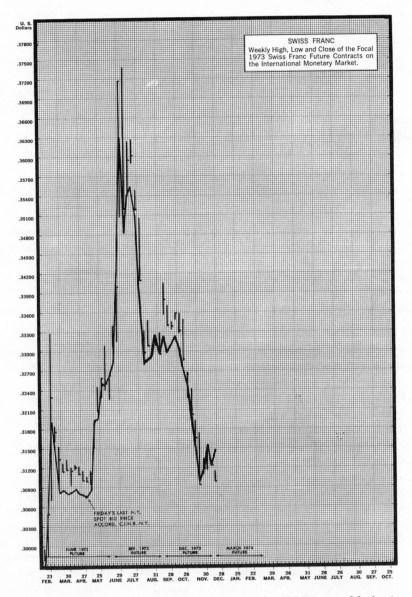

Fig. 63. Swiss franc futures (Source: International Monetary Market.)

the straddled position for another four months before unwinding it turns a short-term gain into a long-term one.

This technique need not be restricted to the foreign-currency market and can, in fact, operate in other commodity markets. Converting a short-term gain into a long-term one does require some skill where spread differences fluctuate widely, and new and old crop months are affected by different demand-supply factors. This technique will not work in the egg futures market, for example. But there are situations where it functions well. With prudence, tax liabilities can be reduced.

Finding an inflation hedge is the object of much investment diversification in these times of turbulence and turmoil. Where all currencies are being inflated, no adequate hedge, over any length of time, exists. Gold is thought to be one of the best hedges. And it probably is! But gold, like all commodities, is influenced by certain factors, other than monetary phenomena, that make any hedge imperfect.

Gold futures are traded on the Winnipeg Commodity Exchange in Canada in contract sizes of 400 ounces. Gold futures are traded in the U.S. in 100-troy ounce contracts on the Chicago Mercantile Exchange and New York Commodity Exchange in 96.45 troy ounces on the Chicago Board of Trade, and 32.15 ounces on the New York Mercantile Exchange. Security deposit is around 7-8 percent; trading volume is light. At time of writing the Pacific Commodities Exchange anticipated adding a silver contract.

How to Buy Silver Coins and Silver Bullion

"Can I use the commodities markets for cash purchases?" Yes! The technique described here may be employed not only in acquiring silver coins or bullion but also foreign currencies (if the amount you desire is fairly large) or even gold or other precious metals.

If you want to own silver bullion because you believe it will appreciate in value, buying a futures contract fifteen months forward locks in the price of silver regardless of how high it rises. When the delivery month arrives, hold onto your long contract, be prepared to pay the entire purchase price, and accept delivery.

Alternatively, you may not wish to consummate the transaction through the futures market. In the second case, close out your position prior to the delivery date, accept your profits, add sufficient funds to the amount, and buy silver from your favorite cash dealer.

What are the advantages of using the futures markets? (1) You may not have enough money now, but a security deposit of 20 percent will control five times that much silver until you have available funds twelve or eighteen months down the road. (2) Interest costs are less because you are borrowing only one-fifth of the cost of the contract for the first twelve to eighteen months. (3) Insurance and storage costs are postponed until you accept actual delivery of the physical good. (4) In real terms, actual cost may be less because you are paying with inflated dollars; a 20 percent inflation rate translates into a considerable reduction one or one and one-half years later.

If price falls instead of rising, won't you have a loss? Of course, but the loss may be even greater if you had owned the cash product throughout the period. Prices always fluctuate. Protect your futures contract with a stop-loss in the event of a price reaction. When the reaction appears to have run its course, prices begin to rebound, initiate a new position at the lower price. This action cuts overall losses.

A disadvantage of the futures market is the fixed contract size. However, with silver, 10,000-ounce units can be purchased on the Commodity Exchange, 5,000-ounce units on the Chicago Board of Trade, and 1,000-ounce units on the MidAmerica Commodity Exchange.[2]

"Junk" silver coins can be purchased by identical methods in $10,000 (face value) units on the New York Mercantile Exchange, in $5,000 units (five bags) on the IMM of the Chicago Mercantile Exchange or Mid-America Commodity Exchange.

Consider this one! Let's say that silver prices are rising and you straddle. Coming into delivery month, lift the short side of the straddle, hold the long side for delivery. Advantages? Accumulate a loss on the short-side—tax deductible! Commission charges—tax deductible! Accept delivery of silver. Gains? *Not* taxable until you have sold or traded the silver. Check this one out, too, with your tax adviser!

The last suggestion is for all of you out there who own silver coins and bullion. Prices do fluctuate, but many owners of actuals ignore shorter-term oscillations and hold for longer-term waves. When prices fluctuate, the value of material wealth varies. The cash product can be hedged similar to a hedged Swiss bank account. When U.S. coin prices are high, sell a contract or two of coin futures against them. This action locks in profits; it protects the value of stored coins.

There are many other techniques, variations of systems, but you are now acquainted with the major means of preserving and increasing your wealth. Those of you who have limited financial resources but are desperate enough to assume large risks and gutsy enough to grab for the brass ring, read on.

2. The Pacific Commodities Exchange anticipates adding a silver contract.

CHAPTER 20
Trading with Little or No Money

If I am working as intelligently, diligently, and rapidly on my own improvement as is within my power, the balance of the problem is in the hand of God. He did not commission me to manage the world, or the U.S.A., or my neighbor. Further, I am unaware that any person has been so endowed or empowered.

—Leonard Read

OF COURSE, TAX SPREADS MEAN LITTLE TO THE INVESTOR WITH ONLY A FEW thousand dollars in risk capital and no gains to postpone. This chapter challenges those who understand and believe the philosophy of this book, but possess limited capital to preserve.

How can a speculator multiply an unimportant sum of money into an important amount? To trade commodity futures requires at least maiden money. The person with only $1,000 or $2,000—even $8,000 or $10,000, for that matter—is handicapped, but he is in no manner excluded from this market.

If you are determined to win in these markets, nothing can stop you! Naturally, launching a program to acquire $1 million with only $5,000, your approach will probably be less conservative than someone commencing with $5,000 who strives to arrogate $10,000. Debuting with $5,000, risk exposure will be greater the more rapidly you accelerate the rate of wealth accumulation.

Nevertheless, there are methods of securing funds to enter the market and to cause your capital to work harder. One of the ensuing plans may suit you.

Starting with $1,000, More or Less

To uncomplicate the following expositions, assume that traded commodities all oblige inaugural security deposits of $1,000.[1] If your hope-chest contains only $1,000, can you open an account with a brokerage company? The answer is probably no.

Most commission houses generally dictate prefatory deposits of $5,000 to $10,000. Some houses demand $2,500 to open an account. Only a few firms have no house rules or grant discretion to the registered representative. If you command only $1,000, can raise no auxiliary money, shop around if you really intend to enter the market with this sum. Somewhere a broker may accept your business.

Of course, there is no margin for error, so you learn your trading lessons well before commencing. You cannot afford to pay a tuition fee. Unfortunately, this type of close-fisted trading may adversely affect your decisions.

If you tense up, most likely you will founder. Your frame of mind will be unsuited to winning. However, if you are a real shooter, can sleep nights, I will show you, in another chapter, how to trade ten contracts when you have only enough margin money for one or two.

But suppose that the house stipulates $3,000. You have only $1,500 but have ferreted out a broker who is eager for new business. He has probably just told you how much money he can generate for you, has urged you to locate an additional $1,500.

Make him this proposition: "Since you are so certain that you can make money for me, I'll open an account with you—I mean jointly with you. I'll put up $1,500 and you put up $1,500 on a fifty-fifty partnership. I'll keep the books, you trade. We'll maintain a joint account until you have either lost half the funds or doubled them."

Ask a sufficient number of brokers, one may accept your proposition. When negotiating special arrangements, you should strictly prospect firms that specialize in commodities (especially small firms), not stock houses. Specialist firms tend to be more flexible.

You can try the same tactic with friends. Two or three can pool funds, form an investment club, a formal partnership, or simply associate for a single purpose (assuming no conflict with state laws). However, friends can create problems. Unless the group is compatible, they may not work together toward common goals.

1. Margin requirements are established by the various commodity exchanges. They are altered frequently, according to trading activity, total value of the contract, and volatility of the commodity. There is no "normal" or "average" security deposit. The above-mentioned $1,000 is only employed for illustrative purposes. In actual practice, recent margin requirements have ranged from $400 per contract to $7,500.

You may interest eight or ten other persons in associating to assemble a fund of $10,000 or $15,000, of which you are appointed "manager" or "secretary-treasurer." If you can convince the other investors of your qualifications, request a "fee" or "salary" for services based upon monthly profits —say, 15 percent.

You will need to acquire the cordial assistance of a well-informed broker to assist in trading decisions. By all means, trade very conservatively to avoid possible problems; document all decisions. If the fund averages $1,000 in monthly profits, $150 off the top is yours plus vested interest according to your original capital contribution.

On the other hand, you may con a relative or in-law into loaning or investing a few dollars with you in this new venture. If you infuse your story of easy riches with inspiring tales of success, dazzle your smitten relative until his whole body wriggles and writhes, and he trembles and tingles to the tips of his fingers with visions of greed, you can stir the very embers of his soul.

Offer to split profits with him on a forty-sixty or twenty-five-seventy-five or whatever basis you can negotiate. Watch his eyes effervesce with greed. When he grabs your arm and begs, "How much do you need, my favorite relative?" get his check (cash is even better) immediately. Once you have his money in hand, he will take up the cudgels for your enterprise with other kinfolk. If you are successful with a few trades, you can probably put the bite on some of them too.

Surely you will conceive of better ways and places to obtain funds according to your circumstances; but if you are really determined to broach commodity trading now, then you do need some capital. Where else can you obtain resources?

Earning 10,000 Percent on Your Capital

You are already aware of the tremendous leverage that commodity trading bestows. If security deposits represent only 10 percent of contract value, then a 1 percent rise in value produces a 10 percent profit on margin money. Now assume that you can also borrow 90 percent of the security deposit. A 1 percent rise in the value of the contract will yield a 100 percent return on your "investment."

A simple example will prove the point. Let's say that one contract of frozen concentrated orange juice (OJ), worth $10,000 at the time you buy it, requires $1,000 as security deposit. A 1 percent increment means that the OJ contract has redoubled by $100 in value. One hundred dollars equals 10 percent of your margin deposit.

But examine what occurs when you borrow $900. Your outlay is only $100. A 1 percent increment equals $100, 100 percent of your original commitment (minus interest charges on your borrowed $900, of course, and commission). A 100 percent increment per contract will return 10,000 percent on your $100 investment. That's like giving a sprat to catch a whale. In fact, by employing a technique I will relate to you in the next part of this chapter, you can generate 10,000 percent if the price of OJ rises by only 33 percent.

By borrowing resources you expand the work power of capital many times over. Naturally, if you err, you can also spawn a huge deficit. In the above OJ contract, a 1 percent fall in price will wipe out your original reserve. But since we are all winners at heart, reversals should not nail our shoes to the floor. Where can you raise funds?

You probably own several assets of value to secure a loan. An insurance policy may be convenient. By pledging the policy, you can still insure your life (should you decide to fall off a tall building) and take advantage of low-cost credit. Stocks, bonds, notes receivable, or similar assets furnish collaterality. This method allows your savings to ply the oars in two places; it affords substantial leverage.

You may be content, and in a position, to touch your banker for an unsecured, short-term advance. But you may experience difficulty in redeeming the note when due. Always think in terms of how debt can be restituted if you dissipate all margin deposit. You may prefer to repay your accommodation monthly—even at a higher interest rate. An installment loan at least accords time to resolve an adverse situation.

Several executive-finance services throughout the country lend up to $25,000 on an unsecured basis with repayment monthly or quarterly over an extended period. Interest rates range from 15 to 20 percent. Another high-cost loan—a second mortgage—may grant a longer payback period. Additionally, there are ethnic funds, private lenders, and even government sources.

For example, a son or daughter in college may qualify for a low-interest accommodation under a government program. Such a loan will free up otherwise committed resources. Look around. Many sources exist; funds can be easily borrowed.

However, I am not advising you to incur liabilities. Commodity trading is a chancy business. All businesses that offer high returns entail risk assumption. Total speculative exposure may increase when you borrow. I do not hold court on how you should manage your life and affairs; my hands are full with my own life. If you pawn your wife's rings and lose them, it was your freedom of choice to assume that chance of loss. I accept no responsibility for your decisions.

Going from $9,000 to $54,000

To open an account necessitates funds. If you do not personally have money, then you will have to use someone else's. After plunging into trading you may discover that you are riding a trend and would like to take advantage of the price rise. (Assume that you initially open your account with $9,000.) How can you add to the position without depositing more money?

Profits accumulated in any trade, although you still hold open contracts, count toward margin required on additional ones. Adding to a position, you can protect accrued profits pyramid-style. This system can best be explicated with an example. Assume trades in New York silver—10,000 ounces. Each one-point change equals $1.

Let's say that the price of silver is $5 per ounce; you expect it to rise and acquire six contracts. When it rises to $5.15, you want to purchase more contracts. The correct strategy is to buy some quantity fewer than six—say, five. Because you already have paper profits of $9,000 ($1,500 per contract times six), you are not solicited for additional security deposit. Paper profits substitute.

If silver continues to rise, add to your position when the price reaches $5.30, for instance. Again, additional contracts will be fewer than the previous acquisition; that is, buy some quantity less than five—for example, four.

Then, at $5.40, you may want to obtain three more. You can continue this process as long as paper profits are adequate to cover margin requirements. At $5.50, you may procure two more contracts and perhaps another one at $5.60. The assemblage will appear as in Figure 64:

You may be thinking, "What difference does it make? Suppose I had inverted the pyramid? Wouldn't that make more sense?" Assuming the same schedule of prices, you would have bought one contract at $5.00 but six when price soared to $5.60. Your pyramid of purchases would rest on its apex as in Figure 65:

Analyze what happens when the price trend reverses. In both exemplifications you have collected a total of twenty-one contracts of silver. In the

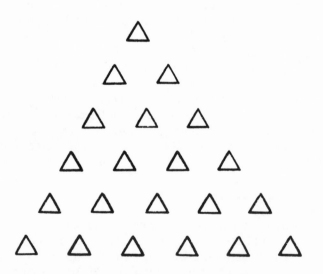

Fig. 64. The contract procurement pyramid

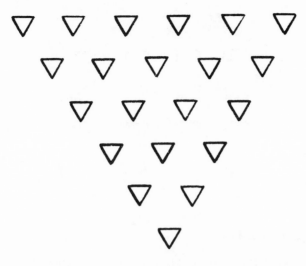

Fig. 65. The contract procurement pyramid, continued

first model, your purchase price averages approximately $5.23; in the second case, your average purchase price is $5.43.

Prices do not rise forever. To predict tops and bottoms of markets is difficult. Assume that the market topped out around $5.60, fell back to $5.50, before liquidating your position.

Having earned profits in both situations, you have failed to safeguard accumulated rewards in the second one. In your second group of acquisitions, you have harvested seven hundred points (or $700) per contract, a total of $14,700. Not bad, eh?

In the first plan gross profits aggregate $54,600. Better yet! When the price rolled back to $5.50, you lost on only one contract; in the second circumstance you lost on six contracts.

Now if price were limit down for a day or two, you might not have been able to close out your position until silver traded at $5.30. You still preserve substantial profits with normal pyramiding, but a $27,300 *loss* in the second set up.

The general rule is: *Never add to your position contracts in greater number than the preceding purchase.*

A variation of the pyramid formula is the block-style plan as shown in Figure 66. You may have purchased six contracts of silver, then four, four, four, and three, and still protect amassed profits in large measure.

The block-style program does not violate the rationale behind pyramiding because you annex no number of contracts greater than the previous acquisition. Nevertheless, no single rule applies to every situation. At times prudence calls for innovation.

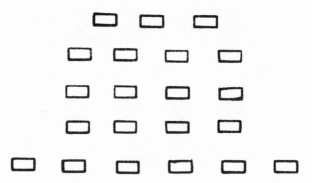

Fig. 66. The block-style plan

Turning $3,000 into $54,000

Having learned a rule, let's break it. In actual practice, few traders consistently pyramid. This system performs best in a slowly trending, predictable market. If the market progresses rapidly, half the swing may already have passed before traders recognize that a bull (or bear) movement is under way.

For example, in August 1973, the December live cattle contract exceeded $60 (price per cwt). Bullish reports, coupled with the anticipated September 12 lifting of the price freeze on beef, convinced some traders that cattle prices were headed sharply higher.

When prices subsequently abated, many considered it a reaction in a bull market. In fact, some traders retained long positions all the way down to $50. Prices did eventually subside to the $40 range, but pyramiding opportunities were already substantially forgone by the time those bulls became bearish.

However, one variation of pyramiding techniques seems more useful on a practical level. It presents the speculator with an opportunity to "test" the market before wading into a heavy obligation. As diagrammed in Figure 67, the system conforms to a Christmas-tree shape. Again assume purchase of twenty-one contracts.

Although acquisitions may occur at price intervals different from previous schemes, no established rule prevails for employing this system. The rationale behind it permits a speculator to pioneer a minor venture when he is uncertain whether a major trend has begun. He can substantially acquire contracts when technical analysis evinces that a major movement is, indeed, under way.

In fact, between prices $5.00 and $5.20, he may be neither aware nor convinced that a pyramiding opportunity exists. After the market shows its true colors, the investor enlarges his stake without violating the basic pyramid principle.

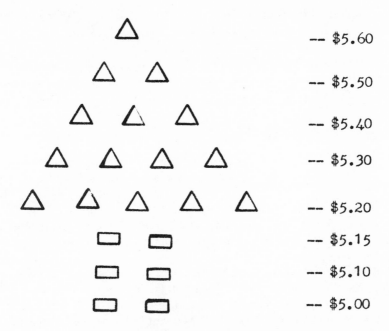

-- $5.60

-- $5.50

-- $5.40

-- $5.30

-- $5.20

-- $5.15

-- $5.10

-- $5.00

Fig. 67. Christmas tree pyramiding technique

Of course, risk exposure is greatest in the $5.20-$5.30 range; presumably he will not establish a major position until quite certain of market facts. In the above mock-up, average price equals $5.26—nearly the same as in our first model.

In all the above exhibits, accumulated profits should be protected with a trailing stop-loss. As price bounces upward, the stop-loss should also be raised, but not within a normal intraday trading range. Building profits is the objective.

Whichever system you adopt, once your stop-loss order has moved into profit areas, gains are reasonably assured. Someone else's money will finance your incremental pyramid or Christmas-tree program.

The above situation also offers the advantage of requiring less security deposit if price dances rapidly enough in your favor. With solicited margin of $1,000 per contract, you can theoretically open an account for $3,000. As long as price does not edge against you, there will be no margin call until you put on five contracts at $5.20. Probably you can safely ignore the margin call for two days; if price climbs enough you will be off call.

Alternatively you can meet margin call. As soon as sufficient paper profits accrue to your account, request a check for the excess. If you operate on borrowed funds, act as soon as profits materialize. Loan repayment takes some pressure off trading.

The purpose of this chapter has been to ventilate marginal means of securing a piece of the future. Some of these methods are not recommended for the unsuccessful competitor. These systems are suitable for the speculator who has studied markets thoroughly, prepared his program soundly, approached trades self-confidently, but temporarily lacks funds to propel himself onto the path of opportunities. However, there is another place where a person with only a few hundred dollars can participate.

Trading in Mini-Contracts

One exchange promises substantially more flexibility, where a speculator with insufficient finances can trade mini-contracts and encounter greater opportunity to pyramid. The MidAmerica Commodity Exchange in Chicago caters futures contracts in multiple units of one thousand bushels of oats, wheat, corn, and soybeans—one-fifth of contract size on other exchanges. Naturally, commissions and security-deposit requirements rate considerably less.

Additionally, in 1968, one-thousand-troy-ounce silver futures began trading—one-fifth of the Chicago Board of Trade contract, one-tenth of the Commodity Exchange contract. Silver coins since 1972, merchant in five-bag units, one-half of the New York Mercantile Exchange's specification; however, in 1973, the IMM also put together a five-bag silver-coins package. Before June 1974, in competition with the Chicago Mercantile Exchange, a half-unit of fifteen thousand pounds of live hogs became available.

The MidAmerica Commodity Exchange is not new—except for the name, which was adopted in 1973. Actually, the exchange traces its history to 1868, when it began trading as Pudd's Exchange in the open air at the corner of Washington and La Salle streets. (I wonder if the cold wind off Lake Michigan invigorated trading.) Surprisingly, it did not come in out of the weather until the 1880s.

In 1880 it was incorporated as the Chicago Open Board of Trade. Finally, in 1973, the Open Board appropriately changed its name to the Mid-America Commodity Exchange. Following nomadic instincts it peregrinated to several locations, finally self-driven to a former home, previously used, between 1914 and 1946, in the heart of Chicago's financial district. The opening-day activities at the new location (May 28, 1974) are shown in Photograph 19.

Although the Open Board was less aggressive in marketing its services, the new MidAmerica has invoked a public-relations consciousness. Nevertheless, this interesting exchange does boast several important firsts. Not only one of the oldest exchanges, in 1882 it also developed the concept of third-party clearing procedures, a practice ultimately adopted by all major exchanges. This step significantly increases liquidity. Otherwise, the original buyer and seller would have to either mutually offset positions or find third parties willing to accept contracts, or make and take delivery of actuals.

Another first, in 1920 the Open Board instituted customer margin requirements. You may long for the good old days, but a security deposit is really a blessing in disguise. Raising and lowering requirements provides indicators of riskiness relative to value, vertiginousness, and villainousness.

And in 1974, it became the first exchange to trade both corn and hogs. In fact, a unique aspect is its single-pit design. Four broad, oak steps surround the huge arena where fleas cross swords with lions. Speculators can easily straddle related commodities, such as corn and hogs (review hog-corn ratio in Chapter 10), or corn and oats, or silver bullion and silver coins, for example.

If you really become serious about these matters, but lack large amounts of capital, you may want to purchase a seat on the MidAmerica Commodity Exchange—if the Windy City's weather is not an important consideration. In 1970, a membership sold for $1,500; most recently the cost has nearly quadrupled to $5,500. Clearing fees are quite low.

There are advantages of smaller, flexible contract sizes, fairly good liquidity (though not comparable to the Chicago Board of Trade, whose volume is unequaled by all other exchanges together). Too, attractive opportunities exist for pit scalpers. Straddling advantages result from all commodities being transacted in a single pit plus arbitrage facilities with other trading floors.

What can you do if your funds are limited? (1) Security deposits are lower on straddles than on net positions. Some offer plenty of action and profit opportunities, as demonstrated in Chapter 15. You can put on a straddle with $400-$500; I advise being overmargined, of course. (2) Several circumstances were mentioned in previous sections of this chapter. One may appeal to you. Or you may prefer speculating in smaller contracts. Competition for business among exchanges invites shopping as contract sizes are altered.

However, if neither (1) nor (2) arouses your interest, then (3) may be your cup of *yerba maté*. Unveiling a relatively new industry in commodities—one that is only in its infancy—the next possibility represents unusual potential.

CHAPTER 21
Investing in
Commodity Mutual Funds

Down to Gehenna or up to the throne, he travels the fastest who travels alone.

—Rudyard Kipling

AN INVESTOR WITH A SMALL SUM OF MONEY, BACKED UP BY CAREFUL RESEARCH and a certain amount of daring, may choose to go it alone and pyramid his investment into a sizable sum. After all, opening an account with $1,000 or $1,500 does not leave much margin for error. An alternative: pool a small sum of money with several others, either in an informal relationship, such as a club, or in a formal arrangement with professional management.

Legal restraints, and implied threats by the "guardians" of the investing public's savings, have thwarted the natural growth of this perfectly legitimate concept—commodity mutual funds. Many small ones are in existence, however, and they generally permit an investor with $500 or more to participate in a speculative, risk-diversification program. Few pool substantial sums for definite objectives.

Commodity mutual funds represent the newest opportunity for the small investor. They offer both advantages and disadvantages. Should you consider this indirect method of participating in these exciting markets? Under certain conditions set forth in this chapter, it may suit your needs. However, at times, joining a commodity mutual fund definitely will be a disadvantage.

The Newest Opportunity for the
Investor with $500 or More

Without implying that mutual funds, club accounts, and other joint endeavors do not already exist, the pooling concept, as applied to commodity trading, is rather limited in scope. Most investors who enter the market for a few skirmishes neither consider nor anticipate alternative systems until they have been directly approached by a friend, broker, or salesman to join together *e pluribus unum.*

Some mention should be made of club accounts. Stock investment clubs, of course, were quite popular during the great bull market. The principal problems of operating a club center on compatibility of interests among the members and concordant management of the club's funds. There are other difficulties as well, but one or both of these problems lie at the bottom of most of them.

Regarding the first complaint, if you are foolish enough to enter into *any* business relationship with that kind of handicap, you are inviting failure. Your interests must come first when choosing a broker, investment adviser, or associates in commodity transactions.

The second one—fund management—is the pitfall difficult to overcome in a club account. Who is in charge of making trading decisions? Ideally they should be joint membership decisions if the purpose of uniting is to be served. Joint decisions imply frequent and continuous contact—business associates or employees in the same firm, for example—and equal contributions to research.

A mastermind group, consisting of a small number of investors, each of whom dedicates himself to a separate phase of research, can bring together an enormous amount of information through spare-time efforts alone, and can build an unequaled management group of analysts who are fomenting their own self-interests through cooperative measures.

The club that meets periodically, invites an outside after-dinner speaker to edify in thirty minutes on the intricacies of trading, then listens to the treasurer's report, will most likely collapse in its efforts. The after-dinner speaker probably does not know a great deal about the markets or else he would not attend without payment of a substantial fee, or he may turn out to be a solicitor. The treasurer's report will probably be a "just wait till next year" appraisal. Seldom satisfactory! Electing a board to turn out decisions for the entire club suggests that the trading committee should devote considerable time to analysis.

Another variation, a small group, one of whom is a broker, maintains contact periodically via the broker, who is responsible for trading decisions. At this point, let me clear up an important point.

Some writers insist that any trader or broker who has a position in the market cannot offer rational or unbiased advice. Further, it is true that some large stock houses will not permit brokers to trade commodities.

(The real reasons obviously have nothing to do with the broker's ability to advise since these large firms maintain substantial research staffs; all trading decisions come anyway from research headquarters.)

A recent study surveyed brokers who do trade and brokers who do not. The evidence is quite contrary to the opinion of a few writers. The broker who trades successfully on his own account tends to have a group of successful clients clustered around him. Whether A attracts B or A makes B successful is not important, but whether A and B together *are successful* is important.

Acting as guide or "manager" of the fund, the broker is in a position to make quick decisions and, it is hoped, profitable ones, since he, too, has a vested interest in winning. Additionally, by concentrating daily on the markets—devoting full time to them—he can bring to the group opinions not easily developed otherwise.

Total success of the club depends, also, upon contributions of information. For example, if one member is in the lumber business, another in the frozen-food business, another in cattle-raising, another a large grain producer, even living in different parts of the country, they can maintain contact via the broker's WATS line and contribute their specialized knowledge while leaving trade timing to the technician's discretion.

The main purpose of this chapter, however, is a discussion of "mutual funds" with specialized and professional management charging a fee for services. Funds may consist of any legal form: closed corporation, general partnership, limited partnership, limited partnership association (in the four states where this form is permitted), or some other appropriate entity. Although they are not truly mutual funds in the sense usually associated with equity investments, the term will be employed here.

The corporate form possesses the advantage of limiting the liability of investors who may be racked with incompetent management. For example, a brokerage firm may not agree to accept the risk of a corporate entity bankrupting; it may demand that an individual also sign responsibility for corporate debts. At the other extreme, a general partnership, the same as a club account, means that recourse to any one or more persons is possible in the event of losses and debit accounts.

I would not want to expose all my personal assets and grant others authority for trading decisions which could seriously affect my personal welfare and total wealth. I believe that prudence suggests either a corporate relationship or a limited partnership.

A limited partnership offers certain advantages. The liability of each investor-partner is limited to the amount of his financial commitment. It may consist only of his initial capital; it may include subsequent contributions or pledges. The general partner assumes risk exposure for losses exceeding investment contributions.

If the general partner and manager of the fund represent the same group of persons, the managing (general) partner is bound to be prudent in his decisions. Safeguarding his own interests he consequently looks after the interests of each and every investor. The system checks and balances, depending upon how management is compensated for its services.

The subject of fees, costs, and charges must not be overlooked. These costs have been the target of complaints. If you are one of those gripers, I must remind you again, friend, of what I wrote at the outset of this book. There is no such thing as something for nothing.

If I seem to overstress this point, it's because so many people have such short memories. In these days of galloping socialism and welfarism, we need to be reminded more frequently than ever that costs are at the heart of everything we do. Even the hermit priest pays a price—he sacrifices social amenities, the comfortable life, to achieve his aims. We, too, must pay for services that others render.

Because federal laws prohibit less expensive means of solicitation and advertising, the cost of grouping investors is higher than need be. The costs of preparing a prospectus, literature, follow-ups by salesmen, are paid by the investor, whether it is real estate, equities, or commodities. Pay the fee. Hope to compensate for the higher cost of doing business with eventual profits.

Trading decisions result from research, statistical compilations, and counsel from advisers—all of whom must be paid. Compensation for management services in stock mutual funds is usually based on a small percentage of the fund's total value—whether profits are earned *or not*.

If a similar management fee is charged against a commodity mutual fund, investors really howl. It is too high! Why? If leverage is in the neighborhood of ten or less for commodities and zero for stocks, then the "value" of open positions must be on the order of six to ten more than cash (including security deposit). If a stock fund charges 0.25 percent or 0.50 percent of the fund's value, then a comparable commodity fund charge should be 2-3 percent of assets, shouldn't it?

Management fees may also include a performance fee. I believe that a commodity fund's management should earn profits based on successful performance. A fair system consists of selling and distribution costs in the neighborhood of 8-10 percent and management fees adequate to cover costs of research and money supervision. If clients earn profits, then the management firm is entitled to participate in the winnings. If management is incompetent, compensation should match. Justice prevails! (I wonder how many other professionals—physicians, lawyers, consultants—would survive on these terms.)

One fund with which I am acquainted absorbs all the above costs. Salesmen are paid by the managing firm, research and analysis expenses are borne by the firm, no management fees are charged. However, if it generates a profit it expects to share heavily.

Additionally, this same fund dons the role of general partner thereby, carrying responsibility for all liabilities (or deficits), while the liabilities of individual investors are limited to inceptive investment. Also, the general partner makes no claim on partnership assets. Neither does it charge any fees. If profits are earned—calculated monthly—50 percent remains with the general partner; the remaining 50 percent is divided among investors on a pro-rata share.

In spite of this overly generous arrangement, some prospective investors protest the profit-sharing arrangement. I also know that some of these so-called investors are the type who only collect "free" information—the kind that is disseminated and digested for everyone, not raw data to be assimilated and analyzed. There isn't a winner among them!

Exiting from the fund involves some costs. In some cases you may be penalized for selling out your interest prematurely. If you have entered into an arrangement, such as a limited partnership, which has a definite legal life for a certain span of years, there may be no way to extract money unless you can locate a willing buyer. The value of a share in the fund can be readily determined at the end of any accounting period.

Investing a sum for a fixed number of years is sound. If you follow the rule that mammon invested in commodity speculation can evaporate and still not affect your style of living or eating habits—in other words, consider the money lost before you even begin—then tying it up for several years is not inconsistent behavior.

In brief, the focus of a commodity fund differs from a stock fund in enough ways that a rootless attitude must prevail. Because most commodity investors have not been exposed to, or have not even though about, the ins and outs of commodity fund management, misunderstandings create tensions that must be resolved.

Why This Concept Has Not Rapidly Spread Before

Added to the myriad of obstacles, hindrances, and contrivances are regulations that impede dissemination of information and hamper the smooth flow of money. Commodities markets are far less controlled than the securities industry, but creeping legislation will soon transmute into extensive control. Some exchanges look askance at every slight innovation in order to preserve the industry's image and postpone the onset of ubiquitous governmental controls.

Promotional literature is interspersed with warnings that an investor can lose money. One exchange recently required that no hint of either profit, potential profit, or even a ratio of risk-to-potential-profit appear in reports and newsletters.

I have pointed out several times that all investments are risky, and I explained the risk-rate-of-return relationship back in Chapter 2. Most investments are far more hazardous than one is led to believe. Rules should be applied equally to every investment vehicle—but as the barnyard

300

revolutionaries learned in George Orwell's *Animal Farm:* "All animals are equal but some animals are more equal than others."

Every piece of fiat money should be inscribed: "Warning: Owning money is a risky investment. The government reserves the right to confiscate up to 100 percent of money's purchasing power through inflationary policies." Every insurance policy, time deposit, and government bond should warn of possible depreciation in value resulting from inflation or default. All stock investors should be put on notice that stock prices fluctuate, that an investor may lose money. Why should such warnings be confined to the investment field?

How about gambling? Imagine a sign above the entrance to every casino, jai alai, dog track, and horse track reading: "Beware: You may lose money if you bet." Maybe we should require labeling all prepackaged goods: "Warning: the contents of this can (package) may not live up to expectations; you may be cheated."

Promoted on a small, local scale, a commodity mutual fund is unlikely to run into difficulties unless it loses money and someone does not want to play the game by the rules. Regulation does more to protect the investor from the industry than the other way around. More than one investor has attempted to reclaim losses through legal proceedings. This type of investor is either plain dishonest or as immature as the little boy who wants to play "keepers" but after losing screams for the return of all his marbles and raises a fuss until his playmates relent.

Seldom will a fund experience difficulties by making profits. However, a major cost of doing business is maintaining a legal contingency fund against irate investors and as protection from pervasive government controls. Due to lack of test cases, the promoter of a large fund is handicapped by not being able to work with clearly defined laws. He must always look over one shoulder while moving forward, which is costly in money and energy. This is still a gray area of legislation; the pioneer of widely sold commodity mutual funds, in the name of self-preservation, must proceed carefully.

Strangely enough, the dishonest promoter stands a better chance of quickly organizing and personally profiting from his enterprises. Laws and practices seem to operate in his favor. The equities industry furnishes ample testimony. In spite of a regulatory network there have been indiscriminate deceptive practices and dishonest deals.

Commodity mutual funds have not become prevalent because of the nature of commodity speculation—its short time horizon, the difficulty of extracting service fees, the existence of nonproductive laws and regulations on one hand, ill-defined legal limits on the other.

Some Advantages of a Speculative Mutual Fund

Participating in the market indirectly via an intermediary—a mutual fund—is an expensive method unless you cannot perform your own research, purchase necessary services, properly manage money. Measured against substitutes, it may furnish the least expensive path. If your risk capital is limited to a few hundred dollars, no stand-in may come forth.

Most funds solicit only a small investment. The minimum is usually $500. One private fund in Florida sells $5,000 participation units. Four or five in Chicago and a couple in New York privately elicit $100,000-$250,000 per respondent. Small clubs may decree less per individual, but I am not aware of any professionally managed fund that accepts less than $500 per investment unit. If risk capital is restricted, fund investing allows you to learn-by-doing one step removed from the action.

Buying into a fund does give the investor the benefits of expensive management and access to extensive analysis that can only be purchased for substantial sums. By spreading these fixed costs over a large number of investors, the average research cost per investor diminishes. Pooling resources, a large number of investors can purchase services jointly at a lower average cost, which enhances the likelihood of making profitable trading decisions.

Another important aspect is money management. This valuable service preserves wealth, allocates capital to different risk levels, provides for reserves and other contingencies. Successful money management, as trading tool and service of the fund, heads the list of winners. Money management also means establishing second, third, and fourth lines of defense against adverse conditions and aggressively tracking profitable ones.

Consolidating small sums into a larger amount creates a better investment attitude. If you have ever suffered the pangs of losses and sleepless nights, or have enjoyed the exaltation of several successive wins, you will immediately recognize that adequate capitalization, coupled with a conservative trading program operated under rational control, can change a defensive approach into an aggressive *plan*, which includes periodic withdrawal from the market.

Diversification usually leads the list of advantages. While it is significant, I rank its importance lower. Diversification is accomplished by scattering investments among different categories of commodities and options, different markets for liquidity, and risk-aversion tactics to reduce total portfolio risk versus potential profit. Diversification also implies exchanging reserve funds for interest-bearing financial instruments, and, at times, even putting most eggs in one basket.

But funds also contribute to individual investment planning. A speculator may decide to dedicate three-fourths of his risk capital to his own system, one-fourth to a mutual fund. This method is like putting most of your money in a one-year certificate of deposit and a smaller portion in an ordinary bank savings account. Both assets pay interest; one pays a higher rate than the other.

When Not to Invest in This Type of Fund

If you prefer doing your own thing, then, of course, mutual funds will hamper your style. I have talked with speculators who frankly told me that investing in a professionally managed fund would be the sensible way to stop their losses, but they enjoy the game's excitement too much to throttle themselves.

Begin by investigating the fund's management capabilities, its research resources, and its ability to perform. Checking its performance record will provide some insight into the past but promises little for the future. Don't be afraid to ask questions, but ask questions that are relevant.

In studying management, do not press for any guarantees of profit. They cannot guarantee a profit. They should, in fact, fully advise you that all of your money can be lost through unprofitable trades. If a fund (or even a broker) *guarantees* a profit, get it in writing. You have nothing to lose as long as the fund is solvent. That is a legal and binding contract. On the other hand, if the fund "guarantees" a profit—a no-risk deal—*caveat emptor.*

Determine management's objectives. Does it specialize in a limited group of commodities? Are the fund's goals compatible with yours? You may, for instance, locate a fund that specializes only in foreign-currency markets, or trades only in spreads and straddles, or concentrates only in grains. If you personally trade only net positions in meats and eggs, putting part of your risk capital in a fund diversifies speculative activities.

Additionally, the facilities of management must relate to its objectives. Complicated, expensive equipment does not necessarily mean better trades. I know of a small fund that operates out of a basement office in a private residence with only a "personal ticker." It has operated very profitably for several years. But you do want to know of the firm's ability to employ economic analysis, technical interpretations, and models, if any.

Finally, carefully examine the terms of the contract. Are fees and charges within the range you are willing to pay? Especially check on the extent of your liability. You should not have to pay in more than your initial obligation if management fails to trade well. This contract feature is many times more important than trading record; a track record can be falsified or manipulated.

Also, does the contract call for investment pledges on a fixed schedule? And what are the penalties if you fail to transmit money on time? When in doubt, don't invest. Look for another fund.

Earning money depends upon correct interpretation of information, analysis, and timing of entry into and exit out of the market. Participation in those earnings depends upon the integrity of the fund's management. But the correct decisions for earning your next $5,000 or $10,000 or $1 million ultimately rest on your shoulders.

SECTION G

Your Next Million Dollars

CHAPTER 22
Secrets of Speculation and Wealth Accumulation

There are no secrets in the commodity markets—only some closely guarded facts.

—A Chicago broker

MAKING A MILLION IN THESE MARKETS IS USUALLY ACHIEVED BY THE LONER. The independent establishes objectives different from those of a mutual fund, which strives for more conservative profit goals. Winners in commodity circles generally fall into one of two categories: the flamboyant plunger and the bookish recluse, with a sufficient number of intervening types.

It is not my prerogative to mend your trading personality. You should already know where you get your kicks. I only set you adrift on possible routes to nirvana; you are the helmsman.

Since we seem to be caught up in that interminable rotation of the wheel of fortune and fate, with control over our own lives always seemingly just beyond our jurisdiction, riches result from taking advantage of opportunities (rather than creating them), regardless of the momentary phase of our manic-depressive cycle. The trick is to hang onto the slimy lucre that so easily slides and slips through our grasping hands.

Real wealth accumulation during a protracted period of our lives surges from exercising substantial control over our own existence. If you still have not made it into the big time, I assume that your total wealth is more or

307

less correlated to the degree of self-discipline and stabilization you have achieved until now. The rules developed in this chapter do not hinge on your biorhythmic cycle. Trading can be done at any time. Keeping losses to a manageable level and retaining wealth become another matter.

Accepting Unprofitable Trades

While the oft-repeated rule of cutting losses and letting profits run is sound advice in theory, how is it converted into dollars and sense?

In the first place, the public usually opts for the opposite appropriation—luxuriant losses, unreplenished profits. All trades are not necessarily profitable. Effective money management will keep you in the game long enough to receive a shot of profit vitamins from time to time.

As a practical matter, effective money management translates into deciding how much to lose, restricting losses on each trade to some proportion of total available risk capital. This attitude may seem negativistic. Since we want to earn profits, the total trading program must be thought of in terms of asset preservation. You may think: "I'm not interested in just preserving my assets. I want my stock of wealth to grow!"

The ordinary person is unaware that individual wealth is not a static thing. He puts money into a savings account. Unmindful of inflation, he expects to draw out the same sum several years later. He buys land. He envisions growth in value with expansion of the city, unmindful that changes in value may be faster or slower in alternative investments. The city may even expand northward instead of southward. He suffers a loss. He pays substantial transaction costs for converting liquid assets into land and back again into a liquid form.

Someone once wrote that a small piece of gold owned two thousand years ago, and compounded at 3 percent annually, today would equal in size all solid celestial bodies seen by the naked eye. I never bothered to check his calculations. Values are ephemeral, and, therefore, so is wealth. Material wealth results from correct anticipation of the whimsical behavior of the human beast in the general marketplace.

Obviously, nothing is forever, especially the tides and fortunes of men (and women). So it is no accident that few emerge wealthy. Two steps are involved: keep from losing what you have already accumulated; and, once you have thoroughly learned this lesson, acquire more at a rate faster than the speed at which you previously stored wealth.

In commodity trading the dilemma is this: big money is most frequently earned by taking advantage of long-term opportunities detected through accurate forecasting, and by possessing the funds and fortitude to stay with the trend. Since not every trade will be a profitable one, how much in losses should be absorbed?

A stop-loss placed too close to the entry price may take you out with a small loss even though your analysis subsequently proves correct. You will have satisfied one part of that famous dictum. Losses have been cut.

But a series of small losses leads to the same place that a few large losses will take you. On the other hand, if you have erred in analysis, failed to employ some stop-loss mechanism, you may end up with a few large losses. A few large losses differ little from many small ones.

Studying several markets you may discover a dozen or so profitable trades in a good year (fewer in a dull year). Most of them will be profitable, if you have done your homework well. A few will not generate profits. Your first decision is to take advantage of *all* of them.

A commodity trader told me about a similar situation. At the time he was manager of a brokerage office in Florida. One of his registered representatives exhibited a phenomenal winning record. The manager developed a simple trading plan: follow the leader. However, he violated an important principle mentioned in Chapter 13. Too many traders, having once developed a successful technique, tend to experiment too soon and gamble too much on the first draft of the scheme.

The manager decided he would selectively follow the leader. Instead of taking advantage of *all* trades he selected only some—the losing ones! How did he manage to lose? Something in his psychological time-frame caused him to desire to lose. Lose he did!

Coattailing, not necessarily easily practiced, requires either a certain degree of expertise or else complete mechanicalness. Of course, the lesson was well learned by the former manager. Today a successful trader, he owns a seat on one of the older exchanges.

Now let's say that the major premise in your trading plan states: "Always go for a major profit move." Where do you put your stop-loss? There are obvious places. Every chartist (and broker) can tell you where. But every chartist and broker can also use the same information to their advantage and to *your* disadvantage. It's another trading plan! Trading on the folly of others!

The fraternity is small enough for both frictions and fraternalism to develop. On one occasion a Merrill Lynch broker had fallen out of favor in one of the pits on a major exchange. Some other brokers decided to hassle the Merrill Lynch broker, so the story goes. An opportunity for a quick shove temporarily set the M-L broker off balance.

His *deck* (cards on which orders are written and filed according to price) went flying. His overhelpful associates immediately retrieved the valuable cards. Of course, they quickly observed prices on stop-loss orders. A flurry of selling followed. The price of the commodity was driven down low enough to trigger Merrill Lynch stop orders. Whatever score was being settled, karmic justice was immediately done.

On the other hand, if you have placed a stop-loss order at the "obvious" chart point, do not be surprised if there is a sell-off and your order is activated. Nothing dishonest has occurred. In fact, you can employ the strategy yourself. One variation would be as follows.

Assume that you hold ten contracts of December eggs at 50.50. The logical stop, according to chart analysis, is 48.00. (If you employ stops, don't place them on even money.) Let's say that fundamentals point toward higher egg prices. Instead of a stop at 48.00, you place an MIT order for another five contracts.

It is a variation of averaging-down—not an especially recommended practice since it violates the principle of adding to a losing position. However, the rationale of your trading plan transcends this rule. It transmutes the practice into a legitimate and logical procedure. In this mockup, if the next level of support is at, say, 44.00, you will want to use a close stop below 48.00 in case the 48¢ support area is penetrated.

If you prefer not to broadcast your plans, resort to a mental stop instead of placing an actual market order. But maintain contact with market events. Even so, how much should you risk losing? Proper perspectives and adequate capital override use of stops so close to the entry point that a minor dip will automatically take you out of the market. Allow amply for basing action if you accumulate positions during an incipient move. (Refer to Chapters 4 and 5 if you cannot recognize basing action.)

One approach to losses focuses on the canvassed security pledge. Using a percentage of initial deposit does defy some of the logic developed in this book. It disciplines the speculator to accept predetermined losses. The deposited token need not equal the minimum margin invited by the exchange or brokerage. I suggest that it match the full sum you underwrite a position with—your engaged capital (but not the entire amount you will sacrifice).

For example, if petitioned security deposit is $1,000 per contract, add 60 percent, or $600, to it. Your stake rounds off to $1,600. If security deposit demands are raised, or if your position deteriorates below maintenance margin, percentage of loss calculations, based on $1,600, will cover these contingencies.

Let's say that strategy allows for losses equivalent to 35 percent of funds ventured ($560 per contract). Your stop-loss will be placed near a point that approximates a $560 loss, consistent with chart formations.

With an original trading fund of $5,000, a $560 loss amounts to 11.2 percent of capital. This stop-loss strategy stresses money-management principles framed earlier in the book. A 11.2 percent loss still leaves plenty of cash with which you can remain in the game.

You understand, I presume, that the nature of stop-losses, for reasons already stated, does not guarantee precise execution of the order. Nevertheless, the technique essays to conserve trading capital.

Market Vane's "Contrary Opinion" service advises not to use close stops when the position is first initiated in order to avoid potential whiplash. Good charting practices can help you escape from a losing position.

A variation of reversal charts, a takeoff on the Trend-Master Method, focuses on changes as a percentage of token money, or sum pledged to a position. You can construct a point-and-figure stop-loss chart by valuing each square 5 percent of earnest money. Using the above $1,600 figure, each chart square equates to $80. A sweep over twenty squares wipes out your complete commitment. Movement over eight squares triggers your stop-loss. Seven squares matches 35 percent, $560 of your original $1,600.

If you prefer using eight-square graph paper, let each square equal 12.5 percent of $1,600. Eight squares bracket $1,600; three squares activate the stop-loss.

The point-and-figure chart of each traded commodity can also be tied into total risk capital—$5,000 in these examples. Denote each square in each commodity as 2 percent of $5,000, or $100. No matter whether you trade shell eggs, silver, greasy wool, and potatoes simultaneously, each square on each chart accommodates $100. A six-square range, 12 percent of trading capital, establishes the amount of losses you are willing to absorb for each commodity traded.

The above chart variations are recommended as a disciplining tool. Shamefully glaring, they telegraph that price is headed the wrong way. For added emphasis, when price wanders in your favor, X each square in black. Unfavorable action merits red. Plainly mark in green, or some other color, where the stop-loss order should be entered.

If these types of charts interest you, I suggest you write to Trend-Master Commodity Forecasts, 4500 Campus Drive, Suite 110, Newport Beach, California 92660, for an introduction to Trend-Master point-and-figure-chart formations.

Ignoring All the Above Rules

A frustrating affair in the lives of many people is to learn a set of rules and subsequently discover that the best results are obtained by breaking hard-learned conventions. Most individuals fail to understand that a system built on human tenets springs from a set of assumptions. As long as assumptions hold, principles will apply. Sometimes referred to as exceptions, going against precepts can fecundate outstanding opportunities.

Mechanically following any tenet leads nowhere. Understanding the original intent or basis for a principle, acting with awareness, separates the thinking person from the automaton. First of all, understand the underlying reasons and assumptions of the recipes you have discovered. Next, interpret maxims according to each situation.

In the pages just preceding, I suggested adding to a losing position—in violation of a good rule—under circumstances, or assumptions, described in that particular case. Suppose, using the figures from page 310, that the price continues its descent to 46¢. Buying more egg contracts at 46¢ is no longer sound, while buying contracts at both 48¢ and 44¢ may be sound, based upon conditions and circumstances thought to exist. In other words, don't be foolish. But take calculated risks if your total speculative portfolio can bear them.

Interpreting rules within a very narrow context, ignoring the role of changing assumptions, will surely produce losses, or, at the very best, only small profits. On the other end, a very liberal interpretation produces no rules at all—investment anarchy. Nevertheless, fully aware of the possible consequences, you may experimentally violate certain rules.

A story about the famous speculator Jesse Livermore illustrates the potency of acting on individual assessment contrary to the senses. One day, during a stock market boom when prices were rising faster than smoke, the famous speculator walked into his broker's office and ordered him to sell short some San Francisco stock. The broker corrected, "You mean 'buy,' don't you, Mr. Livermore? You said 'sell.' " "No, I meant exactly what I said—sell two thousand shares." Exasperated but compelled to comply, the broker sold short two thousand shares of the San Francisco firm.

The next day, Jesse Livermore returned. To the broker he seemed to have an odd expression on his face. When his client shorted another thousand shares the broker insisted: "But, Mr. Livermore, the price of everything is going up. Everybody's buying. Prices are going much higher. Things are booming in San Francisco. You sure you're not making a mistake?" The story goes that although Jesse Livermore was acting somewhat strangely, he still insisted on being short.

On the third day the previous day's performance was repeated. Obviously rumors began circulating that the famous speculator had taken leave of his senses. On the fourth day, the earthquake struck San Francisco; you know who was right. Breaking the rules? It paid off in this instance. Where did Jesse Livermore obtain his information? The next chapter provides the key to all successful speculator's "luck."

Can chart patterns fail the predictive test? You already know the imperfections of the method; however, let me indicate an area which can substantially alter chart formations. If more controls on commodity trading occur—for example, an SEC-type watchdog over commodities markets—look for *changes* in chart patterns caused by the restrictions and limitations placed on professional traders.

Floor brokers, certainly, are targets of impending legislation and ultimate controls. This group furnishes much short-term market action. They contribute to the liquidity of these markets. The absence of their activity will alter trading patterns. Therefore, old interpretations of chart formations will need to be modified.

Each and every principle must be weighed in accordance with the rule's validity, its application to your situation and objectives. Overtrading is undoubtedly a dangerous practice. Yet I recognize its practice in the trading plans of some readers. If trading capital is limited, what other choice do you have? And if you decide on short-term scalping, your outlook—therefore, the plan under which you operate—will differ considerably from the long-termer's horizon.

Scalping for Short-term Profits

Scalpers are brokers in the pit who trade on their own account for very small price changes. An active scalper may be in and out of the market, on both sides of it, several times daily. His clearing fee measures only about one-tenth of your day-trade commission. Keeping alert and dumping a losing position quickly when sentiment in the pit (or ring) changes, he squires small losses. For him a $100 change represents a big move. The terms *uptrend* and *downtrend* are meaningless outside his circle of operations. Scalping may be his principal source of livelihood. Living well means being right.

Day-trading may be your cup of tea. Although you cannot function on the same level with a scalper, you are, nevertheless, competing with him. This information should serve as fair warning. You are competing with professionals, but with several disadvantages.

His transaction costs may be only $2 or $3, while yours may be $20 or $25. He works full time at his endeavor and probably has been for several years. How does that compare with your situation? He is closer to the source of action, which means he not only absorbs the opinions of associates but also senses or feels impending changes in prices, directly observing the behavior of other brokers. He reacts rapidly to new inputs of data.

To day-trade suggests that chart action must be recorded in finer detail than for longer-term trades. One-square reversal charts perform well for this purpose if they are maintained accurately intraday and day-by-day.

Employing a part-time chartist (a college student, for example) will free you of the task of score-keeping to concentrate on strategy. Your competition does. I know of one broker in Chicago who retains three full-time secretaries who chart; he trades only for his own account.

When prices trend well—that is, when they fluctuate within a fairly narrow but well-delineated channel—scalping from point-and-figure charts is fun and profitable. Most profits are generated by bucking the trend. Here I am writing of action within the channel, not the intermediate-term trend.

For example, as prices oscillate upward within a channel, you assume they will reverse at or before they reach the upper resistance line. Place an order in advance to sell if a certain price is touched. (Scalping from a distance can only be accomplished by placing the order in advance. By the time a price is reached and is communicated over your leased equipment, and you then telephone the floor with your order, market action will have shifted price away from the point. You will have missed your chance.) Naturally, you must also predetermine the buy point from your charts in order to make the system viable.

Sooner or later, however, prices will edge or catapult out of the channel. You will have experienced a loss. Then a new channel is formed. New opportunities arise.

One way of reducing risks: day-trade only from one side of the market. For example, if the intermediate trend is ascending, prices will be working back and forth within this up-slanted channel. Forgo opportunities to short. Only accept trades from the long side. When prices break through to oscillate within a newly created channel, your chances of losses are reduced; your chances of larger profits are expanded.

Day-trading does furnish more possibilities to stretch risk capital. Some brokerage firms suggest less security deposit for day-trades because risk exposure is reduced. Some are very strict. They will not permit you to trade without the full amount on deposit. Others may ignore your account balance as long as you are not debit.

Whether it is an advantage or disadvantage, you can swing some big numbers with considerably less capital. And a small profit on many transactions is just as good as a large profit on one speculation.

Most concede that short-term traders usually lose. I'm not convinced that such a distinction is so easily rendered. Furthermore, no established evidence shows whether short-term traders lose because of their time-horizon or because of personality type.

Unless you are a floor broker, you do operate under handicaps. The game is rigged in favor of your competition. But the advantages of being out of the market at the close of each day, the excitement of frequent trading, and the lower capital requirements may offset these short-comings.

Buying and Selling on News

Suppose that everyone possessed perfect information about future demand and supply of commodities. The *raison d'être* of the markets would disappear. They would cease to function unless another group of poorly informed investors came along. So of what value is news about commodities?

News is published in newspapers, but experienced traders act on it when it is initially transmitted by the wire services. Information available to everyone has little or no value. The futures market has an uncanny ability to discount future events well before they are cognized by very many. Someone, somewhere, of course, does know something. He, or they, has acted on that knowledge. Futures prices reflect their actions.

Generally, the future has been discounted back to the present before very many investors find out about important events. By the time the majority learns a piece of news, it is already too late—after the fact. The majority is always wrong.

The exception to the above is when, for some reason, information has not been properly interpreted. Opportunities exist even late in the game.

An example is President Allende's downfall in Chile. Even when it became obvious that Allende's coalition Marxist-radical government was nearing collapse, the price of copper still languished. Traders lacked an understanding of Chilean politics, the debt-ridden Chilean economy, the unlikelihood of reversing expropriation proceedings, the attitudes of Chilean workers, and the actual condition of the chief mines. When news of Allende's suicide came over the wire, the opportunity to buy copper for a quick turn presented itself. Within fifteen minutes copper was priced limit up.

Once again, what are the rules? For prices to change appreciably, some people must know something. Enough of them have acted. If you possess information you should first determine whether the news is unique. If the information is not already in the price, then you must decide whether the news, when it becomes widely disseminated, is significant enough to induce a substantial number of investors to act.

Scouting New Opportunities

Speculative opportunities abound in commodities; they only await discovery. Most of them are not new, however. The combination has probably been examined before. But if you are a recent arrival to this investment form, scout opportunities until you meet with one or several that appeal to your interests. Holding net positions, of course, offers only one trading tactic.

Straddling crude coconut oil and bean oil has been propounded previously. Straddles among substitute products are followed by professionals. The idea may be new to you. Several possibilities were mentioned in Chapter 15. Now let's compare coconut oil and soybean oil prices.

Coconut oil is traded on the Pacific Commodities Exchange, soybean oil on the Chicago Board of Trade. Both contracts consist of sixty thousand pounds; trading hours are the same. Coconut oil is squeezed from copra, the dried meat of the coconut, which yields 62-66 percent oil and 33-34 percent meal. In Chapter 15 you learned that crushing soybeans produces about 18 percent in oil, roughly 80 percent in meal.

These relationships are significant. For example, a $1 fluctuation per short ton of copra meal modifies the cost of coconut oil by less than .03¢ per pound. A $1 change per short ton of soybeans equals approximately .22¢ per pound of soybean oil.

What fundamental factors influence coconut oil's price? On the demand side, three separate markets must be considered. In producing countries it is employed primarily as an edible oil with insignificant competition from other vegetable oils. In Europe, basic use is edible, but it is also important in industrial products. In the United States, consumption is essentially as an industrial raw material. In fact, the U.S. Bureau of the Census and the Department of Agriculture classify it as a "soap oil." Nevertheless, increasing quantities are used in imitation milk products, pastries, and shortening.

Therefore, in producing countries such factors as population growth and

315

income amelioration influence consumption. In Europe, coconut oil competes with other edible oils on a price basis; this market is more sensitive to changes in demand-supply relationships; worldwide adjustments are achieved largely in Europe. In the United States, demand is less elastic; that is, the market is less responsive to price changes. Because not much coconut oil competes directly with other oils, it commands a premium over soybean oil in its noncompeting uses.

Supply is affected by a long-term cycle. Five years pass from infancy to maturity plus one more year from the time the coconut palm blossoms until the nut is harvested. Year-to-year supply, however, can vary sharply due to weather—typhoons and droughts. Therefore, storms and rainfall statistics bear close study. Either of these caprices of nature can affect production for one or two years.

Although the prices of coconut oil and soybean oil tend to move in the same direction, special conditions can cause them to deviate. This presents interesting opportunities to straddle. The chart in Figure 68 summarizes the average prices of both products from January 1960 to May 1974. Generally, coconut oil sells at a premium over soybean oil.

Beginning in early 1960, GSA began selling crude coconut oil from its stockpiles. These sales continued through 1963. In the fall of 1962, major copra-producing areas suffered a drought. The typhoon "Welming" hit East Central Philippines in late 1966, followed by closure of the Suez Canal and the Six-Day War—all were pivotal in the sharp price rise through mid-1968.

Coconut oil prices steadily declined from the latter part of 1970 through the end of 1972. Supplies rose about 40 percent annually. With soybean production expanding, soybean oil prices during 1972 rose to about a 1¢ premium. Copra production leveled off in 1972. It declined in 1973. Figure 68 is a pictograph of the results of demand and supply interacting. Additionally, poor outputs of sunflower oil in Russia, peanut oil in India, and fish oil from Peru created shortages of fats and oils.

Other price factors include crushing margins, already mentioned, and cost of insurance and freight. A freight increase of $14 per long ton on copra will raise the cost of imported coconut oil by 1¢ a pound. A third factor, import duties, is now less significant. Copra is duty free. Preferential treatment for oil ended this year (1974) for the Philippines; a flat import duty of 1¢ per pound is now imposed across the board.

While a straddle between these two markets is beset with risks, the combination of demand and supply factors makes absorbing study. Of course, both markets must be examined, with substitute products taken into account, and it must be realized that while the United States is an importer of coconut oil, it is an exporter of other fats and oils. While the potential is attractive, this situation cannot be entered into haphazardly. You do require information, but . . .

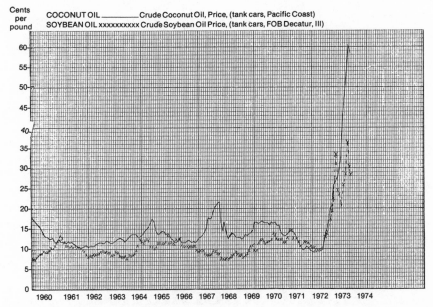

Fig. 68. Comparison of coconut oil and soybean oil prices (Source: Pacific Commodities Exchange, Inc.)

Developing Distrust of Outside Sources

Once you attune yourself to these markets, you will receive an enormous amount of "news" and "information" which can confuse you as much as help you. How much trust should you place in these data? Very little, if any!

If you read much at all, often-conflicting news, commodity letters, and free advice will just get in the way of listening to the voice of the market. You need to know what the market is saying, not the confusion of Babel. No one who puts his decisions in the hands of others succeeds for very long.

Each person, pursuing his own self-interest, is not at all interested in whether you lose or win. Losers are scorned. Winners evoke envy. And if you are receiving a lot of cheap advice, what else can you expect for a nickel?

You do need research tools, however. Purchasing commodity advisory services may cause you to approach an analysis from a different viewpoint. Expect to pay a good price for adequate data. Worthwhile services are worth their price. Nevertheless, the final decision is yours! There is no substitute for making that final act to buy, to sell, to stand aside. All the outside news you acquire can be an important tool in your business. Information on big windfalls, however, comes from the inside.

317

CHAPTER 23
Methods of Developing Inside Information

As soon as you trust yourself, you will know how to live.
—Johann Wolfgang von Goethe

THIS VERY IMPORTANT CHAPTER REPORTS ON THE THIRD KEY TO CONSIST-
ent success. It tells the secret of all speculators' "luck." Some investors
accidentally stumble onto these skills, and in such cases the discoverers
operate intermittently because they do not understand the causal relationships. Others unknowingly exploit these tactics for a brief period, amass
a considerable sum, and arrogantly believe their own superior games-
manship created wealth. Lasting luck, however, is not accidental. It demands continuous dynamism. This chapter particularizes specific instruction
to gain predictive and cognitive skills, so that you can chain the wheel of
fortune and fate.

Trust Yourself

Success in commodity speculation emanates not only from practical
abilities but also from development of a psychological framework that
prompts you to benefit from seizing time's forelock. Abilities evolve from
application to actual cases of many of the techniques described in this book.

Owing to the impatience and restlessness of the budding speculator,
however, experimentation without much study will lead to certain losses;

subsequently, a little more study and purchases of cheap research services, and further defeats and despair follow. Try again if you now recognize the cost of success!

The cheapest way to encounter the practical nature of speculation is through elaborate and extensive paper-trading, maintenance of records, and charting, along with a modest amount of study. Continued attention will give you a deeper desire to develop practical abilities, and finally will lead into theories and discovery of the forces that cause prices to gyrate.

Success, then, centers on acquiring abilities associated with technical and fundamental analysis, self-training to sculpt a winning attitude, and, most importantly, insight to recognize opportunities into whose path you have flung yourself through an ordering of your life.

Harry cannot do it for you. Neither your broker, banker, nor barber can do it for you. You alone are responsible for yourself! No one else can answer for trading decisions made by you or authorized in your name. No one else is responsible for the results when you tot up the score on the bottom line.

Your are now the sum total of all you have ever believed true. You are the creator of profitable conjunctures, not by market manipulation but by organizing your life in a manner that establishes you at the right place and moment to triumph over existing circumstances. Since you have built your providential spaceship, you have earned it—so collect your profits. Sweep out into interstellar space and pluck your riches from among the flocks of stars pasturing on the long savannahs of the blue.

And what source inspires these victories? The great scientist J. C. Bose says creative persons know that "the true laboratory is in the mind, where behind illusions they uncover the laws of truth." What is true for the scientist is equally true for the investor.

Most people exercise only a small fraction of their innate power. In fact, we can readily observe three types of human conditions: the haves, have-nots, and I-don't-cares. Affluence is natural to the investor who comprehends relationships among forces and demonstrated effects on the market.

But most people are satisfied with just getting by. They vegetate in a dream world of gryphons and the Queen of Hearts; or they are stymied by their inability to make decisions and act upon them.

> Anon, to sudden silence won,
>   In fancy they pursue
> The dream-child moving through a land
>   Of wonders wild and new,
> In friendly chat with bird or beast—
>   And half believe it true.[1]

1. Lewis Carroll, *Alice's Adventures in Wonderland* (New York: Modern Library, n.d.), p. xvii.

Even if you have suffered a series of misfortunes, you must refuse to be apprehensive. Diagnose slumps. Sort out your good and bad tendencies. Develop deep calmness. Increase your receptivity of intuition. Match-winning speculators know this source of profitable decision-making although they may refuse to talk about it. Or they may only know that their system works but fail to understand it adequately to articulate it.

The power of self-control, of trusting in yourself after proper and thorough preparation, leads to halcyon days. And once you develop a profitable system, duplicate it. Be slow to change as long as the system is fertile. Experiment cautiously. Until you are able to command yourself to do things that you should but may not want to do, you are not on the way to becoming a master speculator. But once you have learned the way, thrust in the sickle for the harvest is ready for taking.

Train Your Mind

On the other hand, suppose you have already delivered large sums to the commodity markets. Your stomach still flip-flops when you recall the miscarriages. Your wife becomes irate if she even spies you reading the commodity page of the newspaper.

Obviously these markets still fascinate you: You read the paper at the office to keep peace on the homefront; the fact you are reading this book indicates an ongoing interest. But should you ever trade again? I mean for keeps?

A trouncing should stimulate you to try again (and again) until struggles render remedial results. If you hit the wrong target before—whether on one trade or on several—analyze every factor in the situation in order to eliminate all chances that the error may be duplicated in the future. Now I recognize that such laborious exertion is time-consuming, certainly not very exciting. On the other side of the coin, did you actually enjoy taking the last loss on the chin?

If you analyze yourself deeply enough, you may come across a remarkable revelation. You may learn that you have alternately demonstrated prowess and panic in various financial transactions according to your habitual train of thoughts. Answer truthfully, Which in you has prevailed recently—thoughts of winning or thoughts of losing? Yogananda has clearly stated the key: "Success or failure is the just result of what you have done in the past, *plus* what you do now."

Neither is it all Georgia peaches and Wisconsin cream for those who have made it. Some flushed speculators I know have had to contend with bigger problems than failures do. Winners train themselves to reject thoughts of losing *at all times*. Easy to do?

Here is what happened to one trader. He had made $4 million speculating. Last year, getting caught in a squeeze, he lost slightly more than $2 million. How would you have reacted?

It is easy to think: "Oh, if I had only quit when I had the $4 million in hand, I could have comfortably retired." As they say in Central America: "A bird in hand is worth a thousand flying." You may think that the remaining $2 million still represents a lot of bread, but how would you react if 50 percent of *your* capital was wiped out!

The point? Keep your mind unprejudiced and unbiased. Your mind is like a camera. Wriggling a camera with indecisive movements blurs the film; holding it steady—not jerking it around with hasty judgments—produces a clear picture.

How can you become a champion soon? Reaping the harvest is hastened or hampered by habits. Thoughts are mental magnets. Right habits will draw to you correct information, a cooperative and informed adviser, ability to recognize opportunities, and unbiased judgment. That is, people and conditions necessary to feather the nest will be attracted to you according to your habitual thought patterns.

You doubt that? Prove it for yourself if you have money for experimentation. Like the statement set forth in a book advertisement, the author challenges, "Maybe I'm wrong, but what if I'm right?"

Some popular clichés offer "proof" of the efficacy of this system. For instance: The rich get richer but the poor get poorer. Yes, the rich get richer—because once they start the creative force flowing to form a success pattern, they repeat it to breed more triumphs.

The importance of training your mind to claim victory follows from the fact that material manifestations always trail psychological assumptions. If you let your mind accept the thought that you are a loser, you are defeated.

A commodity trader who *fears* he may abort will be led to choose risky trades. He will buck all logic—charts, fundamentals, advice, trend of future prices, information—like Taurus, the bull. If he raps with other traders, they circumambulate in the same circle—a vicious circle at that. Of course, he blames everyone else for his stillborn. The real cause lies in the trader's built-in attitude. He walks, talks, and acts like a nonstarter.

You may be thinking: "I'm not like that man. I feel like a winner. I do my homework and carefully plan each commitment. Still I haven't been very successful. Why is that so?"

Last century the sun-spot theory was propounded as a cause of business fluctuations. The moon's impress on the tides of oceans and people has been popularized. Ionization influences emotional states.

Mysterious sidereal waves do influence the sun and weather as well as the behavior of animals and humans. Studies indicate that certain types of persons react to particular wavelengths. There is a group of common waves; the masses respond to them.

You may not agree with the exact relationships, but different categories of professional people—physicists, botanists, financiers, economists, psychologists, for example—have observed this behavioral kinship. Roy Davis recently wrote: "Creative people know from experience that they are 'led' from opportunity to opportunity and that 'good fortune' just seems to happen to them. All parts of the universe are connected and we draw to ourselves exactly what we are in attitude and consciousnesses."[2]

A few people have mastered the mesmerism caused by these common forces. They have unchained themselves from circumstances that occupy the decisions of the unthinking masses.

Not all manifestations are identical. But the periodicity of events must certainly arouse the curiosity of at least some of our friends. The eighteen-year building cycle and fifty-four-year wholesale-price cycle suggest that different factors are interacting. Further, since not all behavior is identical, responses to the same waves must also differ.

Obviously it is not necessary to comprehend these mysterious forces in order to decide whether to buy rye or barley or sell lead or mercury. But it is necessary to acquire self-discipline and reflect a state of optimism. Tagore, the famous poet, wrote: "Pessimism is a form of mental dipso-mania, it disdains healthy nourishment, indulges in the strong drink of denunciation, and creates an artificial dejection which thirsts for a stronger draught."[3] And the poor get poorer!

Concentrate on Your Trades

After incurring losses, you must carefully plan your strategy, charge it with increasing intensity of attention, and carry it out with dynamic will-power. The natural tendency, of course, is to dwell on setbacks. Analyze liabilities, but focus attention on how they might have increased net worth. In other words, consider the right solution to the problem, not the problem of defeat itself. There is a difference in outlook!

After a time, you will discover that most washouts were actually near-wins. We come surprisingly close to milk and honey. Naturally, careful planning and persistence are major components. Oftentimes a minor alteration of one factor would have put us on the right track. This discovery alone can enable you to tackle the next situation with great vigor.

However, the rewarding technique is to trade correctly the first time. You should transfer your attention from plight to prosperity, from worry over past pain to calmness on your future fortune, from restlessness of mind to energy-producing thoughts, from mental wanderings to concentration.

Unerring investors devote considerable time to deep concentration on matters that concern conservation and growth of wealth. They are not willy-nillys. They do not scatter their energies.

Winners can dive deeply within their minds to float up the best solu-

2. Roy Eugene Davis, *Time, Space, and Circumstance* (New York: Frederick Fell, 1973), p. 105.

3. Rabindranath Tagore, *Sādhanā* (Tucson: Omen Press, 1972), pp. 52-53.

tions for each situation. If you learn to withdraw your attention from all distractions—whether they happen to be mini-skirts, office hubbub, jangling telephones, nagging wife, or noisy kids—and to concentrate on one thing—namely, commodity futures trading—you will learn how to attract the right information at will. But accomplishment does require practice.

Most people, naturally, find it difficult to concentrate in their usual environments. At the office the distractions of business certainly demand attention; at the broker's office the hustle and bustle of activity can cause confusion; late in the evening your body easily succumbs to that tempting demon of escape—sleep. I sympathize with you. It is not a problem easily overmastered.

If you trade frequently, concentration on each situation is imperative. If you trade only occasional special situations, you may find more time and seclusion to deliberate.

One registered representative I know literally closets himself. He carries the telephone into a broom closet and cracks the door just enough to watch the board. Eccentric? Possibly. But not likely at age thirty. He already knows the importance of concentration.

Try to gossip with a pit broker during trading hours; he won't even recall having seen you. Why? There are 168 hours in a week. Roughly twenty of these hours are devoted to making it. Don't you believe those twenty hours merit your full attention? Enough time remains in the other 148 for play.

While you are active in these markets, make everything serve your main objective—to win. If the market charges against you, pay more attention than ever to achieving the best solution. Concentrate on every reasonable alternative. Whenever you withdraw your attention from a situation, you allow it to disintegrate. Concentration on circumstances of good fortune will keep them in existence.

Wherever you direct your attention, you build. You can erect a destructive or constructive framework. The whole trick is to devote all of your willpower to mastering one situation at a time. Do not be a flibbertigibbet and scatter your energies. Neither should you walk away from a new investment once you have committed funds (for real or for practice).

If you experience difficulty in focusing your attention for prolonged periods, I suggest you tackle this problem first. There are several excellent books on the subject. A few months devoted to ironing this kink out of your personality is time well spent. Remember that even in this age of affluence, only 0.1 percent of the American population are inflation-dollar millionaires. The builder of a better mousetrap needs mice to catch in it!

Consult with the Genie

Suppose that you know how to focus attention and conserve energy for speculative needs. Exactly from where does this information purl? "Will I recognize it?" I cannot predict precise channels. But I will relate the personal experiences of others and suggest some techniques; you may wish to experiment with them.

In the last chapter I retold the story about Jesse Livermore. Someone asked him, too, for his source of information on the San Francisco quake. He replied that he had not known about the impending earthquake. But a "voice inside" urged him to short that particular stock.

Many people have mentioned to me this "voice inside." Rarely does it manifest in audibles tones. Usually the individual "hears" it in the same sense when he "talks to himself." Here is the *caveat* of it.

A person who imagines he hears voices is deluding himself. He may as well play the Ouija board; the results would about match. An imagined voice is a feedback from the conscious mind.

I refer to a deeper level—the voice of intuition, which derives its information from sources the conscious mind cannot tap. If you never experience the urging of an intuitive voice, you are not alone. There are other methods to contact this source.

One day last year, at the height of red-meat prices, an analyst walked into his office and announced, "Fellows, we're at the start of a bear market and no one knows it." "How do you know?" was the natural question. He answered, "Last night I dreamed of a bear—a huge bear standing on his hind legs. It was very vivid. I never have dreamed about bears before. The message was clear." His comments met with the expected guffaws. Meat prices went straight down.

If you are a scoffer, let me remind you that I know of a corporation formed a few years ago for the sole purpose of trading on the dreams of one of its corporate officers. They incorporated with $4,000. In slightly more than three months they had driven this sum to $180,000. The strange sequel to this event is that the believers became doubting Thomases. They did not really believe inwardly what they manifested outwardly.

One speculator of the corporation dreamed about a giant move in a commodity. Had they accepted the trade they would have multiplied their investment to nearly $500,000 within another few months. Instead of listening to the intuitively derived dream, they consciously planned. Egoism caused them to take a position opposite to the dream. They promptly dropped $100,000 in the market.

If there were sufficient space I would relate several other brief stories, startling and fantastic. But you will benefit more if I give directions on how to contact these intuitive sources.

There are many methods. I will only mention four which have been successfully experimented with. These methods are not shortcuts. They entail hard work. There is no such thing as something for nothing. Extensive study is still necessary. In fact, studying, charting, analyzing, and reading seem to saturate the mind and trigger this mechanism under the right conditions.

In general, the method requires a long period of concentration during which time the entire issue is stated carefully. Review all the chief facts. Examine the anticipated trade in detail with everything you know about it. State the desired end result, but do not think about means for achieving it. Open the trapdoor of your subconscious mind. Drop the whole ball of wax into it with a command to take care of the matter, believing with complete confidence that it will be. Afterwards, *forget about it.*

It is important not to revive the matter for frequent review. The answer may reveal itself in any one of several ways: A newspaper article may stand out, a statement made by your financial adviser, something read, sudden revelation like a flash in the mind, a dream, or even the sound of an inner voice—all are prototypes in which answers reveal themselves.

If you repeat these steps in a regular place and time, you may force results sooner. Use these steps in each example below. First, employ your talents in the best possible manner. Research adequately, do your homework regularly, study everything about the commodity, understand general market conditions. Second, clearly state the entire issue. A simple statement that you want to trade coconut oil will not suffice. Details! Third, do not expect a free ride. Your subsequent experiences will only equal your mental-consciousness capacity. Fourth, expect successful fulfillment. Fulfillment is natural to the investor who accepts his nature and uses his intelligence and intuition with wisdom.

Try this method in a room where you will neither be distracted by noise nor fear interruptions. Work with lights lit, subdued, or off, as you prefer. If you can cut off the telephones and instruct your secretary not to disturb your period of concentration, the office may briefly provide a quiet sanctuary. A chapel, a private room in a library, or a place in your home may furnish the desired environment.

Follow the steps given above. With a pen and paper in front of you (or a Dictaphone may work), concentrate deep enough, long enough, for answers to come through. When thoughts begin pouring out, record them immediately. Many people besides investors have found this method helpful in solving all major problems.

Or after retiring at night, just prior to sinking into sleep, repeat the above steps. This time, with eyes closed, visualize a blackboard (or chalkboard) in your mind's eye. Be sure that you can "see" the blackboard clearly, in detail. Ask your question so that it can be answered with a short response. Request that the answer be written upon the blackboard. The eeriness of seeing an answer being written on the blackboard may startle you out of your concentration and destroy the vision. Try again only when you are prepared to accept solutions.

The third method is dreams. If you want to develop a talent for investment-related dreams, again duplicate the four steps above. Just before dropping off to sleep, command your subconscious mind to produce the desired type of dream. Ask it to furnish the correct answer. As you slip into a somnolent state, keep echoing "answer, answer, answer . . ." Rehearse every night until you achieve denouement.

The fourth method requires more time. I do not recommend it unless you are prepared for the unusual. Assemble a group of financial advisers (living or dead). Learn about each one thoroughly. Read his biography if it is available. In your mind's eye, during twilight of sleep, imagine that your group of, say, six financial advisers meets to discuss your investments. You must remain chairman of your committee no matter how great are the personalities you have called upon. Imagine them to be real people with facial expressions, animations, and alive in every way.

Call the meeting to order. Thank each one for coming. And then, one by one, request the particular qualities of his that you want impressed on your mind. In other words, choose your advisers so that each has different qualities which you do not possess but would like to acquire. In time, as you energize them, these figures of imagination will take on individual personalities. You will notice a change within yourself as you begin to annex these desired traits. Do not fear the outcome.

An excellent combination of methods is Number 4 followed by Number 3. After you have consulted with your imaginary financial advisers, visualize the blackboard and request a specific answer to your investment question. The combination plan produces good sequels.

Before committing any important sum of money to commodity markets, sit quietly. Think how you can make it grow. Lull all senses and thoughts. It is very important that you disconnect your central mind from incoming trunk lines of your five physical senses. Subdue thoughts until they no longer jump around like a chained monkey. Then concentrate deeply. You will be guided by a great creative power. Afterwards you should utilize all material means to achieve your financial objectives.

Choose Cooperative Consultants

If you select a group of imaginary financial advisers, you expect them to impart certain qualities to you. In the flesh you bank on no less. Build with the mastermind principle.

Speculation requires enlisting the assistance of others. At a minimum you will need a broker to execute your orders. You may add the services of a financial adviser and a tax accountant. You may even create a partnership. Whatever number of people you choose, they must cooperate to achieve your objectives in trading commodity, foreign-currency, or coin futures.

The key to power for such alliance is *harmony*. As Leonard Read would say, dialog is appropriate if the mutual goal is enlightenment; otherwise, each is engaged in useless talk. Unless the work of your consultants harmonizes to achieve what *you* want, they not only are useless to you but their opinions can interfere with your decision-making process.

326

The *raison d'être* of your group of consultants is to furnish you with knowledge, information, experience, training, and native ability that you may not possess. And here a cooperative wife can be a major asset. Wives cooperate well when they do not contribute to pressures during adversity. However, managing this alliance toward a harmonious, productive effort is your responsibility. You must take charge!

Guard Your Secret

Do not expatiate on failure or associate with those who do. Strive to feel and feed a sense of victory. Prating about your investments only scatters energy. It invites negative expressions from people who are envious, stupid, or just plain zeroes or even minuses. Success must be continually fed. You starve the creature when you fail to keep private matters private.

Look at what happened to the individual who gassed about the bear in his dream. Had he kept the matter to himself and confidently acted upon it, the opinions of others would have been unimportant. Not everyone thinks as you do. If you think like everyone else, you are part of the masses; no amount of instruction will convert you into a consistent winner.

If you constantly require reassurance from others, you are not ready to trade. If you must bolster your confidence with garrulity about a position, ignore the trade and wait for another opportunity. Reliance upon crutches and gossip reveals lack of insight.

Furthermore, if you are still deliberating whether to trade and divulge it to others who are not interested in your welfare, negative people can generate and transmit destructive energy. Such forces can interfere with your entire delicate decision-making mechanism. And that is a scientific fact!

This book has outlined the systems of pros. Winning means to develop a champion's profile. Skillful use of analytical tools implies learning techniques—broadly referred to as technical and fundamental analysis. Being consistently right requires contacting paranormal sources. To cap this dissertation, I have decided to write the final chapter on the subject of keeping wealth in your hands, where it should be safest.

CHAPTER 24
Ways of Preserving
Your Assets

The fault, Dear Brutus, is not in our stars, but in ourselves.

—Shakespeare

NOT JUST A FEW INDIVIDUALS WHO HAVE QUICKLY GARNERED MILLIONS in these markets give it all back, plus some, within a year or two through an epidemic of losing trades.

Now we have had epidemics many times before. Various plagues wiped out nearly half of the so-called civilized world. Taking a clue from medicine, the secret of controlling epidemics is to prevent them from flourishing. And if they do loom in one area, isolate, have plenty of vaccines on hand to inoculate generously.

Similarly, financial virulence must be insulated, defense mechanisms established, reliance on inner guidance promoted. Potential epidemics are sanitated through proper money management. Wealth preservation derives from investing in alternative sources. Defense mechanisms include scouting opportunities to not only immunize existing assets but to multiply wealth faster than others take it away. In the futures markets an investor can sterilize, pasteurize, purify, and multiply.

Of course, unless we recognize the source of all wealth and learn to contact that source, we only know that "the wind bloweth where it listeth, and thou hearest the sound thereof, but canst not tell whence it cometh, and whither it goeth" (John 3:8).

As Emerson wrote (see epigraph to Chapter 2), most men gamble with fortune, "and gain all and lose all, as her wheel rolls." Emerson advises us not to become elated when we unwittingly pluck a few thousand out of the market. Don't believe that happy days are here with a few lucky shots. "Nothing can bring you peace but the triumph of Principles."

The Roller-Coaster System

Applied to commodities, currencies, coins, and all other investment forms, Emerson's warning is likened to a roller-coaster. Have you ever been on a joy ride?

After buying a ticket, waiting briefly in line, you are finally seated on the amusement device—up front for thrills, farther back for "safety." The train is slowly dragged upwards by the chain. At times it seems to barely move. But you know it's advancing; the ground sinks farther away. With you expecting the chain to break at any moment to crash to the starting point, the concatenated vehicles finally level off. The top is reached. For a moment you sigh from the accomplishment of battle and the breath-taking view.

Now's the time to pull all stops—to make the big run. But down it spins. People scream. Cool wind rushes past as rapidly as precious gains disintegrate. Your stomach floats to the upper chestline. The first big down took less time than the big up, but, oh, what a sensation! At least you do not return to "Go."

But the wheel of chance rotates again; the coaster rolls upward. Not as far as before—not even a 50 percent retracement. There is a brief sensation that better days are preparing for you. The event raises your spirits. Do not believe it.

And the roller-coaster dips again. Down, up slightly, down again, up once more, then down, down, and the ride is over. The thrill is short-lived.

Thus the adventures of a speculator who wins at first. But the fickle finger of fate flags the high-flyer full flurry forward, falling faster and faster, facing finality.

In Chapter 1, I related the history of a roller-coaster victor. His ups pierced higher levels; his downs were successively higher as well. At least he was learning to speculate profitably and preserve some wealth along the way. Why can't asset accumulation be a smooth one-way street—always up?

The Transition Theory

I explain this disheartening state of affairs with the transition theory. Understanding it may flatten out dampening oscillations of the roller-coaster—a little less thrill and more asset preservation.

Most fortunes appear to be lost at the top of swings, primarily, and secondarily at the bottom of a trend. While patterns are being formed, previously accumulated funds tend to dissipate as the trader fails to recognize that the ride is over. New tickets must be purchased for more exhilaration. Why?

Back in Chapter 7, I mentioned that most models and systems work well only in a strongly trending market. Signals are mixed or false toward the end of a major move. Patterns are incompletely molded. Those just overcoming their psychological threshold begin initiating commitments on the wrong side of the swing. Others reverse positions prematurely. A period of distribution can confuse lions and fleas alike. The results are sad. Is there any protection against these circumstances?

The answer has been echoed in the halls of fame and infamy: when in doubt, stay out; or, picking tops and bottoms is dangerous; or, don't get piggish, etc. If you don't know where the market is headed, put your money in short-term, liquid instruments for a while.

No rule states that you must constantly spin the wheel. Your registered representative, of course, appreciates the commissions; but if you lose your money, he too suffers a setback. You will have to locate more funds; he will have to find a new client to replace you.

Long-term charts are useful in these matters. For example, a 5 X 5 point-and-figure chart records every turn, every bit of movement. A 10 X 30 and 20 X 60 further condense market action. A bar chart summarizes daily ranges with one vertical line. A weekly bar chart, naturally, tends to eliminate minor trends and minimize intermediate ones.

One method for long-term trades, to exclude much interim activity, is a point-and-figure chart based on settlement prices only. You can construct long-term ones from historical records by plotting the nearest option. When one month expires, begin with the next one. To exile some intermediate-term swings, choose for reversal an amount equivalent to 150 percent of daily limit.

For example, if daily limits on grains are 20¢, enter a reversal only when prices move one and one-half times, or 30¢. Long-term reversal charts induce proper judgment—at least furnish answers that may startle you occasionally. They are valuable to both long- and short-term traders.

Let's say a short-term trader in corn maintains a 1 X 3¢ reversal chart (under current conditions of market volatility) plus a 3 X 9 and a long-term, close-only, reversal chart. Intermediate and long-term traders may prefer a 2 X 6¢ plus settlement-price-only reversal chart. It helps to separate silk from tassel.

The One Surefire Method

While transition from uptrend to downtrend, or downtrend to uptrend, can clean out your war chest, the fault for failures lies within us. There are periods of testing our mettle—interim tests before final examination. But the path to the stars is through the brambles. *Per aspera ad astra.*

Until we control our will, direct our energies toward singular destinations, subdue those chancellors of God, cause and effect, our fortunes will mostly ebb, sometimes flow, like those of the mass of mankind. One sure-fire method is to take charge of our affairs. "In brief, Sir, study what you most affect" (Shakespeare).

Over twenty years ago, an individual taught me a system. He employed it to discover periods of euphoria and depression. He tagged his approach "muddying up the windshield." His theory was that ups and downs emerge from outside influences.

To learn when and by whom emotions are stirred, he suggested charting behavior hourly until a pattern develops. Upon discovering that someone is "muddying up the windshield"—causing negative reactions—forever kick him out of your life.

Unfortunately for the gentleman, his own charting pointed toward his wife as his problem. He divorced her after ten years of marriage. One year later his millionaire former father-in-law died, leaving his entire estate to his surviving, and divorced, daughter.

The system is easy to initiate. On graph paper, mark waking hours horizontally. Vertically record estimated emotional state. Halfway up draw a zero line. Above zero record plus one through ten; below register minus one through ten.

A minus ten represents extreme depression—the bridge-jumping point. Plus ten registers frenzied delirium—absolute mania. For many people, emotional states tend to oscillate between minus four and plus seven. However, figures are only guestimates—your personal assessment.

Each hour record how you feel. Periodically write on the chart what you were doing, whom you were with. Especially mark down circumstances causing noticeable deviation from ordinary humdrum rhythm. The results may alert you.

After a period of watching yourself, you may reduce your chart to a daily average of feelings. For the long term, a monthly-average chart reveals how moods change from year to year. Some months exhibit greater weaknesses than others.

I recommend the system for two reasons. Seldom do we actually observe ourselves for more than a few seconds, never more than a few minutes. Then we promptly forget to remember ourselves. We react mechanically most of the time.

Charting emotions allows introspection after the event. Never as adequate as on-the-spot inspection, it slowly increases self-awareness. The next obvious step is self-control. Of course, self-governance is not possible until we know what to direct. The system helps to flatten out the day's gyrations. It improves trading decisions.

The second benefit requires less self-work. Simply, do not trade or make important decisions when you are dominated by emotions (either up or down). The advice is tautologous; scrutinizing reactions means delaying actions.

If you have just suffered a major loss, don't pick up the telephone to place another order in a state of desperation. Believe me, it happens every day. It's frightening to see deliberate self-destruction to the point of writing bad checks, huge deficits, and loss of home, business, and transportation.

On your chart Wednesdays may register low points. Year-end festivities may bring high or low emotions. Stay out of the markets if your decisions are based on impulses. Mismanaged, sentient spontaneity will wreck you.

The win-lose profile in Chapter 2 is no fairy tale. This information sprang from actual study. The great speculators of the past all believed that the study of psychology exceeded statistics in importance.

A study of psychology begins with self, then others. Self-study dredges up experiences painful to remember. But an individual should never be ashamed to own he has erred. One philosopher suggested it means being wiser today than yesterday. Do you want to be a winner? For most readers the starting point is here.

The Second Surefire Method

Probably most readers expected a tip on a never-fail trade. Even if a trade produced successful results for ten consecutive years, the first time you try it, it may fail. One time I overheard a registered representative convincing a prospective client to open an account. "Over the past year, 90 percent of my trades were profitable," he confidently stated. "Well, if you're that good," asked the prospect, "why do you need my $5,000?"

However, there are rare occasions when a special friendship exists among individuals. For example, I know of a Chicago broker who took over speculative activities for some very close friends. Over the past six years he has earned over $500,000 for this family. Such rare friendship is extremely valuable—not for the financial results—for the creative force that flows from such an alliance.

"Never-fail" methods abound. Sometimes they work for one person. Two brothers—both house-painters—wanted to go to Florida and buy a small fishing boat. They correctly decided the fastest way to accumulate funds was commodity futures speculation, about which they knew nothing.

They opened two accounts. The broker, as best he could, gave them a short oral course on commodities and a few pamphlets to read. They developed a simple technique; they traded only silver. Whatever position one took, the other assumed an opposite trade, with close stops. The losing brother was stopped out; the winner stayed with his position. In two months they aggregated $10,000, closed out the accounts, and moved to Florida.

I'm *not* recommending this technique. Two uninformed traders accidentally reached a goal via the silver market. Had they continued speculating, losses would inevitably have occurred.

If you have developed an interesting technique I would welcome your correspondence. I can be reached through my U.S. address: Post Office Box 1266, Miami, Florida 33134.

Over the long haul, you depend upon self-acquired talents. Their acquisition is indispensable to success. There are no shortcuts. After creating a success pattern, duplicate it. No better method exists.

Preservation of assets also requires the same self-discipline. One trader in Chicago has an irrevocable method to retain profits above a certain amount. He places excess funds in an irreversible trust. His friends say that without this unalterable system he would have lost his winnings.

The Method Before and During a Depression

"The principles of successful speculation are based on the supposition that people will continue in the future to make the same mistakes that they have in the past" (Thomas F. Woodlock). The method before and during a depression centers on the folly of others, that uninformed investors continue to ante up.

Two ridiculous propositions usually mentioned with respect to economic collapses need to be discussed. The first proposition states that one should be long during economic booms and short during downswings—common stock-market advice by savants in the 1950s and 1960s. I'd be happy to follow the advice. Which commodities do I short? When does a depression begin?

Aside from the apparent fact that life-cycles of futures options yield substantial profits over fairly short periods, there is no guarantee that all commodities will head in the same direction *pari passu*. As for depression dates, some claim it began in late 1971-72 following various governmental interventions.

On page 127 of Harry Schultz's *Panics and Crashes* (Arlington House), a historical chart plots long-term and intermediate-term cyclical waves. I first made my own predictions privately available eight years ago; circumstances have not caused me to alter my projections.

The second misconception is that the imminent depression will parallel the Great Depression. I doubt that. Comparisons are forever being made between 1929-1933 and some current period. Similarity of circumstances predicts neither the course nor the duration of the next one.

Depressions are government-induced, prolonged according to the extent of interference. We could have high unemployment with low prices, high employment with high prices, higher taxes, severe shortages, and dangers to the life and property of all.

Essentially trading tactics are unchanged. Fundamentals point out the direction of prices; technical aspects assist in timing. I would anticipate thinner trading, possibly considerably less liquidity, in many contracts. As long as markets are allowed to continue functioning, profit opportunities will exist.

Over the next couple of years expect increasing volume in commodity, currency, and coin futures—possibly very dramatic, emotional movements in the market as inexperienced, uninformed investors are attracted into speculative activities. I believe these circumstances will enhance profit opportunities.

In the midst of financial panics, naturally enough, people withdraw from these markets. While many new commodities are being introduced at this time, interest in some will abate. The largest volume will continue in basic foodstuffs. Chart patterns may take longer to form or even acquire different shapes if governmental restrictions alter trading requirements. Swing with circumstances.

Of course, precious metals may take on an entirely new importance in conditions of crises. The first step is to learn to trade and preserve financial assets. The next step is to cause assets to grow. At this point I do believe that financial freedom can only be achieved through international diversification.

I suggest that you employ futures markets for two purposes: (1) to hedge foreign assets in the manner prescribed in previous parts of this book; (2) to use that small portion of your total wealth properly set aside for chancier situations to speculate in futures.

The element of risk is offset by potentially huge returns. The riskiest element of all is you. By now you should know the necessity of controlling and directing your own life, making decisions that are important to you and without which freedom is never possible.

The Royal Road to Financial
Independence and Freedom

Some individuals mistakenly believe that inheriting a huge sum generates freedom. "Man's freedom is never in being saved troubles, but it is the freedom to take trouble for his own good, to make the trouble an element of joy." The same author further advises, "We gain our freedom when we attain our truest nature. The man who is an artist finds his artistic freedom when he finds his ideals of art. Then is he freed from laborious attempts at imitation, from the goadings of popular approbation."[1]

From the beginning I encouraged you to develop your own system, make your own decisions, either create your own circle of advisers or join with others in a club or mutual fund which has common purposes in agreement with your aims.

1. Rabindranath Tagore, *Sādhanā* (Tucson: Omen Press, 1972), pp. 64, 74.

Initially, of course, you will be restricted to imitation. An artist usually begins training by studying the masters, various techniques, different media, tools of the trade, and finally learns to paint by copying famous works or imitating the techniques of those who have gone before.

Gradually, as he blossoms into professionalism, his paintings take on individual style, and unique techniques, and ideas manifest. He becomes a master when he frees himself from the confines of imitation and follows an independent course.

This is less true for commodity speculators; very few are leaders. Champions succeed. Their wealth grows. Their status becomes permanent. Wealth flows to them in seemingly endless fashion.

A slightly larger number follow leaders. They are mechanical men. But they awoke out of their sleep long enough to recognize shortcomings. They are awake enough to follow masters, but not sure enough to develop individually.

The third group, that large mass of humanity in a pitiful state, really believe they are awake, that they know the path to nirvana, that all answers are already in hand. The masses can only do what they are told. Not yet even stirring from their slumber, they cannot even hope to achieve the slightest amount of independence and freedom. "The average man has always been a loser more often than a winner in Wall Street."[2] And not only in Wall Street but in every other kind of investment form.

In the world of the masses, dreams get mixed up with reality. Chinese legend tells us about a philosopher who dreamed he was a butterfly. Since it was such a vivid dream, the philosopher became confused when he awoke. He did not know whether he was a man who had dreamed he was a butterfly or a butterfly who now was dreaming he was a man.

Freedom begins with self-control and positive mental attitude. Expressing this condition means believing it. Believing means having faith. The right course, the best trades to undertake, will manifest as a natural course. "Thus, one by one the resistances of life fade into nothingness for the man who has prepared his mind for self-expression through Faith. Success becomes inevitable."[3]

But the same author tells us that faith without willingness to take risks will not carry us far. "Here, then, is the suggestion of a test by which men may measure their capacity for *active faith!* To be effective it must be based on a willingness to risk whatever the circumstances demand: liberty, material fortune, and life itself. Faith without risk is a passive faith which, as Helen Keller stated, 'is no more a force than sight is in an eye that does not look or search out.'"[4]

2. Christopher Elias, *Fleecing the Lambs* (Chicago: Henry Regnery, 1971), p. 30.
3. Napoleon Hill, *The Master Key to Riches* (Greenwich, Conn.: Fawcett Publications, 1965), p. 127.
4. Ibid., p. 133.

Nevertheless, freedom, even financial independence, does not derive from accumulation of vast assets. In fact, enslavement to wealth differs little from enslavement to poverty. What is the safest asset?

Wealth is measured according to the values of stones, minerals, pieces of paper, or whatever it is we hoard. But values alter. Therefore, wealth and the fortunes of men change.

The greater problem is that everyone else covets your wealth. Most of them spend a great deal of time figuring out how to steal it from you.

Money gives you power over material acquisitions—even over the lives of others. "When I possessed all the money I needed I made the grievous error of believing money to be a permanent source of power. Now came the astonishing revelation that money, without faith, is nothing but inert matter, *of itself possessed of no power whatsoever.*"[5]

Financial losses backed by an attitude of defeat will surely lead you down one road. Recognizing that the greater part of your wealth is locked in the safest asset of all, the royal road to financial independence and freedom lies before you.

> Life has flown and left no trace.
> My soul was in a fever—to go where?
> —Fet[6]

5. Ibid., p. 115.
6. Fet is a pseudonym for the Russian poet A. A. Shensin (1820-1892).

Index

Channel, 313–14

Chart formations: ascending triangle, 63–64, 92–93, 117; bowl. *See* rounded bottom; coil. *See* symmetrical triangle; descending triangle, 64–65, 97–98, 117; dormant bottom. *See* flat bottom; double bottom, 61–63, 99–100; double top, 61–63, 99–100, flag, 64–67, 97–98; flat bottom, 68, 70; head and shoulders, 68, 71–73, 76, 81, 119; inverted bowl. *See* rounded top; inverted V, 68–9; "M". *See* double top; pennant, 64, 66–67; quadrubottom, 97–98, 99–100; rounded bottom, 68, 70, 119; rounded top, 68; saucer. *See* rounded bottom; sideways movements. *See* Trends; symmetrical triangle, 64, 66, 117; triple bottom, 61–63, 97–98; triple top, 61–63, 127; V formation, 68–69, 81, 99, 101; "W". *See* double top. *See also* Gaps; Reversal formations

Chicago Board of Trade, 45, 48n, 52, 167, 179, 188, 229, 238, 270, 284, 294–95, 315

Chicago Mercantile Exchange, 45, 52, 189, 211, 235, 242, 284, 294

Chicago Open Board of Trade, 294–95

Christmas tree plan, 292–93

Clearing fees, 295

Clearing member, 49

Clerks: order, 48, 178; runner, 48, 177

Climax patterns. *See* Reversal patterns

Closing price, 53

Coattailing, 309

Cocoa, 50, 54, 65, 84–85, 90, 97–98, 126, 152, 158–60, 180

Coconut oil, 186, 211, 315–17

Coffee, 67

Commissions, 233, 238, 264, 271, 279–80, 299

Commission houses, 45, 50, 287

Commitments of traders, 122–24

Commodity Exchange, Inc., 50, 53, 203, 270, 278, 284, 294

Commodity Exchange Authority, 116, 124, 169

Commodity Fox Trot, 200, 208

Concentration, 322–23, 325–26

Condon, Lester P., 167

Confirmation notice, 50–51

Congestion area, 64, 84–85

Consensus, 125–26

Consolidation, 64, 73–74, 84–85, 89–90, 92–93

Copper, 50, 53, 66, 71, 90, 97, 99–100, 126, 152, 158–60, 180

Continental Illinois Bank, 265

Consumer Price Index. *See* Indices

N

Narrow range day, 83–84
National Bureau of Economic Research, 172–74
Neckline. *See* Chart formations: head and shoulders
Newcastle's disease, 139
Netherlands, 245
New York Cocoa Exchange, 97, 180, 185
New York Coffee and Sugar Exchange, 46, 52, 180, 184
New York Cotton Exchange, 104
New York Mercantile Exchange, 46, 48, 53, 177–78, 250, 270, 284–85, 194
New York Stock Exchange, 45
Nicaragua, 32
Nickerson, "Nick", 44
Nine-day moving average, 106–07
Nixon, Richard M., 133
Nonregulated markets, 50

O

Oats, 90, 221, 230, 235, 295
Odds, 220–24
Off the board, 230
Offset, 49, 51, 121–22, 208, 291
Onion futures, 52
Open contract, 120
Open interest, 42, 116–18, 120–21
Or better (O.B.). *See* Orders
Orange juice, frozen concentrated, 72, 90, 126
Order clerk. *See* Clerks
Orders: limit, 205, 237; market order, 46, 48, 205, 237; MIT (market-if-touched), 206; MOC (market-on-close), 211; O.B. (or better), 205; stop, 206, 209; stop limit, 206; stop-loss, 92, 99, 205, 210, 284–85, 308–09, 311; trailing stop, 206
Orders to buy/sell, 47
Oscillator, 106–08

P

Pacific Commodities Exchange, 186, 211, 212, 284–85, 315
Perdue, Frank, 148
Pick, Franz, 265
Pit broker. *See* Broker
Pits, trading, 186, 196
Platinum, 46, 61, 126
Plywood, 90, 126, 154, 161, 235
Point and figure charts. *See* Reversal charts

Russian ruble, 260
Russian wheat deal, 167–68

Tariffs, 138
Tax straddles, 228, 278–81
Telser, Lester, 168
Ten-day moving average, 104–05
Tick, 87, 97, 102
Trading plan, 200–05, 207–08
Trailing stop. *See* Orders
Transition Theory, 329–30
Traps, 85
Trendline, 75–76, 92, 99–100
Trends, 60, 74–79, 92–93, 96–97, 104; downtrend, 75–77, 92, 99–100, 116, 121, 313; major, 77, 85; minor, 77–8; sideways, 50, 64, 75, 119; uptrend, 75, 313
Trend acceleration, 78
Trend channel, 77
Trend-Master Commodity Forecasts, 311
Two-day reversal, 80, 82–83
Two-hundred-day moving average, 106–07

U

United Kingdom, 193, 246
U. S. Department of Agriculture, 50, 144, 155, 167, 210. *See also* Commodity Exchange Authority
Unwinding, 226, 279–80, 283
Upper chestline. *See* Chart formations head and shoulders
Upper resistance line, 313
Uptrend. *See* Trends

V

Viscott, David S., 37n
Volume, 42, 61, 116–20
Volume moving average, 120
Volume oscillator, 120

W

Waves, 84–85. *See also* Elliott Wave Theory
Weighted moving average, 105–08
Wheat, 54, 80, 90, 92–93, 116–17, 122–24, 126, 140, 164, 167–68, 221, 230, 235, 238
Winnipeg Commodity Exchange, 284

Y

Yogananda, Paramahansa, 241, 320